FINANCIAL RISK MANAGEMENT
NAVIGATING A DYNAMIC LANDSCAPE

JOHAN VAN ROOYEN

notionpress.com
INDIA • SINGAPORE • MALAYSIA

ISBN 979-8-89632-370-9

Contents

Acknowledgements

I wish to express my deepest gratitude to my wife, Dr. Nitayapa Nandhakwang, whose unwavering support and encouragement have been the bedrock of my journey. Your love, patience, and understanding have been my greatest sources of strength, and this book would not have been possible without you by my side.

To my son, Aden, your infectious laughter, boundless energy, and warm hugs have been my daily inspiration. You remind me of the importance of perseverance and joy, and for that, I am eternally grateful.

A special thank you to Sanjeewa Mahesh, whose silent support have significantly shaped the direction and depth of this work. Your dedication to education especially in risk management were instrumental in bringing this project to life.

I also extend my sincere thanks to the Bankers of Bhutan. Your expert knowledge and the rich experiences you shared were crucial in guiding the research for this book. Your insights provided a unique perspective that has enriched the content and brought a practical edge to the theories discussed.

To all of you, this book is as much yours as it is mine. Thank you for being a part of this journey.

Chapter

01

Introduction to Financial Risk Management

Financial risk refers to the possibility of losing money on investments or business operations. This risk arises from various sources, including fluctuations in market prices, changes in interest rates, credit defaults, and operational failures. In today's complex financial environment, understanding and managing financial risk is essential for organizations to protect their assets, ensure profitability, and achieve long-term strategic goals.

Financial risk can be broadly categorized into the following types

Market Risk

It refers to the potential for financial loss due to fluctuations in the market prices of assets, such as stocks, bonds, currencies, or commodities. These fluctuations can be driven by various factors, including changes in interest rates, economic data releases, geopolitical events, or market sentiment. For instance, consider an investment portfolio heavily weighted in technology stocks. If there is a sudden downturn in the tech sector—perhaps due to disappointing earnings reports or regulatory changes—those stocks might lose significant value, leading to a substantial decline in the portfolio's overall worth. This loss exemplifies market risk, as it directly results from adverse movements in market prices.

Credit Risk

This refers to the possibility of a financial loss occurring when a borrower fails to repay a loan or meet contractual obligations, leading to a default. This risk is particularly significant for lenders, investors, and financial institutions, as it directly affects their ability to recover the principal and interest on loans or investments. Credit risk is assessed by evaluating the creditworthiness of the borrower, which includes analyzing their financial history, credit score, and ability to repay the debt.

Consider a bank that provides a mortgage loan to an individual to purchase a home. If the individual loses their job and is unable to make the mortgage payments, the bank faces credit risk. To mitigate this risk, the bank might require collateral (in this case, the house itself) or charge a higher interest rate to compensate for the potential risk of default. However, if the housing market declines and the value of the home falls below the loan amount, the bank may not fully recover its money even after foreclosing on the property, leading to a financial loss due to credit risk.

Liquidity Risk

It refers to the potential for a company or financial institution to encounter difficulties in meeting its short-term financial obligations due to the inability to quickly convert assets into cash without incurring significant losses. This type of risk arises when an entity holds assets that cannot be easily sold or when there is insufficient cash flow to cover liabilities, leading to potential insolvency.

Consider a manufacturing company that has invested heavily in specialized machinery and equipment. While these assets are valuable, they are not easily converted into cash. If the company suddenly faces an unexpected expense, such as a large legal settlement or a downturn in sales, it might struggle to generate enough cash to cover its immediate obligations, like payroll or supplier payments. If the company cannot sell the machinery quickly without taking a loss, it may face liquidity risk, leading to financial distress or even bankruptcy if the situation is not managed effectively.

Operational Risk

This refers to the potential for financial loss resulting from failures in a company's internal processes, systems, people, or external events. This type of risk can arise from a wide range of sources, including human errors, system breakdowns, inadequate controls, fraud, or disruptions caused by external factors like natural disasters or cyber-attacks. Unlike market or credit risks, operational risk is inherent in the day-to-day functioning of an organization and can impact its ability to operate efficiently and profitably.

Imagine a large retail company that relies heavily on its online platform for sales. If the company's website experiences a prolonged outage due to a technical failure or a cyber-attack, it could lose significant revenue as customers are unable to make purchases. Additionally, the company might face reputational damage, and the cost of repairing the system could be substantial. This scenario illustrates operational risk, where the failure of a critical system directly impacts the company's financial performance and operational capability.

Legal and Regulatory Risk

It refers to the potential for financial loss or reputational damage that a company may face due to non-compliance with laws, regulations, or contractual obligations. This type of risk arises from changes in the legal or regulatory environment, or from the company's failure to adhere to existing rules. Legal and regulatory risks can lead to fines, penalties, legal disputes, or restrictions on business operations, impacting the company's profitability and strategic goals.

Consider a pharmaceutical company that launches a new drug in the market. If the company fails to comply with regulatory requirements set by the Food and Drug Administration (FDA), such as proper labeling, safety testing, or marketing practices, it could face significant legal consequences. For instance, if it is discovered that the drug has harmful side effects that were not disclosed, the company could be subject to lawsuits, fines, and a mandatory recall of the product. Additionally, regulatory agencies might impose sanctions or restrictions on the company's ability to release new products, leading to substantial financial losses and damage to its reputation. This scenario illustrates how legal and regulatory risk can critically affect a company's operations and financial health.

Historical Context and Evolution of Risk Management

The concept of risk management has evolved significantly over time. Traditionally, risk management was focused on protecting physical assets from damage or loss. However, as financial markets and instruments have grown in complexity, the scope of risk management has expanded to include financial risks.

Ancient Risk Management

The origins of risk management can be traced back to ancient civilizations, where early forms of risk-sharing and mitigation practices were developed by traders and merchants to safeguard against potential losses. One of the earliest examples comes from ancient Babylon, where maritime loans were used to protect merchants from the financial risk associated with sea voyages. These loans were a precursor to modern insurance; a merchant would borrow money to finance a trading expedition, with the understanding that if the ship was lost at sea, the loan would be forgiven. This arrangement allowed merchants to share the risk of loss with lenders, reducing the financial burden on any single party.

Similarly, in ancient China, the practice of risk pooling was developed to manage the risk of loss during the transport of goods. Merchants who transported goods along treacherous trade routes would pool their resources to ensure that if any one merchant's goods were lost, the loss would be shared among all participants in the pool. This collective approach to risk management helped stabilize trade and commerce in uncertain and risky environments, laying the groundwork for more sophisticated risk management techniques that would emerge in later centuries.

These early examples of risk management highlight the ingenuity of ancient traders and the fundamental human need to protect against uncertainty and potential loss. While these practices were rudimentary compared to today's standards, they represent the foundational principles of risk-sharing and risk mitigation that continue to underpin modern financial and insurance systems. By distributing risk among multiple parties, ancient merchants were able to engage in trade with greater confidence, fostering economic growth and the expansion of early global trade networks.

Medieval Insurance Practices

During the Middle Ages, the concept of insurance evolved into a more formalized method of managing risk, particularly in the context of maritime trade. As European nations expanded their trading networks across oceans, the risks associated with long-distance sea voyages became increasingly significant. Ships faced numerous hazards, including storms, piracy, and navigational errors, which could lead to the total loss of valuable cargo. To mitigate these risks, merchants and ship owners began to seek financial protection through insurance contracts. These early insurance agreements allowed merchants to pool their risks by paying premiums into a collective fund, from which losses could be compensated if a ship was lost at sea. This system provided a safety net, enabling traders to engage in commerce with greater confidence despite the inherent dangers of maritime travel. One of the most notable developments in medieval insurance practices was the establishment of Lloyd's of London in the late 17th century. Originally a coffeehouse where merchants, ship owners, and underwriters gathered to discuss shipping news and arrange insurance deals, Lloyd's quickly became a central hub for marine insurance. The underwriters at Lloyd's would agree to cover a portion of the risk for a ship's voyage in exchange for a premium, and if the voyage was successful, they would keep the premium. However, if the ship was lost, they would pay out a portion of the agreed value. This model of risk-sharing became the cornerstone of modern insurance practices. Lloyd's of London played a crucial role in standardizing and formalizing insurance practices, turning what had been informal, ad hoc agreements into a structured industry with defined rules and procedures. The underwriting process at Lloyd's also introduced the concept of spreading risk among multiple parties, a practice that continues in today's insurance markets. By creating a reliable mechanism for transferring and managing risk, medieval insurance practices, particularly those developed at Lloyd's, laid the foundation for the complex global insurance industry that exists today. This evolution not only facilitated the growth of international trade but also contributed to the broader development of financial markets by providing a means to manage and mitigate the risks inherent in commercial ventures.

Modern Financial Risk Management

The 20th century marked a significant transformation in the field of financial risk management, driven by the development of advanced financial instruments and the formalization of risk management as a specialized discipline. This era saw the introduction of derivatives—financial contracts whose value is derived from underlying assets like stocks, bonds, or commodities.

Derivatives, such as options, futures, and swaps, became powerful tools for managing risk, enabling investors and corporations to hedge against adverse price movements in financial markets. For instance, an investor could use options to protect against a decline in the value of a stock portfolio or a company could use futures contracts to lock in prices for raw materials, thereby stabilizing costs and reducing uncertainty. These instruments allowed for sophisticated strategies that could mitigate various types of financial risk, including market risk, interest rate risk, and currency risk.

The formalization of risk management as a discipline was further advanced by the development of quantitative models and techniques, such as Value at Risk (VaR), which allowed financial institutions to measure and manage the risk of loss in their portfolios. These models became central to the risk management practices of banks, hedge funds, and other financial entities, allowing them to quantify potential losses and allocate capital more efficiently. However, the growing complexity and widespread use of these instruments also introduced new challenges. The collapse of Long-Term Capital Management (LTCM) in 1998 served as a stark reminder of the dangers associated with excessive leverage and the underestimation of risk. LTCM, a hedge fund that employed highly leveraged strategies using derivatives, suffered catastrophic losses when its models failed to predict the extreme market movements that followed the Russian financial crisis. The near collapse of LTCM threatened the stability of the global financial system and required a coordinated bailout by major financial institutions.

The global financial crisis of 2007-2008 further underscored the importance of robust risk management practices. The crisis was triggered by the widespread failure of mortgage-backed securities, which were thought to be low-risk investments but were, in fact, highly susceptible to defaults in the U.S. housing market. The crisis exposed significant flaws in the risk management frameworks of many financial institutions, particularly their reliance on models that failed to account for the possibility of extreme, systemic events. The resulting collapse of major financial institutions, like Lehman Brothers, and the severe economic downturn that followed, led to a comprehensive overhaul of regulatory frameworks worldwide. Governments and regulators introduced stricter rules on capital requirements, risk disclosure, and the use of derivatives, aiming to reduce the likelihood of such crises in the future. These events highlighted the critical need for a more holistic approach to risk management, one that not only relies on quantitative models but also considers the broader economic and systemic risks that can impact financial stability. The evolution of financial risk management in the 20th century, shaped by both innovation and crisis, has had a profound impact on the way financial institutions operate, emphasizing the need for continuous improvement and vigilance in managing financial risk.

The Basel Accords

A pivotal moment in the evolution of global risk management practices came with the introduction of the Basel Accords, a series of international banking regulations formulated by the Basel Committee on Banking Supervision (BCBS). The Basel Accords were developed to address the growing complexity and interconnectedness of global financial markets, aiming to create a more stable and resilient banking system.

The first of these accords, known as Basel I, was introduced in 1988 and focused primarily on the issue of capital adequacy. It established a framework for determining the minimum amount of capital that banks must hold relative to their risk-weighted assets, effectively linking the capital reserves of financial institutions to the level of risk they assumed. By requiring banks to maintain a buffer of capital based on the riskiness of their assets, Basel I sought to reduce the likelihood of bank failures and protect the broader financial system from systemic crises.

Building on the foundation laid by Basel I, the Basel II Accord, introduced in 2004, represented a more comprehensive and nuanced approach to risk management. Basel II introduced three pillars: minimum capital requirements, supervisory review, and market discipline. It expanded the focus beyond credit risk to include market risk and operational risk, reflecting the increasing complexity of banking activities. Basel II also introduced more sophisticated methods for calculating risk-weighted assets, allowing banks to use internal models to assess risk more accurately. However, the global financial crisis of 2007-2008 exposed significant weaknesses in the Basel II framework, particularly in how banks' internal models underestimated risks, leading to inadequate capital buffers.

In response to the lessons learned from the financial crisis, the Basel III Accord was introduced in 2010. Basel III aimed to strengthen the regulation, supervision, and risk management of banks by increasing the minimum capital requirements, introducing new regulatory capital buffers, and enhancing the quality of the capital held by banks. It also introduced new measures for liquidity risk management and leverage ratios, addressing the shortcomings of previous frameworks. Basel III's focus on ensuring that banks have sufficient high-quality capital to absorb losses during periods of financial stress represented a significant advancement in the regulation of global financial institutions.

The Basel Accords have had a profound impact on the global banking system, setting the standard for risk management and capital adequacy worldwide. By establishing a common regulatory framework, the Basel Accords have facilitated greater consistency and comparability across international banks, reducing the risk of regulatory arbitrage. The implementation of these accords has also prompted banks to adopt more rigorous risk management practices, contributing to the overall stability of the global financial system. However, the evolving nature of financial markets and the emergence of new risks continue to challenge regulators, ensuring that the Basel Accords remain a dynamic and integral part of the ongoing effort to safeguard the integrity of the global banking system.

The Importance of Strategic Risk Management in Finance

Strategic risk management integrates traditional risk management practices with the broader objectives of an organization's strategy. Rather than merely focusing on minimizing losses, strategic risk management aims to align risk management practices with the organization's goals, ensuring that risks are managed in a way that supports the achievement of long-term objectives.

Aligning Risk and Strategy

Effective risk management is integral to achieving an organization's strategic goals, as it ensures that potential risks are identified, assessed, and managed in a way that supports long-term objectives. The alignment of risk management with strategy begins with a thorough understanding of how different types of risks—such as market, credit, operational, and geopolitical risks—can influence the outcomes of strategic initiatives. For instance, a company planning to expand its operations internationally must carefully evaluate risks such as foreign exchange fluctuations, which can affect the profitability of its overseas revenues, and political risks, which can impact the stability of the business environment in the target country. Without incorporating these risks into the strategic planning process, the company might face unexpected challenges that could undermine its expansion efforts.

By integrating risk management into strategic decision-making, companies can make more informed choices that balance potential risks with expected rewards. For example, consider a U.S.-based manufacturing firm that plans to establish a subsidiary in a country with a volatile currency. The firm recognizes that foreign exchange risk could significantly erode its profit margins if the local currency depreciates against the U.S. dollar. To mitigate this risk, the firm could use hedging strategies such as forward contracts or options to lock in exchange rates for future transactions. Additionally, the firm might diversify its operations across multiple countries to reduce its exposure to any single currency's fluctuations.

Another crucial aspect of aligning risk and strategy involves understanding the broader geopolitical risks that could impact the company's global operations. For instance, the firm might be entering a market where political instability poses a threat to business continuity. In such a case, the company could develop contingency plans, such as establishing alternative supply chains or securing insurance against political risks, to protect its investments.

The benefits of aligning risk management with strategy are multifaceted. Not only does it help in safeguarding the company's assets and revenue streams, but it also enhances the organization's ability to capitalize on opportunities. When risk management is integrated into the strategic framework, decision-makers can weigh the risks and rewards of various options more effectively, enabling the company to pursue growth opportunities with greater confidence. This proactive approach to risk management ultimately leads to more resilient and adaptable strategies that are better equipped to navigate the uncertainties of the global business environment.

Enhancing Competitive Advantage

Companies that strategically manage risk are not only protecting themselves from potential losses but are also positioning themselves to gain a significant competitive advantage. Effective risk management enables these companies to navigate uncertainties with greater confidence, allowing them to capitalize on opportunities that less-prepared competitors might avoid. For example, a firm that excels at managing credit risk can offer

more favorable terms to its customers, such as extended payment periods or lower interest rates, without exposing itself to excessive risk. By providing these attractive terms, the firm can differentiate itself in the marketplace, attracting more customers and increasing its market share. This competitive edge is particularly valuable in industries where customer loyalty and financial stability are crucial for long-term success.

Moreover, companies that are adept at managing operational risks can streamline their processes, reduce downtime, and minimize the likelihood of disruptions. For instance, a manufacturing company that implements robust operational risk management practices, such as regular maintenance of equipment, rigorous quality control, and comprehensive employee training, can ensure more consistent production and higher quality products. This reliability not only reduces costs associated with operational failures but also strengthens the company's reputation for dependability. Customers and partners are more likely to trust and prefer doing business with a company that consistently meets its commitments and delivers on its promises.

Consider the case of a global logistics company that has developed a sophisticated risk management strategy to address potential disruptions in its supply chain. By using advanced data analytics and predictive modeling, the company can anticipate and mitigate risks such as transportation delays, natural disasters, or geopolitical tensions. As a result, it can guarantee timely delivery of goods even in challenging circumstances, providing a level of service that competitors might struggle to match. This reliability becomes a key selling point, allowing the company to secure long-term contracts with major clients and command premium pricing.

In addition, companies that integrate risk management into their strategic planning are often better equipped to innovate and respond to changing market conditions. By understanding and mitigating risks associated with new ventures, these companies can pursue innovative projects with reduced fear of failure. For example, a technology firm that carefully manages the risks related to research and development might be more willing to invest in cutting-edge projects that could lead to breakthrough products. Successfully bringing these innovations to market before competitors can significantly enhance the firm's competitive position.

Ultimately, the ability to manage risk strategically is a powerful tool for enhancing competitive advantage. It allows companies to not only survive in a volatile business environment but to thrive by making smarter decisions, building stronger relationships, and continuously improving their operations. In today's rapidly changing world, where risks are ever-present and often unpredictable, the companies that can navigate these challenges effectively are the ones that will lead their industries and set the standard for others to follow.

Case Study

Toyota's Strategic Risk Management

Toyota's long-standing success in the global automobile market is a testament to its exemplary strategic risk management practices. The company has developed a comprehensive risk management framework that integrates risk mitigation into every aspect of its operations, particularly in its supply chain management. Toyota's approach to risk management is characterized by meticulous planning, redundancy, and continuous improvement, all of which have been crucial in minimizing operational risks and ensuring the company's resilience in the face of disruptions. A prime example of Toyota's strategic risk management in action occurred during the 2011 earthquake and tsunami in Japan, a catastrophic event that severely disrupted supply chains across various industries.

The disaster caused widespread damage to infrastructure and halted production for many companies, particularly those with a heavy reliance on just-in-time manufacturing processes, which are highly efficient but vulnerable to disruptions. However, Toyota's strategic risk management framework allowed the company to recover more quickly than many of its competitors. This resilience was largely due to Toyota's proactive approach to risk management, which included diversifying its supplier base, maintaining higher levels of critical inventory, and establishing alternative production sites outside of the most vulnerable regions.

In the years leading up to the 2011 disaster, Toyota had already recognized the risks associated with over-dependence on single suppliers or regions. As a result, the company had implemented a strategy of dual sourcing for critical components, meaning that it sourced essential parts from multiple suppliers in different geographical locations. This strategy ensured that if one supplier or region was affected by a disruption, Toyota could quickly shift production to another supplier, minimizing the impact on its overall operations. Additionally, Toyota invested in creating a global network of production facilities, allowing the company to relocate production as needed and reduce the risk of significant operational downtime.

Furthermore, Toyota's culture of continuous improvement, known as "Kaizen," played a crucial role in its ability to respond to the crisis. The company's commitment to constantly refining its processes and learning from past experiences meant that it was better prepared for unexpected events. In the aftermath of the 2011 disaster, Toyota swiftly implemented contingency plans, reorganized its supply chain, and worked closely with its suppliers to restore production as quickly as possible. While other automakers struggled with prolonged disruptions, Toyota was able to resume production relatively quickly, maintaining its competitive edge in the global market.

Toyota's response to the 2011 earthquake and tsunami illustrates the critical importance of strategic risk management in sustaining business operations and achieving long-term success. By anticipating potential risks and embedding risk management into its strategic planning, Toyota has built a resilient organization capable of withstanding even the most severe disruptions. This case study highlights the value of a proactive and comprehensive approach to risk management, demonstrating that companies that invest in understanding and mitigating risks are better positioned to navigate challenges and maintain their leadership in the market.

Key Concepts and Definitions

To effectively manage financial risks, it's crucial to understand the key concepts and terminology used in the field. Here are some foundational definitions:

- **Risk Appetite:** The level of risk an organization is willing to accept in pursuit of its objectives. It reflects the company's tolerance for risk and guides decision-making processes.
- **Risk Tolerance:** The acceptable variation in outcomes related to specific risks. It defines the boundaries within which the organization is comfortable operating.
- **Risk Assessment:** The process of identifying, analyzing, and evaluating risks to determine their potential impact on the organization.
- **Risk Mitigation:** The strategies and actions taken to reduce the likelihood or impact of risks. This can include transferring risk through insurance, diversifying investments, or implementing robust internal controls.
- **Hedging:** A risk management strategy used to offset potential losses by taking an opposite position in a related asset. For example, a company might hedge against foreign exchange risk by entering into a forward contract to lock in exchange rates.
- **Value at Risk (VaR):** A statistical measure that estimates the potential loss in value of a portfolio over a defined period for a given confidence interval. VaR is widely used to assess market risk.

Practical Examples and Exercises

Example 1: Hedging Foreign Exchange Risk

Imagine a U.S.-based company that exports goods to Europe. The company is concerned that a depreciation of the Euro against the U.S. Dollar could reduce the value of its Euro-denominated revenue. To hedge against this risk, the company enters into a forward contract to sell Euros and buy U.S. Dollars at a fixed rate in the future, thereby locking in the exchange rate and protecting against unfavorable currency movements.

Exercise 1: Assessing Risk Appetite

Consider a scenario where you are the CFO of a mid-sized manufacturing firm. Your company is considering expanding into a new market, which presents both opportunities and risks.

- How would you determine the company's risk appetite for this expansion?
- What factors would you consider, and how would you communicate your findings to the board of directors?

Example 2: Diversification as a Risk Mitigation Strategy

A financial advisor is managing a client's investment portfolio. To reduce market risk, the advisor diversifies the portfolio across different asset classes, such as stocks, bonds, and real estate. By spreading investments across various assets that are not perfectly correlated, the advisor reduces the overall risk of the portfolio.

Exercise 2: Risk Identification and Assessment

- Using the above example of the U.S.-based company exporting to Europe, identify and assess the different types of risks the company faces (e.g., market risk, credit risk, operational risk).
- For each type of risk, suggest possible mitigation strategies and assess their potential impact on the company's strategic goals.

Example 3: Strategic Risk in Mergers and Acquisitions

A large technology firm is considering acquiring a smaller software company. The acquisition could provide strategic benefits, such as access to new technology and markets. However, it also presents risks, including integration challenges, cultural differences, and potential legal liabilities. To manage these risks, the acquiring firm conducts thorough due diligence and develops a detailed integration plan that aligns with its strategic objectives.

Exercise 3: Strategic Risk Management Planning

You are part of the strategic planning team for a multinational corporation. The company is exploring opportunities to enter a new geographic market.

- Develop a strategic risk management plan that identifies potential risks, assesses their impact, and outlines mitigation strategies.
- Consider how these risks align with the company's overall strategic goals.

Chapter

02

Types of Financial Risks

In this chapter, we explore the various types of financial risks that organizations encounter and the strategies to manage them effectively. Understanding these risks is crucial for developing a robust risk management framework that supports the organization's strategic objectives.

Credit Risk

What it is

Credit risk is the potential for financial loss that occurs when a borrower or counterparty fails to meet its obligations to repay a loan or fulfill a financial contract. This failure could result in the lender or creditor losing some or all of the principal and interest, leading to a direct negative impact on their financial position. Credit risk is one of the most significant and pervasive risks in the financial world, particularly for banks, financial institutions, and companies that extend credit to customers or engage in various financial transactions.

Credit risk arises in a variety of contexts. In its most straightforward form, it occurs when a borrower defaults on a loan. For example, if an individual takes out a mortgage to buy a house and then fails to make the scheduled payments, the bank that issued the loan faces credit risk. This risk is not limited to individual borrowers; it can also arise in corporate lending, where businesses might fail to repay loans due to poor financial performance, mismanagement, or adverse economic conditions.

In addition to traditional lending, credit risk is present in other financial activities, such as the issuance of bonds, trade credit, derivatives, and other credit-sensitive transactions. For instance, when a company issues bonds to raise capital, investors who purchase those bonds are exposed to the risk that the company might not be able to make the promised interest payments or repay the principal at maturity. Similarly, when a company extends trade credit to its customers by allowing them to pay for goods or services at a later date, it assumes the risk that those customers might not fulfill their payment obligations.

The impact of credit risk can be severe, leading to significant financial losses for the lender or creditor. This risk can also trigger a chain reaction of adverse effects, particularly in the banking sector, where high levels of loan defaults can undermine the stability of the entire financial system. The global financial crisis of 2007-2008 is a stark example of how widespread credit risk can lead to systemic failures. The crisis was precipitated by the collapse of the U.S. subprime mortgage market, where lenders had extended credit to borrowers with poor credit histories, resulting in a massive wave of defaults that destabilized financial institutions worldwide.

To manage credit risk effectively, financial institutions employ various strategies and tools. These include conducting thorough credit assessments before issuing loans, setting appropriate interest rates to compensate for risk, requiring collateral, and diversifying their loan portfolios to spread risk across different sectors and geographic regions. Additionally, financial institutions often use credit derivatives, such as credit default swaps (CDS), to transfer credit risk to other parties willing to assume it.

Credit risk management is a critical component of a financial institution's overall risk management framework. It involves continuous monitoring of borrowers' creditworthiness, regularly assessing the risk of loan portfolios, and implementing measures to mitigate potential losses. For example, banks use credit scoring models to evaluate the likelihood of a borrower defaulting on a loan, and they may adjust credit terms or limit exposure to high-risk borrowers accordingly.

In the context of corporate finance, companies must also manage credit risk when dealing with their customers and suppliers. This involves assessing the financial health of counterparties, setting credit limits, and closely monitoring outstanding receivables. Companies may also use credit insurance to protect against potential losses from customer defaults.

In summary, credit risk is an inherent part of financial activities that involves lending, borrowing, or extending credit. It poses significant challenges for financial institutions and corporations alike, as failure to manage this risk effectively can lead to substantial financial losses and, in extreme cases, systemic crises. By understanding the nature of credit risk and implementing robust risk management practices, organizations can better protect themselves against the uncertainties associated with credit exposures and maintain financial stability in a volatile economic environment.

Practical Example

Imagine a bank that provides a mortgage loan to a borrower. If the borrower loses their job and is unable to make the mortgage payments, the bank faces credit risk. To mitigate this risk, the bank might require the borrower to provide collateral, such as the house itself, or it might conduct thorough credit assessments before approving the loan.

Exercise 1

Consider a company that sells products on credit to customers.

- How should the company assess the creditworthiness of its customers, and what measures can it take to minimize the risk of non-payment?

Market Risk

What it is

Market risk, also known as systematic risk, refers to the potential for financial loss that arises from fluctuations in the market prices of financial assets. These assets can include stocks, bonds, currencies, commodities, and other financial instruments. Market risk is inherent in any investment or trading activity where the value of an asset can change due to a variety of external factors. Unlike specific risks that can be mitigated or diversified away, market risk affects the entire market or a significant portion of it, making it unavoidable for investors and financial institutions.

Market risk is driven by a wide range of factors that can cause asset prices to move unpredictably. These factors include changes in interest rates, economic data releases, inflation, political events, geopolitical tensions, natural disasters, and shifts in investor sentiment. Because these drivers are often beyond the control of individual investors or companies, market risk is considered a fundamental aspect of participating in financial markets.

Key Components of Market Risk

- Interest Rate Risk: Interest rate risk is the risk that changes in interest rates will affect the value of financial instruments. For example, when interest rates rise, the prices of existing bonds typically fall because new bonds are issued at higher rates, making the older, lower-yielding bonds less attractive. This inverse relationship between interest rates and bond prices is a critical aspect of market risk for bond investors. Similarly, changes in interest rates can affect the cost of borrowing for companies and consumers, influencing economic activity and, consequently, stock prices.
- **Equity Price Risk:** Equity price risk is the risk of loss due to fluctuations in the prices of stocks or equity indices. Stock prices are influenced by a variety of factors, including company performance, earnings reports, macroeconomic conditions, and investor sentiment. For instance, a downturn in the economy can lead to a broad decline in stock prices, affecting the value of equity investments across the board. Additionally, specific events, such as corporate scandals or changes in industry regulations, can lead to sharp declines in the stock prices of affected companies.
- **Currency Risk:** Currency risk, also known as exchange rate risk, arises from changes in the value of one currency relative to another. This risk is particularly relevant for companies and investors involved in international trade or cross-border investments. For example, if a U.S.-based company generates significant revenue in euros, but the euro depreciates against the U.S. dollar, the company's reported earnings in dollars will decline, even if its sales in euros remain constant. Currency risk can also impact the value of foreign investments, as fluctuations in exchange rates can lead

to gains or losses when converting foreign returns back into the investor's home currency.

- **Commodity Price Risk:** Commodity price risk is the risk that changes in the prices of commodities, such as oil, gold, or agricultural products, will affect the value of investments or the costs for businesses. For example, an airline company that relies heavily on jet fuel is exposed to commodity price risk, as a sharp increase in oil prices would raise operating costs and potentially reduce profitability. Conversely, investors in commodity futures may face losses if prices move against their positions.

Practical Examples of Market Risk

- **Interest Rate Risk:** Consider a bank that holds a large portfolio of fixed-rate bonds. If interest rates rise unexpectedly, the value of these bonds will decrease because new bonds issued at higher rates will offer better returns. As a result, the bank may incur significant losses when it marks its bond portfolio to market, reflecting the lower market value of the bonds. To manage this risk, the bank might use interest rate swaps or other hedging strategies to protect against adverse movements in interest rates.
- **Equity Price Risk:** An investment firm that holds a diversified portfolio of stocks is exposed to equity price risk. If the stock market experiences a broad decline due to an economic recession, the value of the firm's equity portfolio will likely fall, leading to potential losses. To mitigate equity price risk, the firm might use options, such as protective puts, to limit downside exposure or diversify its investments across different asset classes.
- **Currency Risk:** A U.S.-based multinational corporation with substantial operations in Japan faces currency risk due to fluctuations in the exchange rate between the U.S. dollar and the Japanese yen. If the yen weakens relative to the dollar, the corporation's earnings in yen will translate into fewer dollars, reducing its overall profitability. To hedge against this risk, the company could use

forward contracts to lock in exchange rates for future transactions or diversify its revenue sources across multiple currencies.

- **Commodity Price Risk:** A food manufacturing company that relies on agricultural commodities, such as wheat and corn, is exposed to commodity price risk. If the prices of these commodities rise sharply due to supply shortages or increased demand, the company's production costs will increase, potentially squeezing profit margins. To manage this risk, the company might enter into futures contracts to lock in prices for these commodities, reducing the impact of price volatility on its operations.

Managing Market Risk

Given the inherent nature of market risk, it cannot be entirely eliminated, but it can be managed through various strategies. Diversification is one of the most common methods for managing market risk. By spreading investments across different asset classes, industries, and geographic regions, investors can reduce the impact of adverse price movements in any single area.

Hedging is another important strategy for managing market risk. Financial instruments such as options, futures, and swaps allow investors and companies to offset potential losses from market movements. For example, an investor concerned about a potential decline in the stock market might purchase put options on a stock index, which would increase in value as the market falls, helping to offset losses in the investor's stock portfolio.

Regular monitoring and analysis of market conditions are also crucial for managing market risk. By staying informed about economic indicators, geopolitical developments, and market trends, investors and companies can make more informed decisions and adjust their risk management strategies as needed.

Conclusion

Market risk is a fundamental aspect of investing and financial management that affects all participants in financial markets. While it cannot be completely avoided, understanding its sources and implementing effective risk management strategies can help mitigate its impact. By carefully managing market risk, investors and companies can protect their portfolios and operations from the adverse effects of market volatility and position themselves for long-term success in an unpredictable financial environment.

Practical Example

Suppose a U.S.-based company has significant investments in foreign currencies. If the U.S. dollar strengthens against these foreign currencies, the value of the company's investments may decline, leading to a financial loss. To manage this market risk, the company might use hedging strategies, such as forward contracts, to lock in exchange rates.

Exercise 2

A company invests in both stocks and bonds.

- How can the company diversify its portfolio to reduce market risk?
- Discuss the role of asset allocation in managing market risk.

Liquidity Risk

What is it

Liquidity risk refers to the potential for an organization to face financial difficulties or even insolvency because it is unable to meet its short-term financial obligations as they come due. This risk arises when a company or financial institution is unable to convert its assets into cash quickly or without incurring significant losses. Liquidity risk is a critical concern for businesses and financial institutions because it can lead to a cascading series of problems, including defaults on obligations, a loss of investor and creditor confidence, and in extreme cases, bankruptcy.

Liquidity risk is often categorized into two main types

- **Funding Liquidity Risk:** This type of risk occurs when an organization is unable to secure funding to meet its immediate cash flow needs. It can result from a sudden withdrawal of deposits, a credit crunch, or a decline in market confidence. Funding liquidity risk is particularly relevant for banks and financial institutions, which rely on a steady flow of funds to finance their operations and obligations.
- **Market Liquidity Risk:** This risk arises when an organization cannot sell its assets quickly or at a fair market price due to a lack of market activity or demand. Market liquidity risk is more likely to affect companies with significant holdings in illiquid assets, such as real estate, specialized equipment, or large blocks of securities that cannot be easily sold without causing a significant drop in their market value.

Key Drivers of Liquidity Risk

- **Asset-Liability Mismatch:** One of the primary causes of liquidity risk is an asset-liability mismatch, where the maturity profiles of assets and liabilities are not aligned. For example, a company might have long-term investments in real estate or machinery, which are illiquid, but its liabilities, such as short-term loans or accounts payable, require immediate cash payments. If the company cannot liquidate its assets quickly enough to meet these obligations, it faces liquidity risk.
- **Market Conditions:** Adverse market conditions, such as a financial crisis or a sudden downturn in an industry, can exacerbate liquidity risk. During such periods, even assets that are normally considered liquid may become difficult to sell without taking a significant discount, as buyers become scarce and market confidence wanes.

- **Operational Disruptions:** Operational issues, such as supply chain disruptions, cyberattacks, or natural disasters, can lead to liquidity problems. For instance, a manufacturing company might face a liquidity crunch if a key supplier fails to deliver critical components on time, delaying production and sales, and thereby affecting the company's cash flow.
- **Credit Rating Downgrades:** A downgrade in a company's credit rating can increase liquidity risk by making it more expensive or difficult to access external financing. Creditors and investors may become hesitant to lend to or invest in a company with a lower credit rating, forcing the company to rely more heavily on its existing cash reserves.

Practical Examples of Liquidity Risk

- **The 2008 Financial Crisis:** The global financial crisis of 2007-2008 serves as a stark example of liquidity risk on a massive scale. During the crisis, many financial institutions faced severe liquidity challenges as the value of mortgage-backed securities plummeted and interbank lending froze. Lehman Brothers, one of the largest investment banks at the time, was unable to meet its short-term obligations due to a lack of liquid assets and was forced to file for bankruptcy. This event underscored the critical importance of maintaining sufficient liquidity buffers and highlighted the dangers of over-reliance on short-term funding sources.
- **Corporate Example:** Consider a real estate development company that has invested heavily in a large commercial property project. The company financed the project with a combination of equity and short-term loans, expecting to repay the loans with revenue generated from leasing or selling the property. However, if the real estate market experiences a downturn and the company is unable to sell or lease the property quickly, it may struggle to generate the cash needed to service its debt. This situation illustrates market

liquidity risk, as the company's assets are not easily convertible into cash without significant losses, putting its financial stability at risk.

- **Retail Example:** A large retail chain relies on just-in-time inventory management to minimize storage costs and improve cash flow. However, if there is an unexpected disruption in the supply chain, such as a strike by transport workers or a natural disaster, the company might not receive inventory in time to meet customer demand. This delay could lead to lost sales and a sudden cash flow shortage, making it difficult for the company to pay suppliers, employees, and other short-term obligations. This scenario demonstrates how operational disruptions can lead to liquidity risk.

Managing Liquidity Risk

Effective liquidity risk management is essential for maintaining financial stability and ensuring that an organization can meet its obligations under all circumstances. Several strategies can help manage liquidity risk:

- **Maintaining Adequate Liquidity Reserves***:* Organizations should maintain sufficient liquid assets, such as cash and cash equivalents, to cover short-term liabilities. This liquidity buffer acts as a safety net, allowing the company to meet its obligations even during periods of financial stress.
- **Diversifying Funding Sources:** Relying on a single source of funding can increase liquidity risk, especially if that source becomes unavailable or expensive. Companies and financial institutions should diversify their funding sources by using a mix of short-term and long-term debt, equity, and credit lines from multiple financial institutions.
- **Aligning Asset and Liability Maturities:** To avoid asset-liability mismatches, organizations should strive to match the maturity profiles of their assets and liabilities. For example, a company with long-term investments should finance those investments with

long-term debt, rather than short-term loans that might need to be repaid before the assets can be liquidated.

- **Stress Testing and Scenario Analysis:** Regular stress testing and scenario analysis can help organizations assess their vulnerability to liquidity shocks and identify potential weaknesses in their liquidity management strategies. By simulating various adverse scenarios, such as a sudden drop in asset prices or a credit market freeze, companies can better prepare for unexpected liquidity challenges.
- **Liquidity Contingency Planning:** Developing a liquidity contingency plan is crucial for managing liquidity risk. This plan should outline the steps the organization will take in the event of a liquidity crisis, including identifying alternative sources of funding, prioritizing payments, and communicating with stakeholders.
- **Monitoring and Reporting:** Continuous monitoring of liquidity ratios, cash flow forecasts, and market conditions is essential for managing liquidity risk. Organizations should establish clear reporting lines and protocols to ensure that liquidity risks are identified and addressed promptly.

Conclusion

Liquidity risk is a fundamental challenge that all organizations must manage to ensure their long-term viability. The inability to meet short-term obligations can lead to severe financial difficulties, damage to reputation, and even bankruptcy. By understanding the sources of liquidity risk and implementing effective risk management strategies, organizations can protect themselves against the uncertainties of financial markets and operational disruptions, ensuring they have the resources needed to meet their obligations and continue operations even in challenging times.

Practical Example

Consider a manufacturing company that has invested heavily in specialized machinery and equipment. While these assets are valuable, they are not easily converted into cash. If the company suddenly faces an unexpected expense, such as a legal settlement, it might struggle to generate enough cash to cover its obligations, leading to liquidity risk.

Exercise 3

- Analyze the liquidity position of a hypothetical company by reviewing its balance sheet.
- Identify the liquid and illiquid assets and suggest strategies the company can implement to improve its liquidity.

Operational Risk

What is it

Operational risk refers to the potential for financial loss or damage to a company's reputation due to failures in internal processes, systems, people, or external events. Unlike market or credit risks, which are often external in nature, operational risk arises from within the organization and can be influenced by a wide range of factors, including human error, technological failures, inadequate internal controls, fraud, and unexpected external events such as natural disasters or cyberattacks. Managing operational risk is critical because it directly impacts a company's ability to conduct its day-to-day operations effectively and maintain its financial health.

Key Components of Operational Risk

- **Process Failures:** Process failures occur when established procedures or workflows do not function as intended. This can happen due to poorly designed processes, lack of clarity in roles and responsibilities, or inefficiencies that lead to delays, errors, or bottlenecks. For instance, a financial institution may face operational risk if its loan approval process is not properly standardized, leading to inconsistent evaluations and increased chances of approving high-risk loans.

- **System Failures:** System failures refer to the breakdown or malfunctioning of critical IT systems, software applications, or infrastructure that a company relies on to operate. For example, if a bank's online banking platform experiences a prolonged outage, customers may be unable to access their accounts, resulting in financial losses, customer dissatisfaction, and reputational damage. System failures can also expose the company to cybersecurity risks, as outdated or poorly maintained systems may be more vulnerable to cyberattacks.
- **Human Errors:** Human errors are mistakes made by employees or management that can lead to operational disruptions, financial losses, or regulatory breaches. These errors can range from data entry mistakes to more serious issues like failing to follow established procedures or making poor decisions due to lack of training or oversight. For example, an employee who accidentally sends a confidential email to the wrong recipient may cause a data breach, leading to potential legal and financial consequences for the company.
- **Inadequate Controls:** Inadequate internal controls are a significant source of operational risk. When a company lacks effective control mechanisms—such as proper checks and balances, segregation of duties, or regular audits—there is a greater likelihood of errors, fraud, or non-compliance with regulations. For instance, a company that does not implement adequate controls over financial reporting may issue inaccurate financial statements, resulting in regulatory penalties and loss of investor confidence.
- **Fraud and Misconduct:** Fraud and misconduct by employees or management represent a severe form of operational risk. This can include embezzlement, insider trading, bribery, or falsifying records to meet performance targets. Fraud not only leads to direct financial losses but can also severely damage a company's reputation

and result in legal and regulatory consequences. An example of this is the infamous Enron scandal, where fraudulent accounting practices by top executives led to the company's collapse and a significant loss of trust in corporate governance.

- **External Events:** External events, such as natural disasters, political instability, or pandemics, can disrupt business operations and expose companies to operational risk. These events are often beyond the control of the organization but can have profound impacts on its ability to function. For example, a manufacturing company with factories in a region prone to earthquakes may face significant operational risks if a major earthquake damages its facilities, halting production and leading to financial losses.

Practical Examples of Operational Risk

- **System Failure Example:** A large retail company operates an extensive online sales platform that generates a significant portion of its revenue. During a peak shopping season, the company's website crashes due to an unexpected surge in traffic. The outage lasts for several hours, during which time customers are unable to complete purchases, resulting in substantial lost sales and a wave of customer complaints. This incident highlights the operational risk associated with system failures and underscores the importance of robust IT infrastructure and contingency planning.
- **Human Error Example:** In a financial services firm, a junior employee accidentally inputs incorrect data into a risk management system, causing the system to underestimate the risk exposure of certain investment portfolios. As a result, the firm makes investment decisions based on flawed risk assessments, leading to significant financial losses. This example demonstrates how human error can introduce operational risk and emphasizes the need for proper training, oversight, and verification processes to minimize such risks.

- **Fraud Example:** A senior manager at a manufacturing company manipulates inventory records to hide theft of raw materials over several years. The fraud is eventually uncovered during an internal audit, revealing significant financial discrepancies and leading to the dismissal of several employees involved. The company also faces legal action from investors who claim that the company's financial statements were misleading. This case illustrates the severe impact that fraud and inadequate internal controls can have on a company's financial health and reputation.
- **External Event Example:** A global logistics company with operations in multiple countries is hit by a major hurricane that devastates one of its key distribution centers. The disaster disrupts supply chains, delays deliveries, and forces the company to reroute shipments, incurring additional costs and customer dissatisfaction. The incident highlights the operational risk posed by external events and the importance of having disaster recovery and business continuity plans in place.

Managing Operational Risk

Given the broad and diverse nature of operational risk, managing it requires a comprehensive approach that includes identifying, assessing, mitigating, and monitoring potential risks across all areas of the organization. Key strategies for managing operational risk include:

- **Risk Identification and Assessment:** The first step in managing operational risk is identifying potential risks across the organization's processes, systems, and activities. This involves conducting regular risk assessments, process mapping, and root cause analysis to understand where vulnerabilities may exist. Risk assessments should consider both internal and external factors that could impact the organization's operations.
- **Implementing Strong Internal Controls:** Effective internal controls are critical for reducing operational risk. This includes establishing clear policies and procedures, implementing checks

and balances, ensuring proper segregation of duties, and conducting regular internal audits. By strengthening internal controls, organizations can minimize the likelihood of errors, fraud, and non-compliance.

- **Training and Awareness:** Training employees on risk management practices, operational procedures, and ethical standards is essential for reducing human errors and preventing fraud. Ongoing training programs should be tailored to different roles within the organization and include practical scenarios to help employees recognize and respond to potential risks.
- **Investing in Technology and Systems:** Robust IT systems and technology are vital for managing operational risk, particularly in areas such as data management, cybersecurity, and business continuity. Organizations should regularly update and test their systems to ensure they are resilient to failures and protected against cyber threats. Additionally, implementing automation and digital tools can help reduce the risk of human error.
- **Developing Contingency Plans:** Contingency planning is crucial for managing the impact of external events, system failures, or other disruptions. Organizations should develop and regularly update business continuity plans, disaster recovery plans, and crisis management protocols to ensure they can respond quickly and effectively to operational disruptions.
- **Monitoring and Reporting:** Continuous monitoring of key operational metrics, risk indicators, and control effectiveness is essential for identifying emerging risks and ensuring that risk management strategies remain effective. Regular reporting to senior management and the board of directors helps maintain transparency and accountability in managing operational risk.

Conclusion

Operational risk is an inherent part of running a business and can arise from a wide range of internal and external factors. While it cannot be entirely eliminated, organizations can significantly reduce their exposure to operational risk by implementing strong internal controls, investing in technology, training employees, and developing comprehensive contingency plans. By proactively managing operational risk, companies can protect their financial stability, maintain operational resilience, and build trust with stakeholders, ultimately contributing to long-term success and sustainability in an increasingly complex business environment.

Practical Example

A large retail company relies heavily on its online platform for sales. If the company's website experiences a prolonged outage due to a cyber-attack, it could lose significant revenue, damage its reputation, and incur costs to repair the system. This scenario illustrates operational risk.

Exercise 4

Identify potential operational risks in a hypothetical e-commerce company.

- Propose measures to mitigate these risks, focusing on improving internal processes, strengthening cybersecurity, and enhancing employee training.

Legal and Regulatory Risk

What is it

Legal and regulatory risk refers to the potential for financial loss, operational disruption, or reputational damage that a company may face as a result of failing to comply with laws, regulations, industry standards, or contractual obligations. This type of risk arises from the legal and regulatory environment in which a company

operates, including changes in laws, interpretations of regulations, enforcement actions by regulatory bodies, and legal disputes. Legal and regulatory risk is a critical concern for organizations across all sectors, as non-compliance can lead to significant financial penalties, legal costs, restrictions on business activities, and a loss of trust among stakeholders.

Key Components of Legal and Regulatory Risk

- **Compliance Risk:** Compliance risk arises when a company fails to adhere to the laws and regulations that govern its operations. This can include violations of labor laws, environmental regulations, financial reporting standards, data protection laws, or industry-specific regulations. Non-compliance can result in fines, sanctions, and legal action, as well as damage to the company's reputation. For example, a pharmaceutical company that fails to comply with the stringent requirements of the Food and Drug Administration (FDA) for drug approval could face costly recalls, lawsuits, and a loss of market share.
- **Contractual Risk:** Contractual risk occurs when a company fails to fulfill its obligations under a contract or when another party breaches a contract. This type of risk can lead to financial losses, legal disputes, and damage to business relationships. For instance, if a supplier fails to deliver goods on time as stipulated in a contract, the purchasing company may incur additional costs to source the goods elsewhere and may also face legal action to recover damages.
- **Regulatory Change Risk:** Regulatory change risk arises when new laws or changes to existing regulations affect a company's operations, products, or services. This risk is particularly relevant in highly regulated industries, such as finance, healthcare, and energy, where regulatory changes can have a profound impact on business models and profitability. For example, the introduction of stricter emissions regulations in the automotive industry could require car manufacturers to invest heavily in new technologies, significantly altering their cost structures and competitive dynamics.

- **Litigation Risk:** Litigation risk refers to the potential for legal action against a company, either from external parties such as customers, suppliers, competitors, or regulatory authorities, or from internal parties such as employees. Litigation can be costly, time-consuming, and damaging to a company's reputation. For instance, a technology company might face litigation from a competitor over intellectual property rights, leading to legal expenses, potential damages, and disruptions to its business operations.
- **Reputational Risk:** Reputational risk is closely linked to legal and regulatory risk, as non-compliance with laws or involvement in legal disputes can harm a company's reputation. Negative publicity, customer dissatisfaction, and loss of stakeholder trust can have long-lasting effects on a company's brand and market position. For example, a financial institution involved in a money laundering scandal may suffer significant reputational damage, leading to customer attrition and increased scrutiny from regulators.
- **Operational Disruption Risk:** Legal and regulatory issues can also cause operational disruptions, particularly if a company is required to halt or modify its operations to comply with legal requirements. This type of risk is evident in situations where regulatory bodies impose restrictions on a company's activities, such as suspending a business license or mandating the shutdown of facilities until compliance is achieved.

Practical Examples of Legal and Regulatory Risk

- **Compliance Risk Example:** A multinational corporation operating in multiple countries faces compliance risk as it must adhere to the varying labor laws, tax regulations, and environmental standards in each jurisdiction. If the company fails to comply with the labor laws in one of its markets—such as by not providing the legally required benefits to employees—it could face legal action, fines, and damage to its reputation. To mitigate this risk, the company would need to implement a robust compliance program that ensures adherence to local regulations and regularly updates its practices in response to legal changes.

- **Contractual Risk Example:** A construction firm enters into a contract with a property developer to complete a large-scale building project by a specific deadline. However, due to unforeseen delays in obtaining necessary permits, the construction firm is unable to meet the deadline, leading to a breach of contract. The property developer sues the construction firm for damages, and the firm faces significant legal costs and potential financial losses. This scenario illustrates the importance of carefully managing contractual obligations and having contingency plans in place to address potential delays or disruptions.
- **Regulatory Change Risk Example:** A financial services company that offers investment products to retail customers is impacted by new regulations introduced by the Securities and Exchange Commission (SEC) aimed at enhancing consumer protection. The new rules require the company to implement stricter disclosure practices and modify its product offerings to meet the regulatory standards. These changes result in increased compliance costs and may also limit the company's ability to offer certain high-margin products, affecting its profitability. The company must quickly adapt to the new regulatory environment by updating its compliance procedures, retraining staff, and potentially restructuring its product portfolio.
- **Litigation Risk Example:** A large technology company faces a class-action lawsuit from consumers who claim that the company's product is defective and has caused widespread harm. The litigation results in extensive legal expenses, a potential settlement, and negative media coverage that damages the company's brand. In response, the company must enhance its product quality controls, improve customer communication, and strengthen its legal defenses to minimize the impact of future litigation.
- **Reputational Risk Example:** A prominent bank is involved in a high-profile regulatory investigation for allegedly facilitating

money laundering activities. The investigation leads to significant fines, regulatory sanctions, and negative media coverage, severely damaging the bank's reputation. As a result, the bank loses customers, faces increased regulatory scrutiny, and sees a decline in its stock price. This example underscores the interconnectedness of legal, regulatory, and reputational risks and the importance of maintaining strong ethical standards and compliance practices.

Managing Legal and Regulatory Risk

Given the complex and evolving nature of legal and regulatory requirements, managing legal and regulatory risk requires a proactive and comprehensive approach. Key strategies for managing this type of risk include:

- **Developing a Robust Compliance Program:** A strong compliance program is essential for managing legal and regulatory risk. This program should include clear policies and procedures for ensuring compliance with all relevant laws and regulations, as well as regular training for employees on compliance issues. The program should also include mechanisms for monitoring compliance, such as internal audits and compliance assessments, and processes for reporting and addressing potential compliance violations.
- **Staying Informed of Regulatory Changes:** Companies must stay informed of changes in laws and regulations that could impact their operations. This requires continuous monitoring of regulatory developments, engaging with industry associations, and maintaining relationships with legal advisors and regulatory experts. By staying ahead of regulatory changes, companies can anticipate potential risks and make the necessary adjustments to their operations and strategies.
- **Implementing Strong Contract Management Practices:** Effective contract management is critical for reducing contractual risk. This involves carefully reviewing and negotiating contract terms to ensure that they are clear, fair, and enforceable. Companies should also maintain detailed records of all contractual agreements and

establish procedures for monitoring contract performance and addressing any potential breaches.

- **Investing in Legal Expertise:** Companies should invest in legal expertise to manage legal risks effectively. This may involve building an in-house legal team, retaining external legal counsel, or both. Legal experts can provide valuable guidance on navigating complex legal and regulatory environments, handling disputes, and mitigating litigation risks.
- **Enhancing Reputational Management:** Managing reputational risk requires a proactive approach to public relations, stakeholder communication, and corporate governance. Companies should establish a crisis management plan to address potential reputational threats and ensure that they respond quickly and transparently to any legal or regulatory issues that arise.
- **Engaging with Regulators:** Building a positive relationship with regulators can help companies manage regulatory risk more effectively. Companies should engage with regulators to understand their expectations, seek guidance on compliance issues, and demonstrate their commitment to operating within the law. This proactive engagement can also provide opportunities for companies to influence regulatory developments and advocate for favorable regulatory outcomes.
- **Conducting Regular Risk Assessments:** Regular risk assessments are crucial for identifying potential legal and regulatory risks and evaluating their impact on the organization. These assessments should be integrated into the company's broader risk management framework and should involve input from legal, compliance, and operational teams.

Conclusion

Legal and regulatory risk is an ever-present challenge for companies operating in today's complex and dynamic business environment. The consequences of non-compliance can be severe, ranging from financial penalties and legal disputes to operational disruptions and reputational damage. To effectively manage legal and regulatory risk, companies must adopt a proactive approach that includes robust compliance programs, continuous monitoring of regulatory developments, effective contract management, and strong legal expertise. By doing so, organizations can protect themselves from the uncertainties of the legal and regulatory landscape, maintain their operational integrity, and safeguard their reputation in the marketplace.

Practical Example

A pharmaceutical company launches a new drug but fails to comply with regulatory requirements set by the Food and Drug Administration (FDA). If the drug has undisclosed harmful side effects, the company could face lawsuits, fines, and a mandatory recall of the product, leading to substantial financial losses and damage to its reputation.

Exercise 5

Consider a multinational corporation expanding into a new market with stringent regulations.

- What steps should the company take to ensure compliance with local laws and regulations?
- Discuss the role of a legal compliance team in managing regulatory risk.

Strategic Risk and Business Model Risk

What is it

Strategic risk refers to the potential adverse effects on a company's long-term goals and overall business strategy due to changes in the market environment, competitive dynamics, or internal weaknesses. These risks can arise from various factors, such as shifts in consumer preferences, technological advancements, regulatory changes, or failures in strategic execution. Strategic risk directly impacts a company's ability to achieve its objectives and maintain its competitive position in the market.

Business model risk, a specific subset of strategic risk, involves the risk that a company's business model—its core way of generating revenue and delivering value to customers—may become obsolete or fail to perform as expected. Business model risk can arise due to disruptive innovations, changes in industry standards, or shifts in customer behavior that render the existing business model less effective or irrelevant. Companies that fail to recognize and adapt to these risks may struggle to sustain their revenue streams and competitive advantage over time.

Key Components of Strategic and Business Model Risk

- **Market Environment Changes:** One of the primary drivers of strategic risk is the evolving market environment. Changes in economic conditions, customer preferences, and technological advancements can all significantly impact a company's strategic objectives. For example, a global economic downturn might reduce consumer spending, affecting a company's sales and profitability. Similarly, the emergence of new technologies can disrupt existing markets and create opportunities for competitors to gain an edge.
- **Competitive Landscape Shifts:** The competitive landscape is constantly changing as new entrants join the market, existing competitors innovate, and industry dynamics evolve. Strategic risk arises when a company fails to anticipate or respond effectively to these shifts. For instance, a company that maintains a traditional brick-and-mortar retail model might face strategic risk as online retailers capture market share through more convenient and cost-effective shopping experiences.

- **Internal Weaknesses:** Internal weaknesses, such as poor management decisions, lack of innovation, or inadequate resource allocation, can also contribute to strategic risk. These weaknesses may hinder a company's ability to execute its strategy effectively or adapt to changes in the external environment. For example, a company with a rigid organizational structure may struggle to innovate or respond quickly to market changes, putting its strategic objectives at risk.
- **Technological Disruption:** Technological disruption is a significant source of both strategic and business model risk. Companies that fail to keep pace with technological advancements may find their products or services becoming outdated or irrelevant. For example, the rise of digital streaming services has significantly disrupted traditional media and entertainment companies that relied on physical media sales or cable subscriptions. Companies that fail to embrace digital transformation may face declining revenues and market share.
- **Regulatory and Policy Changes:** Changes in regulations and government policies can introduce strategic risk by altering the business environment in which a company operates. For instance, new environmental regulations might require a company to invest in cleaner technologies, increasing operational costs. Alternatively, changes in trade policies or tariffs can affect supply chains and market access, impacting a company's ability to compete globally.
- **Disruptive Business Models:** Disruptive business models introduced by new entrants or competitors can pose a significant risk to established companies. A disruptive business model often offers a new way of delivering value to customers that is more efficient, cost-effective, or aligned with changing consumer preferences. For example, the rise of ride-sharing platforms like Uber and Lyft disrupted the traditional taxi industry by offering a more convenient and affordable alternative. Established companies that fail to adapt to such disruptions risk losing market share and relevance.

- **Strategic Execution Failures:** Even a well-conceived strategy can fail if not executed effectively. Strategic execution failures occur when a company is unable to implement its strategy as planned due to issues such as poor communication, lack of alignment among departments, or insufficient resources. These failures can lead to missed opportunities, operational inefficiencies, and ultimately, failure to achieve strategic goals.

Practical Examples of Strategic and Business Model Risk

- **Retail Industry Example:** A traditional department store chain faces strategic risk as e-commerce continues to grow and consumer preferences shift toward online shopping. The company's existing business model, which relies heavily on physical store sales, becomes less effective as more customers choose to shop online for convenience and better pricing. To address this risk, the company must adapt its strategy by investing in e-commerce capabilities, optimizing its supply chain for online fulfillment, and reconsidering its brick-and-mortar footprint. Failure to do so could result in declining sales, reduced market share, and potential obsolescence.
- **Technology Industry Example:** A leading software company that has historically dominated the market with its on-premises software solutions faces business model risk as cloud computing gains popularity. Customers are increasingly adopting cloud-based solutions for their flexibility, scalability, and lower upfront costs. The company's traditional licensing model, which relies on large, upfront payments for software installations, becomes less attractive in comparison to subscription-based cloud services. To mitigate this risk, the company must pivot to a cloud-first strategy, developing and offering cloud-based versions of its software products and transitioning to a subscription revenue model.
- **Automotive Industry Example:** An established automaker that has built its business model around internal combustion engine (ICE) vehicles faces both strategic and business model risk as

the industry shifts toward electric vehicles (EVs). Regulatory pressures to reduce carbon emissions, coupled with growing consumer demand for environmentally friendly vehicles, threaten the company's traditional product lineup. To remain competitive, the automaker must invest heavily in EV technology, develop new supply chains for battery components, and reposition its brand to appeal to environmentally conscious consumers. Failing to do so could result in lost market share to competitors that have successfully transitioned to EVs.

- **Media Industry Example:** A traditional print newspaper company encounters strategic risk as digital news platforms and social media become the primary sources of news consumption. The company's business model, which relies on print subscriptions and advertising revenue, becomes increasingly unsustainable as readership declines and advertisers shift their budgets to digital platforms. To survive, the newspaper must develop a digital strategy that includes online subscriptions, digital advertising, and multimedia content. If the company fails to adapt, it risks becoming irrelevant in the rapidly changing media landscape.

Managing Strategic and Business Model Risk

Managing strategic and business model risk requires a forward-looking approach that includes continuous monitoring of market trends, proactive innovation, and the ability to pivot when necessary. Key strategies for managing these risks include:

- **Strategic Planning and Scenario Analysis:** Effective strategic planning involves assessing potential risks to the business strategy and conducting scenario analysis to explore how different market conditions or competitive developments might impact the company. By considering various scenarios, companies can develop contingency plans and identify strategic pivots that may be necessary to address emerging risks.

- **Market Research and Customer Insights:** Regular market research and deep understanding of customer needs and preferences are essential for managing strategic risk. By staying attuned to shifts in consumer behavior, companies can anticipate changes in demand and adjust their business models accordingly. For example, a company might conduct customer surveys, analyze purchasing trends, and monitor competitor activity to identify early signs of market shifts.
- **Innovation and R&D Investment:** Investing in research and development (R&D) and fostering a culture of innovation are critical for mitigating business model risk. Companies must continuously explore new technologies, products, and business models to stay ahead of industry disruptions. For example, a company in a rapidly changing industry like technology might establish innovation labs, partner with startups, or invest in emerging technologies to remain competitive.
- **Agile and Flexible Business Models:** Developing agile and flexible business models allows companies to adapt more quickly to changes in the market environment. This might involve diversifying revenue streams, adopting a modular approach to product development, or creating scalable business processes that can be adjusted as market conditions evolve. For instance, a company might develop multiple revenue models, such as subscription services, licensing, and direct sales, to reduce reliance on any single source of income.
- **Diversification:** Diversification is a key strategy for managing both strategic and business model risk. By diversifying their product lines, customer base, and geographic presence, companies can reduce their exposure to risks associated with any single market or industry. For example, a consumer goods company might expand into new international markets or develop products that appeal to different customer segments to mitigate the risk of declining demand in its core market.
- **Leadership and Organizational Alignment:** Strong leadership and organizational alignment are essential for executing strategic

initiatives and managing strategic risk. Companies must ensure that their leadership teams are capable of making informed decisions, communicating the strategic vision clearly, and aligning the organization's resources and efforts toward achieving strategic goals. Regular communication, performance monitoring, and cross-functional collaboration are critical to successful strategy execution.

- **Regular Strategic Reviews:** Conducting regular strategic reviews allows companies to assess the effectiveness of their current strategies and identify emerging risks. These reviews should include evaluations of market conditions, competitive dynamics, and internal performance metrics. Based on the findings, companies can make informed adjustments to their strategies and business models to better align with changing circumstances.

Conclusion

Strategic risk and business model risk are critical challenges that every company must navigate to achieve long-term success. As markets evolve, consumer preferences shift, and new technologies emerge, companies must remain vigilant and adaptable to mitigate these risks. By continuously monitoring the external environment, fostering innovation, and maintaining flexibility in their strategies and business models, organizations can protect themselves against the adverse effects of strategic risk and position themselves for sustained growth and competitive advantage. Failing to address these risks can lead to obsolescence, lost market share, and ultimately, the decline of the business. Effective management of strategic and business model risk is therefore essential for any company seeking to thrive in today's dynamic and competitive landscape.

Practical Example

A traditional brick-and-mortar retailer faces strategic risk as consumer preferences shift toward online shopping. If the company fails to adapt its business model to incorporate e-commerce, it risks losing market share to competitors who have successfully integrated online sales channels.

Exercise 6

- Evaluate the strategic risks faced by a hypothetical company in the technology industry. Consider factors such as market competition, technological advancements, and changing consumer preferences.
- Propose strategies the company can implement to mitigate these risks and adapt its business model.

Chapter

03

Risk Management Frameworks and Standards

In this chapter, we delve into the essential frameworks and standards that guide risk management practices across organizations. These frameworks provide the structure and guidelines necessary for effectively identifying, assessing, and mitigating risks, ensuring that businesses can achieve their strategic objectives while maintaining long-term stability.

Basel Accords and Regulatory Frameworks

The Basel Accords are a series of international banking regulations developed by the Basel Committee on Banking Supervision (BCBS) to promote stability and reduce risk within the global banking system. These accords provide a standardized approach for managing credit, market, and operational risks, with a strong emphasis on maintaining adequate capital reserves. The evolution of the Basel Accords from Basel I to Basel III reflects the growing complexity of financial markets and the lessons learned from past financial crises.

Basel I: The Foundation of Modern Banking Regulation

Introduced in 1988, Basel I was the first set of regulations that established a formal framework for managing credit risk in the banking sector. The key contribution of Basel I was the introduction of the concept of Risk-Weighted Assets (RWA), which provided a standardized method for calculating the minimum capital requirement that banks must hold relative to the risks associated with their asset portfolios.

Risk-Weighted Assets (RWA)

Risk-Weighted Assets are calculated by assigning different risk weights to various types of assets held by a bank. The riskier the asset, the higher the risk weight. The total RWA is used to determine the minimum amount of capital that a bank must hold to protect against potential losses.

Formula

Capital Adequacy Ratio (CAR) = Tier 1 Capital + Tier 2 Capital / Risk -Weighted Assets × 100

Example Calculation

Let's consider a bank with the following balance sheet items:

- Tier 1 Capital: $200 million

- Tier 2 Capital: $50 million
- Risk-Weighted Assets (RWA): $2.5 billion

Step 1: Calculate the Capital Adequacy Ratio (CAR)

- CAR = $200 million + $50 million / $2.5 billion × 100
- CAR = $250 million / $2.5 billion × 100 = 10%

Answer and Explanation

- The Capital Adequacy Ratio (CAR) for the bank is 10%, which is above the minimum requirement of 8% set by Basel I. This indicates that the bank has sufficient capital to cover its risk-weighted assets.

Basel II: Expanding the Scope of Risk Management

Basel II, introduced in 2004, expanded on the foundation laid by Basel I by incorporating market and operational risks into the regulatory framework. Basel II introduced the concept of the "Three Pillars," which provided a more comprehensive approach to risk management.

Three Pillars of Basel II

- Pillar 1: Minimum Capital Requirements – Banks must hold a minimum amount of capital to cover credit, market, and operational risks.
- Pillar 2: Supervisory Review Process – Regulatory authorities assess the internal risk management processes of banks to ensure they are adequate.
- Pillar 3: Market Discipline – Banks are required to disclose their risk management practices and capital adequacy, promoting transparency and allowing market participants to assess the risk profile of banks.

Example of Operational Risk under Pillar 1

Operational risk refers to the risk of loss resulting from inadequate or failed internal processes, people, systems, or external events. Under Basel II, banks are required to hold capital against operational risks.

Formula for Operational Risk Capital Charge

One method to calculate the capital charge for operational risk is the Basic Indicator Approach (BIA): Operational Risk Capital Charge = $\alpha \times$ Gross Income

where α is a fixed percentage (usually 15%)

Example Calculation

Assume a bank has an annual gross income of $500 million.

Step 1: Calculate the Operational Risk Capital Charge

- Operational Risk Capital Charge = 0.15 × $500 million = $75 million

Answer and Explanation

- The bank is required to hold $75 million in capital to cover potential operational risks.
- This calculation shows how Basel II expands risk management beyond credit risk to include operational risks, ensuring a more holistic approach to risk management.

Basel III: Strengthening the Global Banking System

In response to the 2007-2008 global financial crisis, Basel III was introduced to address the weaknesses in the regulatory framework highlighted by the crisis. Basel III focused on improving the quality of capital held by banks, increasing capital requirements, introducing liquidity standards, and reducing leverage in the banking system.

Key Components of Basel III

- **Capital Adequacy Ratio (CAR):** Basel III raised the minimum CAR and introduced stricter definitions for Tier 1 and Tier 2 capital.
- **Leverage Ratio:** Basel III introduced a leverage ratio to prevent excessive borrowing by banks.
- **Liquidity Coverage Ratio (LCR):** Basel III introduced the LCR to ensure that banks maintain a sufficient level of high-quality liquid assets (HQLA) to withstand a 30-day liquidity stress scenario.

Formulae for Basel III

- **Capital Adequacy Ratio (CAR):**

CAR = Tier 1 Capital + Tier 2 Capital / Risk-Weighted Assets × 100

- **Leverage Ratio:**

Leverage Ratio = Tier 1 Capital / Total Exposure × 100

- **Liquidity Coverage Ratio (LCR):**

LCR = High-Quality Liquid Assets (HQLA) / Total Net Cash Outflows over 30 Days × 100

Example Calculation

Let's consider a bank with the following financial details:

- Tier 1 Capital: $300 million
- Tier 2 Capital: $100 million
- Risk-Weighted Assets (RWA): $3 billion
- Total Exposure (including off-balance-sheet exposures): $10 billion
- High-Quality Liquid Assets (HQLA): $1 billion
- Total Net Cash Outflows over 30 Days: $800 million

Step 1: Calculate the Capital Adequacy Ratio (CAR)

- CAR = $300 million + $100 million / $3 billion × 100
- CAR = $400 million / $3 billion × 100 = 13.33%

Step 2: Calculate the Leverage Ratio

- Leverage Ratio = $300 million / $10 billion × 100 = 3%

Step 3: Calculate the Liquidity Coverage Ratio (LCR)

- LCR = $1 billion / $800 million × 100 = 125%

Answer and Explanation

- The Capital Adequacy Ratio (CAR) of 13.33% is well above the minimum requirement, indicating that the bank has sufficient capital to cover its risk-weighted assets.
- The Leverage Ratio of 3% meets the Basel III requirement, preventing excessive borrowing relative to the bank's capital.
- The Liquidity Coverage Ratio (LCR) of 125% exceeds the 100% minimum, ensuring that the bank has enough liquid assets to handle a 30-day liquidity stress scenario.
- These calculations demonstrate how Basel III strengthens the resilience of banks by requiring them to hold higher-quality capital, maintain prudent leverage levels, and ensure adequate liquidity.

Enterprise Risk Management (ERM)

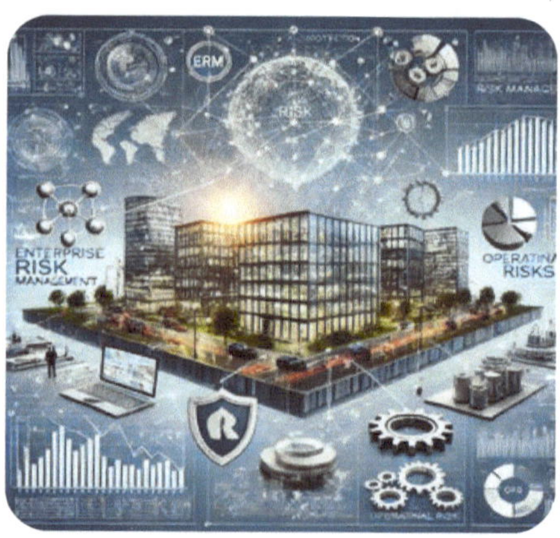

Enterprise Risk Management (ERM) is a comprehensive and integrated approach to identifying, assessing, managing, and monitoring risks across an entire organization. Unlike traditional risk management practices that often focus on specific types of risks in isolation, ERM provides a holistic view, allowing organizations to understand and address the full spectrum of risks they face. By integrating risk management into strategic planning and day-to-day operations, ERM helps organizations align their risk management efforts with their overall business objectives, ensuring long-term sustainability and resilience.

Key Components of ERM

Risk Identification

Risk identification is the process of systematically identifying potential risks that could impact an organization's ability to achieve its objectives. This includes recognizing risks across all areas of the organization, such as strategic, financial, operational, compliance, and reputational risks.

Example: A retail company identifies the following risks:

- **Strategic Risk:** Competitors launching similar products at a lower price point.
- **Financial Risk:** Currency fluctuations affecting the cost of imported goods.
- **Operational Risk:** Disruptions in the supply chain due to supplier bankruptcies.
- **Compliance Risk:** Non-compliance with data protection regulations.
- **Reputational Risk:** Negative publicity from product recalls.

Exercise

For each risk identified above, determine the potential sources and the areas of the organization that could be affected.

Risk Assessment

Risk assessment involves evaluating the likelihood and potential impact of identified risks. The goal is to prioritize risks based on their significance to the organization, allowing for effective allocation of resources to manage them.

Quantitative Risk Assessment

Risks can be assessed quantitatively by assigning probabilities and potential financial impacts to each risk. The product of these values gives an Expected Loss (EL) that helps in prioritizing risks.

Formula

Expected Loss (EL) = Probability of Risk Occurrence × Impact of Risk

Example Calculation

Assume a manufacturing company faces the following risks:

- Supply chain disruption with a 20% probability, leading to an estimated loss of $1 million.
- Regulatory fines with a 10% probability, leading to an estimated loss of $500,000.
- Currency fluctuation with a 30% probability, leading to an estimated loss of $700,000.

Step 1: Calculate the Expected Loss for each risk.

- Supply Chain Disruption EL: 0.20 × $1,000,000 = $200,000
- Regulatory Fines EL: 0.10 × $500,000 = $50,000
- Currency Fluctuation EL: 0.30 × $700,000 = $210,000

Step 2: Prioritize the risks based on Expected Loss

- Currency Fluctuation: $210,000
- Supply Chain Disruption: $200,000
- Regulatory Fines: $50,000

Answer and Explanation

The company should prioritize managing currency fluctuation risk and supply chain disruption risk, as they represent the highest expected losses.

Risk Mitigation

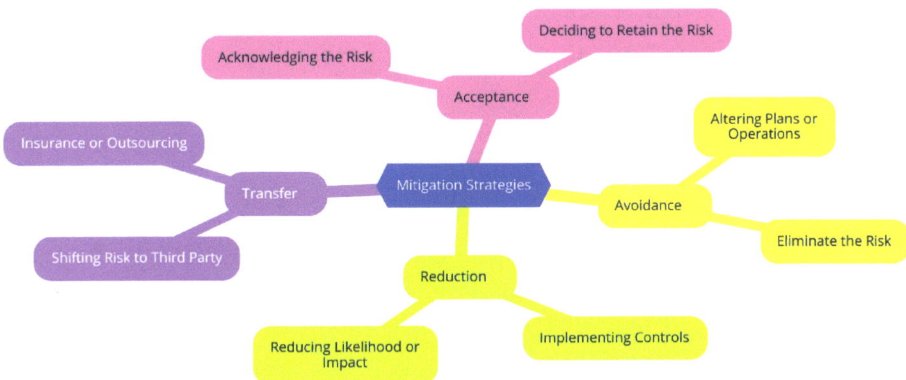

Risk mitigation involves developing strategies and implementing actions to reduce the likelihood or impact of risks. Mitigation strategies can include risk avoidance, reduction, transfer (e.g., insurance), and acceptance.

Mitigation Strategies

- **Avoidance:** Altering plans or operations to eliminate the risk.
- **Reduction:** Implementing controls or processes to reduce the risk's likelihood or impact.
- **Transfer:** Shifting the risk to a third party, such as through insurance or outsourcing.
- **Acceptance:** Acknowledging the risk and deciding to retain it without taking specific actions to mitigate it.

Practical Example

A company concerned about supply chain disruptions might:

- Diversify suppliers to reduce reliance on a single source (Reduction).

- Invest in inventory management technology to better forecast demand and manage stock levels (Reduction).
- Purchase business interruption insurance to cover losses from supply chain disruptions (Transfer).

Exercise

Develop a risk mitigation plan for a retail company facing the risk of data breaches. Consider strategies for reducing the likelihood and impact of a data breach.

Risk Monitoring

Risk monitoring is the continuous process of tracking identified risks, reassessing their impact, and evaluating the effectiveness of mitigation strategies. This ensures that risk management remains dynamic and responsive to changes in the organization's environment.

Key Activities

- Regular risk assessments to identify new or emerging risks.
- Monitoring key risk indicators (KRIs) to detect early signs of risk.
- Reviewing and updating risk mitigation plans as necessary.

Example

A financial institution monitors key risk indicators such as market volatility, changes in interest rates, and credit default rates to manage its portfolio risk. If a significant change is detected in any of these indicators, the institution reviews its risk exposure and adjusts its mitigation strategies accordingly.

Exercise

- Identify three key risk indicators for a hypothetical technology company that is heavily reliant on cloud-based services.
- Explain how these indicators can help in monitoring the company's risk profile.

Risk Reporting

Risk reporting involves communicating identified risks, risk assessments, and the effectiveness of risk management activities to stakeholders, including senior management, the board of directors, and external stakeholders.

Importance of Risk Reporting

- Ensures transparency and accountability in risk management practices.
- Facilitates informed decision-making by providing stakeholders with accurate and timely information about risks.
- Supports regulatory compliance by documenting the organization's risk management processes.

Example

A multinational corporation prepares a quarterly risk management report for its board of directors. The report includes a summary of key risks, changes in the risk environment, the status of risk mitigation efforts, and recommendations for further action. The board uses this information to guide strategic decisions and resource allocation.

Exercise

Create a risk reporting template for a hypothetical healthcare company. The template should include sections for risk identification, assessment, mitigation strategies, monitoring updates, and recommendations.

Healthcare Company	
Executive Summary	**Overview of Report**: Briefly summarize the key risks identified, their potential impact, and the overall risk status of the organization. **Objective**: Outline the purpose of the report and the specific time period covered.

Risk Identification	**Risk ID**: Unique identifier for each risk. **Risk Description**: Detailed description of each identified risk. **Category**: (e.g., Operational, Financial, Compliance, Strategic) **Source of Risk**: (e.g., External factors, Internal processes) **Date Identified**: When the risk was first identified. **Owner**: Person or team responsible for managing the risk.
Risk Assessment	**Likelihood:** Assessment of the probability that the risk will occur **Impact**: Potential impact on the organization if the risk materializes **Risk Level**: Combination of likelihood and impact to determine overall risk level **Vulnerability**: Areas where the organization is particularly susceptible to this risk.
Mitigation Strategies	**Mitigation Plan**: Detailed description of actions planned or taken. **Strategy Type**: (e.g., Avoidance, Reduction, Transfer, Acceptance) **Implementation Timeline**: Timeframe for executing the mitigation plan. **Current Status**: Status of the mitigation efforts **Resources Required:** Any resources needed to implement the mitigation.

Monitoring Updates	**Monitoring Frequency**: How often the risk and mitigation efforts are reviewed **Latest Update**: Summary of the most recent monitoring activities and findings. **Changes in Risk Profile**: Any changes in the likelihood or impact since the last report. **Effectiveness of Mitigation**: Evaluation of how effective the mitigation strategies have been so far.
Recommendations	**Further Actions:** Additional actions recommended based on the current risk assessment and monitoring updates. **Resource Allocation**: Suggestions for allocating resources to address any new or emerging risks. **Strategic Adjustments**: Recommendations for any strategic changes needed to manage the risks effectively. **Next Steps**: Outline of immediate next steps, including timelines and responsible parties.
Appendix	**Supporting Documents**: Any additional documentation, such as detailed risk matrices, charts, or process diagrams. **Glossary:** Definitions of key terms used in the report.

ERM Frameworks

COSO ERM Framework

The COSO ERM Framework, developed by the Committee of Sponsoring Organizations of the Treadway Commission (COSO), is widely recognized as a leading standard for risk management. It emphasizes the integration of risk management with corporate governance and strategic planning, helping organizations align their risk management efforts with their overall business objectives.

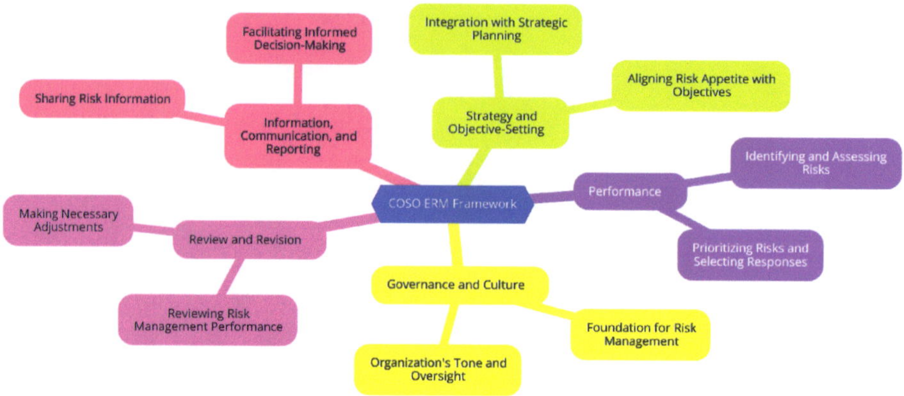

Key Components

- **Governance and Culture:** Establishing the foundation for effective risk management by setting the organization's tone, reinforcing the importance of risk management, and establishing oversight responsibilities.
- **Strategy and Objective-Setting:** Ensuring that risk management is integrated into the strategic planning process, aligning the organization's risk appetite with its objectives.
- **Performance:** Identifying and assessing risks that could affect the achievement of objectives, prioritizing risks, and selecting risk responses.
- **Review and Revision:** Reviewing risk management performance and making necessary adjustments to improve the effectiveness of the risk management process.
- **Information, Communication, and Reporting**: Sharing risk information across the organization to facilitate informed decision-making and accountability.

Example

A global consumer goods company uses the COSO ERM Framework to align its risk management practices with its strategic goals of market expansion and innovation. By embedding risk management into its strategic planning process, the company identifies potential risks related to entering new markets, assesses their impact, and develops mitigation strategies such as local partnerships and market research.

Exercise

- Using the COSO ERM Framework, identify and assess the top five risks facing a hypothetical retail company expanding into international markets.
- Develop a risk mitigation plan for one of the identified risks.

ISO 31000: A Global Standard

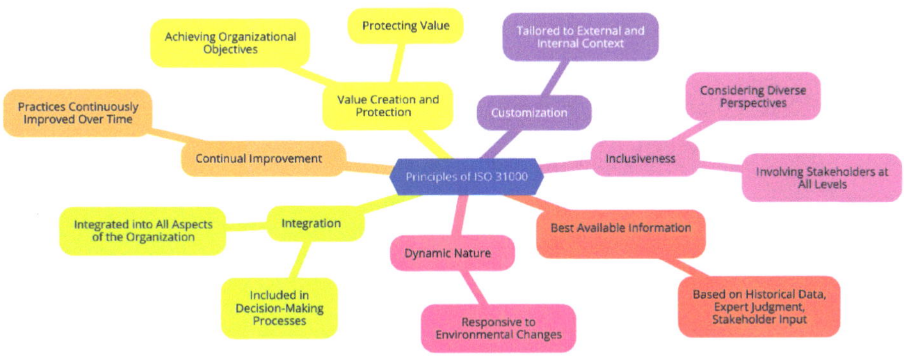

ISO 31000 is an international standard that provides guidelines for implementing risk management within an organization. It offers a structured approach to managing risks by establishing principles, frameworks, and processes that can be applied to any organization, regardless of its size, industry, or geographic location.

Principles of ISO 31000

- **Value Creation and Protection:** Risk management should contribute to the achievement of organizational objectives and the protection of value.
- **Integration:** Risk management should be integrated into all aspects of the organization, including decision-making processes.

- **Customization:** Risk management practices should be tailored to the organization's external and internal context.
- **Inclusiveness:** Risk management should involve stakeholders at all levels to ensure that diverse perspectives are considered.
- **Dynamic Nature:** Risk management should be responsive to changes in the organization's environment.
- **Best Available Information:** Decisions should be based on the best available information, including historical data, expert judgment, and stakeholder input.
- **Continual Improvement:** Risk management practices should be continually improved over time.

Example

A technology company adopts ISO 31000 to enhance its risk management practices, focusing on cybersecurity, data privacy, and compliance with international regulations. The company establishes a risk management framework that aligns with ISO 31000 principles, ensuring that risks are identified, assessed, and managed in a systematic and consistent manner.

Exercise

Develop a risk management plan for a hypothetical financial services company using the ISO 31000 framework. The plan should include risk identification, assessment, mitigation strategies, and monitoring activities.

Practical Examples

Implementing ERM in a Manufacturing Company

Scenario

A manufacturing company faces several risks related to supply chain disruptions, regulatory changes, and market competition. The company decides to implement an ERM framework to manage these risks and align risk management with its strategic objectives.

Step 1: Risk Identification

- **Supply Chain Disruption:** Risk of supplier bankruptcy leading to production delays.
- **Regulatory Changes:** Risk of new environmental regulations increasing production costs.
- **Market Competition:** Risk of losing market share to competitors offering lower prices.

Step 2: Risk Assessment

- **Supply Chain Disruption:** Probability: 30%, Impact: $2 million.
- **Regulatory Changes:** Probability: 20%, Impact: $1.5 million.
- **Market Competition:** Probability: 40%, Impact: $3 million.

Step 3: Risk Mitigation

- **Supply Chain Disruption:** Diversify suppliers, establish contingency contracts, and maintain safety stock.
- **Regulatory Changes:** Invest in environmentally friendly technologies and engage with regulators to influence policy development.
- **Market Competition:** Enhance product differentiation through innovation and improve cost efficiency.

Step 4: Risk Monitoring

- **Supply Chain Disruption:** Monitor supplier financial health and track lead times.
- **Regulatory Changes:** Stay informed about upcoming regulations and participate in industry forums.
- **Market Competition:** Track competitor pricing strategies and market trends.

Step 5: Risk Reporting

- **Risk Reporting:** The company prepares a quarterly risk management report for senior management, outlining the top risks, mitigation efforts, and any changes in the risk environment.

Answer and Explanation

- By implementing an ERM framework, the manufacturing company systematically identifies, assesses, and mitigates its key risks, ensuring that it remains resilient in the face of challenges.
- The company's ability to monitor risks and report on them regularly also supports informed decision-making and helps align risk management with its overall strategic goals.

Exercise 2: ERM for a Hypothetical Retail Company

Scenario

A retail company is planning to expand its operations into international markets. The company uses the COSO ERM Framework to identify and assess the top five risks it might face.

Step 1: Risk Identification

- **Currency Fluctuations:** Risk of exchange rate volatility affecting profit margins.
- **Regulatory Compliance:** Risk of non-compliance with foreign regulations.
- **Supply Chain Disruptions:** Risk of delays in international shipping.
- **Market Competition:** Risk of local competitors offering similar products at lower prices.
- **Cultural Differences:** Risk of product offerings not aligning with local consumer preferences.

Step 2: Risk Assessment

- **Currency Fluctuations:** Probability: 25%, Impact: $1 million.
- **Regulatory Compliance:** Probability: 20%, Impact: $500,000.
- **Supply Chain Disruptions:** Probability: 30%, Impact: $800,000.
- **Market Competition: Probability:** 35%, Impact: $1.2 million.
- **Cultural Differences: Probability:** 20%, Impact: $600,000.

Step 3: Risk Mitigation Plan for Currency Fluctuations

- **Hedging:** Use financial instruments such as forward contracts or options to hedge against currency risk.
- **Diversification:** Spread operations across multiple countries to reduce exposure to any single currency.
- **Pricing Strategies:** Adjust pricing in international markets to account for potential exchange rate fluctuations.

Answer and Explanation

By identifying and assessing the top five risks, the retail company can prioritize its risk management efforts and allocate resources effectively. The mitigation plan for currency fluctuations provides specific strategies to manage this risk, ensuring that the company's profit margins are protected as it expands into new markets.

Conclusion

Enterprise Risk Management (ERM) offers a comprehensive framework for identifying, assessing, mitigating, monitoring, and reporting risks across an organization. By integrating ERM into their strategic planning and daily operations, companies can better align their risk management practices with their overall business objectives, ensuring long-term success and resilience. Through practical examples, calculations, and exercises, this chapter has provided insights into how organizations can implement and benefit from ERM, making it a vital tool for navigating the complexities of the global business environment.

ISO 31000 Risk Management Standard

ISO 31000 is an internationally recognized standard that provides guidelines for effective risk management practices. It is designed to help organizations develop a systematic, structured, and comprehensive approach to managing risks, ensuring that risk management is embedded in all aspects of the organization. The goal of ISO 31000 is to enhance an organization's ability to achieve its objectives by identifying and managing risks in a way that is integrated with its overall strategy and operations.

Key Principles of ISO 31000

ISO 31000 is built on a set of core principles that guide organizations in developing effective risk management practices:

Integrated

Risk management should be an integral part of all organizational processes, including strategic planning, decision-making, and daily operations.

Example: A manufacturing company integrates risk management into its product development process by conducting risk assessments at each stage of the product lifecycle, from design to production to market launch.

Structured and Comprehensive

The risk management approach should be systematic, structured, and comprehensive, ensuring that all relevant risks are identified, assessed, and managed effectively.

Example: A financial institution implements a structured risk assessment process that includes quantitative models for assessing credit risk, market risk, and operational risk, ensuring a comprehensive evaluation of its risk profile.

Customized

Risk management practices should be tailored to the organization's specific external and internal context, including its size, industry, and risk appetite.

Example: A small technology startup tailors its risk management approach to focus on cybersecurity risks and intellectual property protection, which are critical to its business model.

Inclusive

All relevant stakeholders should be involved in the risk management process to ensure diverse perspectives and comprehensive risk identification.

Example: A healthcare company involves its clinical staff, IT department, legal team, and senior management in its risk management process to address risks related to patient safety, data privacy, regulatory compliance, and financial performance.

Dynamic

Risk management should be responsive to changes in the internal and external environment, allowing the organization to adapt to emerging risks and opportunities.

Example: A retail company continuously monitors changes in consumer behavior and adjusts its risk management strategies to address risks associated with evolving market trends and economic conditions.

Best Available Information

Risk management decisions should be based on the best available information, including historical data, expert judgment, and stakeholder input.

Example: A pharmaceutical company uses clinical trial data, market research, and expert opinions to assess the risks associated with launching a new drug, ensuring that decisions are informed by the most reliable and relevant information.

Human and Cultural Factors

Risk management should consider human behavior and cultural factors, recognizing that these elements can significantly influence risk perceptions and responses.

Example: A global corporation tailors its risk management approach to account for cultural differences in risk tolerance and decision-making practices across its international offices.

Continuous Improvement

Risk management processes should be continually improved over time, incorporating lessons learned from past experiences and adapting to changes in the organization's environment.

Example: A construction company regularly reviews and updates its risk management practices based on feedback from project teams, incident reports, and industry developments, ensuring that its approach remains effective and relevant.

ISO 31000 Process

ISO 31000 outlines a structured process for managing risks that includes the following key steps:

Establishing the Context

Establishing the context involves understanding the organization's internal and external environment, including its objectives, stakeholders, and the factors that influence its risk profile.

Steps

- Define the organization's objectives and risk appetite.
- Identify internal and external factors that could impact the organization's ability to achieve its objectives.
- Establish the criteria for evaluating risks, including the likelihood and impact of different risk events.

Example

A technology company establishes the context for its risk management process by identifying its key objectives (e.g., market expansion, product innovation) and the internal and external factors that could influence these objectives (e.g., cybersecurity threats, regulatory changes).

Risk Assessment

Risk assessment is the process of identifying, analyzing, and evaluating risks to determine their potential impact on the organization and prioritize them based on their significance.

Steps

- **Risk Identification:** Identify potential risks that could impact the organization's objectives.
- **Risk Analysis:** Analyze the likelihood and impact of each identified risk.
- **Risk Evaluation:** Evaluate and prioritize risks based on their potential impact and the organization's risk appetite.

Quantitative Risk Assessment Example

A financial services company conducts a risk assessment to identify and evaluate cybersecurity risks. The company uses historical data on cyber incidents and expert judgment to assess the likelihood and impact of various threats.

Formula for Risk Calculation

- Risk Level = Probability of Risk Occurrence × Impact of Risk

Calculation Example

- Cybersecurity Threat: Probability: 25%, Impact: $2 million

Risk Level = 0.25 × $2,000,000 = $500,000

- Data Privacy Breach: Probability: 15%, Impact: $3 million

Risk Level = 0.15 × $3,000,000 = $450,000

Answer and Explanation

The risk level for a cybersecurity threat is $500,000, while the risk level for a data privacy breach is $450,000. The company should prioritize addressing the cybersecurity threat due to its higher risk level.

Risk Treatment

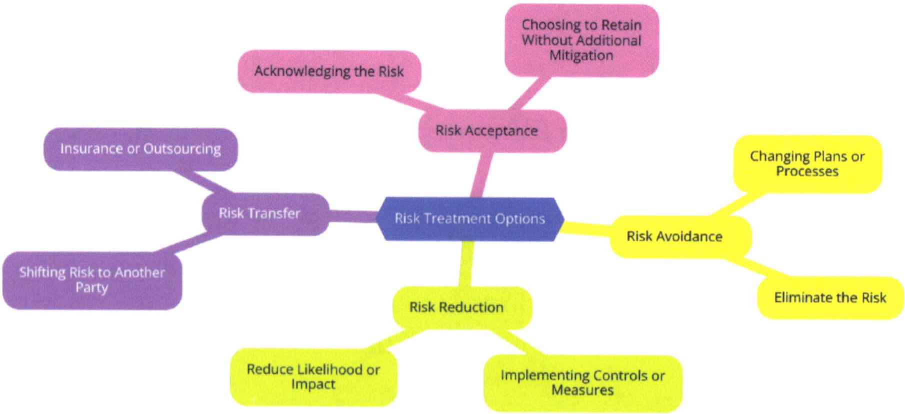

Risk treatment involves selecting and implementing strategies to mitigate, transfer, avoid, or accept risks based on their assessed level of impact and the organization's risk appetite.

Risk Treatment Options

- **Risk Avoidance:** Changing plans or processes to eliminate the risk.
- **Risk Reduction:** Implementing controls or measures to reduce the likelihood or impact of the risk.
- **Risk Transfer:** Shifting the risk to another party, such as through insurance or outsourcing.
- **Risk Acceptance:** Acknowledging the risk and choosing to retain it without additional mitigation efforts.

Example

A technology company facing a high risk of data breaches decides to implement the following risk treatment strategies:

- **Risk Reduction:** Invest in advanced cybersecurity tools and employee training to reduce the likelihood of data breaches.
- **Risk Transfer:** Purchase cyber liability insurance to transfer the financial impact of a potential breach.
- **Risk Acceptance:** Accept the residual risk of minor data breaches that fall within the company's risk appetite.

Monitoring and Review

Monitoring and review involve continuously tracking the effectiveness of risk management strategies and making necessary adjustments to address changes in the organization's environment.

Key Activities

- Monitor key risk indicators (KRIs) to detect early signs of emerging risks.
- Review the effectiveness of risk treatment strategies and adjust them as needed.
- Conduct regular audits and assessments to ensure that risk management practices remain relevant and effective.

Example

A healthcare company regularly monitors patient safety indicators and reviews its risk management practices to ensure compliance with regulatory standards. The company adjusts its risk treatment strategies based on audit findings and changes in industry regulations.

Communication and Consultation

Communication and consultation involve engaging with stakeholders throughout the risk management process to ensure transparency, gather input, and build support for risk management initiatives.

Key Activities

- Communicate risk management objectives, processes, and outcomes to internal and external stakeholders.
- Consult with stakeholders to gather feedback and incorporate diverse perspectives into the risk management process.
- Foster a risk-aware culture by educating employees and stakeholders about the importance of risk management.

Example

A multinational corporation communicates its risk management policies to employees across all levels of the organization. The company also consults with external experts and regulators to ensure that its risk management practices align with industry best practices and regulatory requirements.

Practical Example: Implementing ISO 31000 in a Financial Services Company

Scenario

A financial services company adopts ISO 31000 to enhance its risk management practices, particularly in the areas of cybersecurity, data privacy, and regulatory compliance.

Step 1: Establishing the Context

- **Objectives:** The company's objectives include protecting customer data, ensuring compliance with financial regulations, and maintaining market trust.
- **Internal Factors:** The company's reliance on digital platforms, employee awareness of cybersecurity, and the robustness of internal controls.
- **External Factors:** Regulatory requirements, cyber threats, and evolving customer expectations.

Step 2: Risk Assessment

- **Cybersecurity Threats:** Probability: 30%, Impact: $4 million.
- **Data Privacy Breach:** Probability: 20%, Impact: $3 million.
- **Regulatory Non-Compliance:** Probability: 15%, Impact: $2.5 million.

Calculation of Risk Levels

- **Cybersecurity Threat**: Risk Level = 0.30 × $4,000,000 = $1,200,000
- **Data Privacy Breach:** Risk Level = 0.20 × $3,000,000 = $600,000
- **Regulatory Non-Compliance:** Risk Level = 0.15 × $2,500,000 = $375,000

Answer and Explanation

The cybersecurity threat has the highest risk level ($1.2 million), followed by the data privacy breach ($600,000) and regulatory non-compliance ($375,000). The company should prioritize addressing the cybersecurity threat.

Step 3: Risk Treatment

- **Cybersecurity Threat:** Implement advanced encryption and intrusion detection systems (Risk Reduction) and purchase cyber insurance (Risk Transfer).

- **Data Privacy Breach:** Strengthen data access controls and conduct regular audits (Risk Reduction).
- **Regulatory Non-Compliance:** Establish a compliance team to monitor regulatory changes and conduct regular compliance training for employees (Risk Reduction).

Step 4: Monitoring and Review

- Regularly monitor cybersecurity alerts and incidents.
- Review and update data privacy policies based on audit findings.
- Track regulatory updates and adjust compliance strategies as needed.

Step 5: Communication and Consultation

- Communicate risk management policies and procedures to all employees.
- Consult with legal and cybersecurity experts to ensure alignment with best practices.
- Engage with regulators to stay informed about upcoming regulatory changes.

Exercise 3: Developing a Risk Management Plan Using ISO 31000

Scenario

A hypothetical technology company is facing significant risks related to cybersecurity, data privacy, and regulatory compliance. Using the ISO 31000 framework, the company needs to develop a comprehensive risk management plan.

Step 1: Establishing the Context

- **Objectives:** Protect intellectual property, ensure compliance with data protection laws, and safeguard customer trust.
- **Internal Factors:** Use of cloud-based services, employee access to sensitive data, and internal security protocols.

- **External Factors:** Cyber threats, data protection regulations, and industry standards.

Step 2: Risk Assessment

- **Cybersecurity Threat:** Probability: 25%, Impact: $2 million.
- **Data Privacy Breach:** Probability: 20%, Impact: $1.5 million.
- **Regulatory Non-Compliance:** Probability: 10%, Impact: $1 million.

Step 3: Risk Treatment

- **Cybersecurity Threat:** Implement multi-factor authentication and continuous monitoring systems (Risk Reduction).
- **Data Privacy Breach:** Conduct regular employee training on data protection and enforce strict data access controls (Risk Reduction).
- **Regulatory Non-Compliance:** Hire a compliance officer to oversee regulatory adherence and conduct regular audits (Risk Reduction).

Step 4: Monitoring and Review

- Continuously monitor cybersecurity threats and update response strategies.
- Review data privacy policies and controls quarterly.
- Stay informed about changes in data protection laws and adjust compliance practices accordingly.

Step 5: Communication and Consultation

- Educate employees on cybersecurity risks and data protection responsibilities.
- Consult with external cybersecurity firms for advanced threat assessments.
- Engage with legal advisors to ensure ongoing compliance with data protection regulations.

Answer and Explanation

By following the ISO 31000 framework, the technology company can develop a structured and comprehensive risk management plan that addresses its most significant risks. The plan includes specific risk treatment strategies, monitoring and review processes, and communication efforts to ensure that risks are effectively managed and aligned with the company's strategic objectives.

Conclusion

ISO 31000 provides a robust framework for organizations to manage risks systematically and comprehensively. By adhering to the key principles and process outlined in the standard, organizations can ensure that their risk management practices are integrated with their overall strategy and operations. Through practical examples, calculations, and exercises, this chapter has demonstrated how ISO 31000 can be applied in various contexts, helping organizations enhance their resilience and achieve their objectives in an increasingly complex and uncertain environment.

Strategic Risk Management (SRM) Frameworks

Strategic Risk Management (SRM) is a critical component of an organization's overall risk management framework, focusing specifically on managing risks that could impact the achievement of strategic objectives. SRM frameworks help organizations identify, assess, prioritize, and mitigate strategic risks, ensuring that they can navigate uncertainties and maintain their competitive edge over the long term. Effective SRM is essential for aligning risk management with the organization's strategic planning process, thereby

safeguarding the company's future and ensuring that its long-term goals are met.

Key Components of Strategic Risk Management (SRM)

Strategic Risk Identification

Strategic risk identification involves systematically identifying risks that could affect the organization's ability to achieve its strategic objectives. These risks can arise from various sources, including market dynamics, competitive threats, technological disruptions, regulatory changes, and shifts in consumer behavior.

Steps

- **Analyze Market Dynamics:** Identify external factors such as economic trends, industry shifts, and changes in customer preferences that could impact the organization's strategic goals.
- **Monitor Competitive Landscape:** Assess potential threats from existing competitors, new entrants, and substitute products or services.
- **Evaluate Technological Disruptions:** Consider the impact of emerging technologies that could render existing products or business models obsolete.
- **Assess Regulatory Environment:** Identify potential regulatory changes that could affect the organization's operations, profitability, or market access.

Example: A pharmaceutical company identifies the following strategic risks

- **Market Change:** A shift in consumer preference toward personalized medicine.
- **Competitive Threat:** Entry of a new competitor with a groundbreaking drug.

- **Technological Disruption:** Advances in biotechnology that could replace traditional drug development methods.

Risk Assessment and Prioritization

Risk assessment and prioritization involve evaluating the likelihood and impact of identified strategic risks and determining their significance to the organization. This process helps prioritize risks based on their potential impact on strategic objectives, enabling the organization to focus its resources on the most critical risks.

Quantitative Risk Assessment

Risks can be assessed quantitatively by assigning probabilities and potential financial impacts to each risk. The product of these values gives an Expected Risk Impact (ERI) that helps in prioritizing risks.

Formula

Expected Risk Impact (ERI) = Probability of Risk Occurrence × Financial Impact of Risk

Calculation Example

Assume the pharmaceutical company has identified the following strategic risks:

- **Market Change:** Probability: 40%, Financial Impact: $10 million.
- **Competitive Threat:** Probability: 30%, Financial Impact: $15 million.
- **Technological Disruption:** Probability: 20%, Financial Impact: $25 million.

Step 1: Calculate the Expected Risk Impact (ERI) for each risk.

- **Market Change ERI:** 0.40 × $10,000,000 = $4,000,000
- **Competitive Threat ERI:** 0.30 × $15,000,000 = $4,500,000
- **Technological Disruption ERI:** 0.20 × $25,000,000 = $5,000,000

Answer and Explanation

The ERI calculations reveal that the technological disruption risk has the highest expected impact ($5 million), followed by the competitive threat ($4.5 million) and market change ($4 million). The company should prioritize its strategic risk management efforts on mitigating the technological disruption risk.

Risk Mitigation Strategies

Risk mitigation involves developing and implementing strategies to reduce the likelihood or impact of strategic risks. These strategies can include actions such as diversifying revenue streams, investing in innovation, forming strategic partnerships, or entering new markets.

Risk Mitigation Options

- **Diversification:** Spread risk by diversifying the company's product offerings, customer base, or geographic presence.
- **Innovation:** Invest in research and development to stay ahead of technological disruptions and maintain competitive advantage.
- **Strategic Alliances:** Form partnerships or alliances to enhance capabilities and reduce exposure to competitive threats.
- **Market Entry:** Explore new markets to offset risks associated with market saturation or declining demand in existing markets.

Example

To mitigate the risk of technological disruption, the pharmaceutical company could:

- **Invest in Biotechnology:** Allocate resources to develop expertise in emerging biotechnologies that could complement or replace traditional drug development methods.
- **Acquire Startups:** Acquire or partner with biotech startups to accelerate innovation and gain access to cutting-edge technologies.
- **Expand R&D Efforts:** Increase investment in research and development to explore new drug delivery systems or personalized medicine solutions.

Calculation of Mitigation Costs and Benefits

Assume the company decides to invest $3 million in biotechnology to mitigate the risk of technological disruption.

Step 1: Estimate the reduction in the financial impact of the risk

- **Post-mitigation Financial Impact:** $20 million (reduced from $25 million)
- **New ERI:** 0.20 × $20,000,000 = $4,000,000

Step 2: Calculate the net benefit of the mitigation strategy

- **Net Benefit:** $5 million (original ERI) - $4 million (new ERI) - $3 million (cost of mitigation) = ($2 million)

Answer and Explanation

The net benefit calculation suggests that while the mitigation strategy reduces the risk impact, it may not provide a positive return on investment in the short term. The company must consider whether the strategic importance of mitigating technological disruption justifies the cost or explore alternative mitigation strategies.

Integration with Strategic Planning

Integration with strategic planning ensures that risk management is aligned with the organization's strategic objectives and is embedded in the strategic decision-making process. This alignment allows organizations to proactively manage risks while pursuing their long-term goals.

Steps

- **Incorporate Risk Assessment in Strategic Planning:** Ensure that risk assessments are a core component of the strategic planning process.
- **Align Mitigation Strategies with Strategic Goals:** Develop risk mitigation strategies that support the organization's overall strategic objectives.
- **Monitor Strategic Risks Continuously:** Regularly review and update the risk management plan to address changes in the internal and external environment.

Example

The pharmaceutical company integrates its strategic risk management efforts with its broader strategic plan by:

- **Incorporating Risk Assessments:** Regularly conducting strategic risk assessments as part of its annual strategic planning process.
- **Aligning Innovation with Strategy:** Aligning its investment in biotechnology with its long-term goal of becoming a leader in personalized medicine.
- **Monitoring Competitive Landscape:** Continuously monitoring competitor activities and technological developments to adjust its strategy as needed.

Practical Example: Implementing SRM in a Global Automotive Company

Scenario

A global automotive company is managing the strategic risks associated with the industry-wide transition to electric vehicles (EVs). The company uses an SRM framework to identify, assess, and mitigate these risks while aligning its risk management efforts with its strategic goal of becoming a leader in the EV market.

Step 1: Strategic Risk Identification

- **Regulatory Changes:** Risk of stricter emissions regulations increasing production costs for internal combustion engine (ICE) vehicles.
- **Consumer Preferences:** Risk of declining demand for ICE vehicles as consumers shift toward EVs.
- **Technological Disruption:** Risk of falling behind competitors in EV technology development.

Step 2: Risk Assessment and Prioritization

- **Regulatory Changes:** Probability: 50%, Financial Impact: $100 million.
- **Consumer Preferences:** Probability: 40%, Financial Impact: $150 million.
- **Technological Disruption:** Probability: 30%, Financial Impact: $200 million.

Calculation of Expected Risk Impact (ERI)

- **Regulatory Changes ERI:** 0.50 × $100,000,000 = $50,000,000
- **Consumer Preferences ERI:** 0.40 × $150,000,000 = $60,000,000
- **Technological Disruption ERI:** 0.30 × $200,000,000 = $60,000,000

Answer and Explanation

The ERI calculations indicate that consumer preferences and technological disruption pose the highest risks, each with an expected impact of $60 million. The company should prioritize mitigating these risks to protect its strategic objectives.

Step 3: Risk Mitigation Strategies

- **Regulatory Changes:** Invest in EV production to reduce reliance on ICE vehicles and meet emissions standards (Diversification).
- **Consumer Preferences:** Launch marketing campaigns to promote the benefits of EVs and expand EV product offerings (Market Entry).
- **Technological Disruption:** Increase R&D investment in battery technology and autonomous driving systems (Innovation).

Step 4: Integration with Strategic Planning

- **Incorporate Risk Assessments:** Incorporate the assessment of regulatory, consumer, and technological risks into the company's strategic planning process.
- **Align Mitigation with Strategy:** Align the shift toward EV production with the company's strategic goal of becoming a market leader in sustainable transportation.
- **Monitor Industry Trends:** Continuously monitor industry trends, such as advancements in battery technology and changes in consumer behavior, to refine the company's strategic approach.

Exercise 4: Developing an SRM Plan for a Hypothetical Pharmaceutical Company

Scenario

A pharmaceutical company faces significant strategic risks related to market changes, competitive threats, and technological disruptions. Using an SRM framework, the company needs to develop a strategic risk management plan that aligns with its long-term goals.

Step 1: Strategic Risk Identification

- **Market Changes:** Risk of increasing demand for generic drugs reducing the profitability of branded drugs.
- **Competitive Threats:** Risk of a competitor launching a more effective drug for a key therapeutic area.
- **Technological Disruptions:** Risk of new drug development technologies rendering existing methods obsolete.

Step 2: Risk Assessment and Prioritization

- **Market Changes:** Probability: 35%, Financial Impact: $50 million.
- **Competitive Threats:** Probability: 25%, Financial Impact: $75 million.
- **Technological Disruptions:** Probability: 20%, Financial Impact: $100 million.

Calculation of Expected Risk Impact (ERI)

- **Market Changes ERI:** 0.35 × $50,000,000 = $17,500,000
- **Competitive Threats ERI:** 0.25 × $75,000,000 = $18,750,000
- **Technological Disruptions ERI:** 0.20 × $100,000,000 = $20,000,000

Answer and Explanation

The technological disruptions risk has the highest ERI ($20 million), followed by competitive threats ($18.75 million) and market changes ($17.5 million). The company should focus on mitigating the technological disruption risk while also addressing competitive threats.

Step 3: Risk Mitigation Strategies

- **Market Changes:** Diversify product offerings by developing a portfolio of both branded and generic drugs (Diversification).

- **Competitive Threats:** Increase investment in R&D to accelerate the development of new drugs (Innovation).
- **Technological Disruptions:** Partner with biotech firms to integrate cutting-edge drug development technologies (Strategic Alliances).

Step 4: Integration with Strategic Planning

- **Incorporate Risk Assessments:** Include strategic risk assessments in the company's annual strategic planning process.
- **Align Mitigation with Strategy:** Align the development of generic drugs and investment in new technologies with the company's long-term goal of maintaining leadership in key therapeutic areas.
- **Monitor Technological Advances:** Continuously monitor advancements in drug development technologies and adjust the company's strategy accordingly.

Answer and Explanation

By following the SRM framework, the pharmaceutical company can effectively manage its strategic risks while aligning its risk management efforts with its long-term goals. The plan includes specific risk mitigation strategies, integration with strategic planning, and continuous monitoring to ensure the company remains resilient and competitive in a rapidly evolving industry.

Conclusion

Strategic Risk Management (SRM) frameworks provide organizations with the tools and processes needed to identify, assess, and mitigate risks that could impact their strategic objectives. By integrating SRM into the strategic planning process, organizations can ensure that risks are managed proactively and that their long-term goals are safeguarded. Through practical examples, calculations, and exercises, this chapter has demonstrated how SRM frameworks can be applied to various industries, helping organizations navigate uncertainties and maintain their competitive advantage in a complex and dynamic environment.

Integrating Risk Management into Corporate Strategy

Integrating risk management into corporate strategy is essential for organizations to ensure that risks are considered in strategic decision-making and that risk management practices are aligned with the organization's long-term goals. This integration helps organizations navigate uncertainties, capitalize on opportunities, and safeguard their strategic objectives.

Steps to Integrate Risk Management into Corporate Strategy

Align Risk Management with Strategic Objectives

Aligning risk management with strategic objectives ensures that risk management practices support the organization's overall mission and goals. This alignment requires a clear understanding of the organization's strategic priorities and the risks that could impact them.

Steps

- **Identify Strategic Objectives:** Clearly define the organization's strategic objectives, such as market expansion, innovation, or cost leadership.
- **Map Risks to Objectives:** Identify risks that could directly or indirectly affect the achievement of these objectives.
- **Prioritize Risks:** Assess the potential impact of identified risks on strategic objectives and prioritize them based on their significance.

Example

A technology company with a strategic objective of becoming a leader in artificial intelligence (AI) identifies key risks, such as rapid technological changes, data privacy concerns, and regulatory hurdles. The company prioritizes these risks based on their potential impact on its AI strategy.

Calculation Example

Assume the following strategic objectives and associated risks:

- **Objective 1: Market Expansion into AI**
- Risk: Technological Obsolescence
- Impact: $50 million
- Probability: 20%
- **Objective 2: Innovation in AI-driven Products**
- Risk: Regulatory Compliance Issues
- Impact: $30 million
- Probability: 25%
- **Objective 3: Cost Leadership in AI Solutions**
- Risk: High R&D Costs
- Impact: $40 million
- Probability: 30%

Step 1: Calculate the Expected Risk Impact (ERI) for each risk.

- Technological Obsolescence ERI: 0.20 × $50,000,000 = $10,000,000
- Regulatory Compliance Issues ERI: 0.25 × $30,000,000 = $7,500,000
- High R&D Costs ERI: 0.30 × $40,000,000 = $12,000,000

Answer and Explanation

The ERI calculations indicate that High R&D Costs pose the highest risk ($12 million), followed by Technological Obsolescence ($10 million) and

Regulatory Compliance Issues ($7.5 million). The company should focus on managing the risks associated with R&D costs to ensure cost leadership in AI solutions.

Embed Risk Management into Strategic Planning

Embedding risk management into strategic planning ensures that risks are identified, assessed, and addressed during the development of strategic plans. This integration allows organizations to proactively manage risks that could impact their long-term goals.

Steps

- **Conduct Risk Assessments:** Perform risk assessments during the strategic planning process to identify potential risks to strategic initiatives.
- **Incorporate Risk Mitigation:** Develop risk mitigation strategies and include them in the strategic plan.
- **Align Resources:** Allocate resources to manage prioritized risks, ensuring that the organization is well-equipped to handle potential challenges.

Example

An energy company planning to expand into renewable energy markets conducts a risk assessment to identify risks such as fluctuating energy prices, regulatory changes, and technological advancements. The company develops a strategic plan that includes risk mitigation strategies, such as securing long-term supply contracts and investing in R&D for new technologies.

Calculation Example

Assume the energy company has identified the following risks for its strategic initiative to enter the solar energy market:

- **Risk: Fluctuating Energy Prices**
- Impact: \$20 million
- Probability: 40%
- **Risk: Regulatory Changes**
- Impact: \$15 million
- Probability: 30%
- **Risk: Technological Advancements**
- Impact: \$25 million
- Probability: 25%

Step 1: Calculate the Expected Risk Impact (ERI) for each risk.

- Fluctuating Energy Prices ERI: 0.40 × \$20,000,000 = \$8,000,000
- Regulatory Changes ERI: 0.30 × \$15,000,000 = \$4,500,000
- Technological Advancements ERI: 0.25 × \$25,000,000 = \$6,250,000

Step 2: Incorporate Mitigation Strategies

- **Fluctuating Energy Prices:** Secure long-term contracts to lock in prices (Risk Transfer).
- **Regulatory Changes:** Engage with regulators to stay informed about potential changes and adjust strategies accordingly (Risk Reduction).
- **Technological Advancements:** Invest in R&D to keep pace with technological changes (Risk Reduction).

Answer and Explanation

The risk assessment reveals that Fluctuating Energy Prices is the most significant risk (\$8 million ERI). The company decides to secure long-term contracts to mitigate this risk, ensuring price stability and reducing exposure to market volatility.

Develop a Risk-Aware Culture

Developing a risk-aware culture involves fostering an environment where employees at all levels understand the importance of risk management and are encouraged to identify, report, and manage risks. A risk-aware culture ensures that risk management is embedded in the organization's daily operations.

Steps

- **Educate Employees:** Provide training and resources to help employees understand risk management principles and practices.
- **Encourage Risk Reporting:** Establish channels for employees to report risks without fear of retribution.
- **Promote Accountability:** Hold employees accountable for managing risks within their areas of responsibility.

Example

A financial services company develops a risk-aware culture by conducting regular risk management workshops, establishing a whistleblower policy, and integrating risk management responsibilities into employee performance evaluations.

Calculation Example

Assume the company implements a risk management training program with the following metrics:

- Number of Employees Trained: 500
- Training Cost per Employee: $200
- Total Training Cost: 500 × $200 = $100,000
- Expected Reduction in Risk Impact due to Improved Risk Awareness: 10%

Step 1: Estimate the reduction in the overall risk impact for a risk with an initial impact of $10 million

- New Risk Impact: $10,000,000 × (1−0.10) = $9,000,000
- Net Benefit of Training Program: $10,000,000 - $9,000,000 = $1,000,000

Answer and Explanation

The training program is expected to reduce the overall risk impact by $1 million, demonstrating a positive return on investment in fostering a risk-aware culture.

Monitor and Review Strategic Risks

Continuous monitoring and review of strategic risks ensure that risks are effectively managed, and that the organization remains on track to achieve its strategic objectives. Regular monitoring helps identify emerging risks and adjust strategies as needed.

Steps

- **Track Key Risk Indicators (KRIs):** Identify and monitor KRIs that signal changes in the risk environment.
- **Conduct Regular Reviews:** Periodically review the effectiveness of risk management strategies and adjust them based on new information.
- **Update Risk Assessments:** Reassess risks as the organization's internal and external environments evolve.

Example

A healthcare company monitors KRIs such as changes in healthcare regulations, technological advancements, and patient outcomes to manage strategic risks. The company conducts quarterly reviews to evaluate the effectiveness of its risk management strategies and make necessary adjustments.

Calculation Example

Assume the company identifies a KRI related to regulatory changes with the following metrics:

- Initial Risk Impact: $15 million
- Reduction in Risk Impact after Monitoring: 15%

Step 1: Calculate the new risk impact after monitoring

- New Risk Impact: $15,000,000 × (1–0.15) = $12,750,000
- Net Benefit of Monitoring: $15,000,000 – $12,750,000 = $2,250,000

Answer and Explanation

Monitoring the KRI related to regulatory changes is expected to reduce the risk impact by $2.25 million, highlighting the importance of continuous monitoring in managing strategic risks.

Communicate Risks to Stakeholders

Communicating risks to stakeholders ensures transparency and accountability in risk management. Regular communication helps stakeholders understand the organization's risk profile, the effectiveness of risk management strategies, and the potential impact of risks on strategic objectives.

Steps

- **Regular Reporting:** Provide regular risk management reports to the board of directors, senior management, and other key stakeholders.
- **Stakeholder Engagement**: Engage with stakeholders to gather input on risk management practices and address their concerns.

- **Transparency:** Ensure that risk communication is clear, accurate, and accessible to all stakeholders.

Example

A multinational corporation communicates its risk management activities to stakeholders through quarterly risk management reports, which include updates on key risks, mitigation strategies, and any changes in the risk environment. The company also holds annual risk management meetings with stakeholders to discuss emerging risks and strategic priorities.

Calculation Example

Assume the company produces a quarterly risk management report with the following costs:

- Cost of Report Preparation: $10,000 per quarter
- Number of Stakeholders Engaged: 50
- Cost per Stakeholder: $10,000 / 50 = $200

Step 1: Estimate the value of improved decision-making due to enhanced risk communication

- Expected Reduction in Risk Impact due to Better Stakeholder Engagement: 5%
- Initial Risk Impact: $20 million
- New Risk Impact: $20,000,000 × (1–0.05) = $19,000,000
- Net Benefit of Enhanced Communication: $20,000,000 – $19,000,000 = $1,000,000

Answer and Explanation

The enhanced risk communication is expected to reduce the overall risk impact by $1 million, demonstrating the value of effective stakeholder engagement in managing strategic risks.

Practical Example: Integrating Risk Management into the Corporate Strategy of a Multinational Energy Company

Scenario

A multinational energy company is expanding its operations into renewable energy markets. To ensure the success of this strategic initiative, the company integrates risk management into its corporate strategy.

Step 1: Align Risk Management with Strategic Objectives

- **Strategic Objective:** Achieve market leadership in renewable energy.
- **Identified Risks:** Market volatility, technological advancements, regulatory changes.

Step 2: Embed Risk Management into Strategic Planning

- **Risk Assessment:** Conduct risk assessments for each strategic initiative, such as the development of new solar and wind energy projects.
- **Risk Mitigation:** Allocate resources for R&D in renewable technologies and engage with regulators to influence policy development.

Step 3: Develop a Risk-Aware Culture

- **Training:** Implement a risk management training program for employees involved in renewable energy projects.
- **Reporting:** Establish channels for employees to report risks related to renewable energy operations.

Step 4: Monitor and Review Strategic Risks

- **KRIs:** Monitor KRIs such as changes in renewable energy regulations, technological advancements, and market demand for renewable energy.

- **Reviews:** Conduct biannual reviews of the company's risk management strategies and adjust them based on new developments.

Step 5: Communicate Risks to Stakeholders

- **Reporting:** Provide quarterly risk management reports to the board of directors, focusing on risks related to renewable energy expansion.
- **Engagement:** Hold annual meetings with stakeholders to discuss the company's progress in the renewable energy market and address any concerns.

Answer and Explanation

By integrating risk management into its corporate strategy, the energy company can proactively manage risks associated with its expansion into renewable energy markets. The company's approach includes aligning risk management with strategic objectives, embedding risk assessments into strategic planning, fostering a risk-aware culture, continuously monitoring risks, and effectively communicating with stakeholders.

Exercise 5: Developing a Plan to Integrate Risk Management into the Corporate Strategy of a Hypothetical Energy Company

Scenario

A hypothetical energy company is planning to diversify its operations by entering the offshore wind energy market. The company needs to develop a plan to integrate risk management into its corporate strategy to ensure the success of this strategic initiative.

Step 1: Align Risk Management with Strategic Objectives

- **Objective:** Establish a strong presence in the offshore wind energy market.
- **Identified Risks:** Regulatory changes, environmental impact concerns, high capital costs.

Step 2: Embed Risk Management into Strategic Planning

- **Risk Assessment:** Conduct a comprehensive risk assessment for the offshore wind energy project, focusing on regulatory, environmental, and financial risks.
- **Risk Mitigation:** Develop strategies to manage identified risks, such as securing regulatory approvals, conducting environmental impact assessments, and exploring financing options.

Step 3: Develop a Risk-Aware Culture

- **Training:** Provide risk management training to project teams involved in the offshore wind energy initiative.
- **Reporting:** Encourage employees to report risks and suggest mitigation strategies.

Step 4: Monitor and Review Strategic Risks

- **KRIs:** Identify and monitor KRIs such as changes in offshore wind energy regulations, environmental impact assessments, and project financing.
- **Reviews:** Conduct quarterly reviews to evaluate the effectiveness of risk management strategies and make necessary adjustments.

Step 5: Communicate Risks to Stakeholders

- **Reporting:** Develop a risk management communication plan to keep stakeholders informed about the progress and risks associated with the offshore wind energy project.
- **Engagement:** Organize stakeholder meetings to discuss risk management strategies and gather input on project-related risks.

Answer and Explanation

The energy company's plan to integrate risk management into its corporate strategy ensures that risks associated with the offshore wind energy project are effectively managed. By aligning risk management with strategic objectives, embedding risk assessments into strategic planning, fostering a risk-aware culture, continuously monitoring risks, and communicating with stakeholders, the company can navigate uncertainties and achieve its goal of becoming a leader in the offshore wind energy market.

Chapter

04

Risk Identification and Assessment

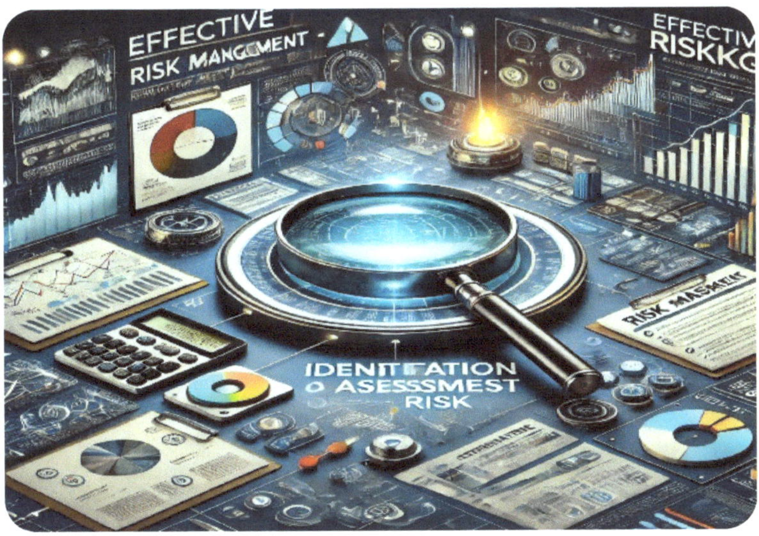

Effective risk management begins with the identification and assessment of potential risks. This chapter explores various techniques and methodologies for identifying and assessing risks, focusing on both qualitative and quantitative approaches. We will also delve into scenario analysis, stress testing, and the strategic implications of risk assessment, with practical examples and exercises to enhance understanding.

Techniques for Identifying Risks

Risk identification is the foundational step in the risk management process, where potential risks that could impact an organization's objectives are systematically identified. This process is crucial because it sets the stage for subsequent risk assessment, mitigation, and monitoring activities. By effectively identifying risks, organizations can proactively address potential challenges and capitalize on opportunities, ensuring they are well-prepared to achieve their strategic goals.

Key Techniques for Risk Identification

Brainstorming

Brainstorming is a collaborative technique where a group of stakeholders comes together to generate a comprehensive list of potential risks. The goal is to encourage open discussion and creative thinking, allowing participants to identify a wide range of risks that might not be immediately obvious.

Steps

- **Assemble a Diverse Group:** Include stakeholders from different departments and levels of the organization to ensure a broad perspective.
- **Set Clear Objectives:** Define the focus of the brainstorming session, such as identifying risks for a specific project, process, or strategic initiative.

- **Encourage the Free Flow of Ideas:** Create an open environment where participants feel comfortable sharing their ideas without judgment.
- **Record All Ideas:** Document every risk mentioned, regardless of how unlikely or insignificant it may seem.

Practical Example

A manufacturing company is planning to launch a new product line and organizes a brainstorming session to identify potential risks. The session includes representatives from production, marketing, supply chain, and finance. The group identifies risks such as:

- **Supply Chain Disruptions:** Delays in receiving raw materials from suppliers.
- **Quality Control Issues:** Potential defects in the new product.
- **Market Competition:** Competitors launching similar products at a lower price point.
- **Regulatory Compliance:** Changes in regulations affecting product safety standards.
- **Customer Acceptance:** Uncertainty about how well the new product will be received by customers.
- **Analysis:** The brainstorming session allows the company to identify a comprehensive list of risks that could impact the success of the new product line. By involving stakeholders from different areas of the business, the company gains a more holistic understanding of potential challenges.

Exercise

- Conduct a brainstorming session for a hypothetical technology startup planning to enter the mobile app market.
- Identify at least five risks the startup might face, such as competition, technical issues, user adoption, regulatory hurdles, and cybersecurity threats.

Checklists

Checklists involve using predefined lists of common risks to ensure that all potential risks are considered during the identification process. Checklists are particularly useful for organizations with established risk management processes or for projects that are similar to previous ones.

Steps

- **Select or Develop a Checklist:** Choose a relevant checklist based on industry standards, past projects, or organizational experience.
- **Review Each Item:** Go through each item on the checklist and evaluate its relevance to the current project or initiative.
- **Identify Additional Risks:** Use the checklist as a starting point and encourage participants to identify any risks not listed.

Practical Example

A construction company uses a checklist to identify risks associated with building a new commercial complex. The checklist includes risks such as:

- **Site Conditions:** Unexpected ground conditions requiring additional excavation.
- **Environmental Regulations:** Compliance with local environmental laws.
- **Worker Safety:** Potential accidents on-site.
- **Project Delays:** Delays due to weather or supply issues.
- **Budget Overruns:** Costs exceeding the project budget.
- **Analysis:** The checklist helps the construction company systematically identify risks that are commonly encountered in similar projects. By using a checklist, the company ensures that no

key risks are overlooked, even those that might seem routine or less obvious.

Exercise

Develop a checklist of risks for a hypothetical financial services company planning to launch a new online banking platform. Consider risks related to technology, security, compliance, customer service, and market competition.

Interviews and Surveys

Interviews and surveys involve engaging with various stakeholders, including employees, customers, suppliers, and other relevant parties, to gather insights into potential risks. This technique leverages the knowledge and experience of individuals who are directly involved in or affected by the organization's activities.

Steps

- **Identify Stakeholders:** Determine who should be interviewed or surveyed, considering their roles and perspectives.
- **Develop Questions:** Prepare a set of open-ended questions or survey items designed to elicit information about potential risks.
- **Conduct Interviews/Distribute Surveys:** Engage with stakeholders through one-on-one interviews, group discussions, or online surveys.
- **Analyze Responses:** Compile and analyze the responses to identify common themes and specific risks.

Practical Example

A retail company planning to expand into a new geographic market conducts interviews with key stakeholders, including regional managers, suppliers, and local government officials. The interviews reveal risks such as:

- **Supply Chain Reliability:** Challenges in establishing reliable logistics networks in the new market.
- **Regulatory Barriers:** Local regulations that could delay the expansion.
- **Cultural Differences:** Potential difficulties in marketing products to a different cultural demographic.
- **Economic Conditions:** The risk of economic downturns affecting consumer spending in the new market.
- **Analysis:** By conducting interviews, the retail company gains valuable insights into risks that may not have been identified through internal brainstorming or checklists. The input from local stakeholders is particularly valuable in understanding region-specific challenges.

Exercise

Design a survey for a hypothetical healthcare organization planning to implement a new electronic health record (EHR) system. The survey should focus on identifying risks related to system implementation, data security, patient privacy, and staff training.

SWOT Analysis

SWOT Analysis is a strategic planning tool used to identify an organization's internal Strengths and Weaknesses, as well as external Opportunities and Threats. By analyzing these four elements, organizations can identify risks that may arise from internal vulnerabilities or external challenges.

Steps

- **Strengths:** Identify internal factors that give the organization a competitive advantage.
- **Weaknesses:** Identify internal factors that may hinder the organization's performance or objectives.
- **Opportunities:** Identify external factors that the organization can leverage to its advantage.
- **Threats:** Identify external factors that could pose risks or challenges to the organization.

Practical Example

A software development company uses SWOT analysis to assess the risks associated with launching a new cloud-based service. The analysis reveals:

- **Strengths:** Strong in-house development team and innovative technology.
- **Weaknesses:** Limited experience in cloud service deployment.
- **Opportunities:** Growing demand for cloud solutions among small businesses.
- **Threats:** Potential data breaches and competition from established cloud providers.
- **Analysis:** SWOT analysis helps the software development company identify both internal and external risks. By understanding its weaknesses and the external threats it faces, the company can develop strategies to mitigate these risks and capitalize on its strengths and opportunities.

Exercise

- Conduct a SWOT analysis for a hypothetical renewable energy company planning to develop a new wind farm.

- Identify at least three risks related to internal weaknesses and external threats.

Cause-and-Effect Analysis (Fishbone Diagram)

Cause-and-Effect Analysis, often represented by a Fishbone Diagram, is a visual tool used to identify the root causes of potential risks. By mapping out the causes and their effects, organizations can better understand the origins of risks and develop strategies to address them at their source.

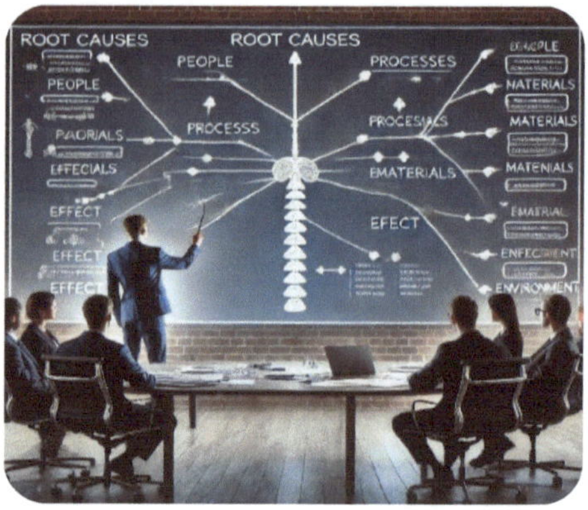

Steps

- **Define the Risk:** Clearly state the risk or problem that needs to be analyzed.
- **Identify Major Categories:** Determine the main categories of causes, such as people, processes, equipment, materials, environment, and management.
- **Brainstorm Possible Causes:** For each category, brainstorm potential causes that could contribute to the risk.
- **Analyze the Diagram:** Review the diagram to identify the most likely root causes and prioritize them for action.

Practical Example

A pharmaceutical company uses a Fishbone Diagram to identify the causes of potential delays in its drug development process. The diagram reveals the following categories and causes:

- **People:** Lack of skilled researchers and high employee turnover.
- **Processes:** Inefficient clinical trial procedures and delays in regulatory approvals.

- **Equipment:** Outdated laboratory equipment leading to testing delays.
- **Materials:** Shortage of critical raw materials and delays in supplier deliveries.
- **Environment:** Regulatory changes and unexpected weather events affecting supply chains.
- **Analysis:** The Fishbone Diagram helps the pharmaceutical company identify the root causes of potential delays in its drug development process. By addressing these root causes, the company can reduce the likelihood of delays and ensure timely product development.

Exercise

- Create a Fishbone Diagram for a hypothetical manufacturing company experiencing high defect rates in its production line.
- Identify and analyze the root causes related to people, processes, equipment, and materials.

Practical Example: Risk Identification for a Manufacturing Company

Scenario

A manufacturing company is planning to launch a new product line and needs to identify potential risks that could impact its success. The company decides to use multiple techniques to ensure comprehensive risk identification.

Step 1: Brainstorming Session

The company conducts a brainstorming session with representatives from production, marketing, supply chain, and finance. The session identifies risks such as:

- **Supply Chain Disruptions:** Potential delays in receiving raw materials.
- **Quality Control Issues:** Possible defects in the new product.

- **Market Competition:** Competitors launching similar products.
- **Regulatory Compliance:** Changes in regulations affecting product safety.
- **Customer Acceptance:** Uncertainty about customer reception.

Step 2: Checklist Review

The company uses a checklist to ensure all common risks are considered. The checklist adds risks such as:

- **Intellectual Property Issues:** Potential patent disputes.
- **Environmental Impact:** Compliance with environmental regulations.
- **Labor Shortages:** Difficulty in hiring skilled workers.

Step 3: SWOT Analysis

The company conducts a SWOT analysis, revealing:

- **Strengths:** Established brand and efficient production processes.
- **Weaknesses:** Limited experience with new product technology.
- **Opportunities:** Growing demand in the target market.
- **Threats:** Economic downturns affecting consumer spending.

Step 4: Fishbone Diagram

To further analyze the risk of supply chain disruptions, the company creates a Fishbone Diagram, identifying root causes such as:

- **Supplier Reliability:** Dependence on a single supplier.
- **Transportation Issues:** Potential delays due to shipping bottlenecks.
- **Inventory Management:** Insufficient inventory levels leading to stockouts.

Analysis

By using multiple risk identification techniques, the manufacturing company identifies a comprehensive list of risks that could impact the success of its new product line. The insights gained from these techniques allow the company to prioritize risks and develop effective mitigation strategies.

Exercise 1: Risk Identification for a Hypothetical Technology Startup

Scenario

A hypothetical technology startup is planning to enter the mobile app market. The startup needs to identify potential risks that could impact its initial market entry.

Instructions

- **Brainstorming:** Conduct a brainstorming session with key stakeholders (e.g., founders, developers, marketing team) to identify potential risks. Consider risks related to product development, market entry, competition, and customer acquisition.
- **SWOT Analysis:** Perform a SWOT analysis to identify the startup's internal strengths and weaknesses, as well as external opportunities and threats. Focus on identifying risks that could arise from internal vulnerabilities or external challenges.

Expected Outcome

The startup should identify at least five risks, such as:

- **Competition:** High competition from established app developers.
- **Technical Issues:** Potential bugs or glitches in the app.
- **Market Demand:** Uncertainty about user adoption and market demand.
- **Regulatory Compliance:** Compliance with app store policies and data privacy regulations.
- **Cybersecurity Threats:** Risk of data breaches or hacking attempts.

Answer and Explanation

By using brainstorming and SWOT analysis, the startup can identify a comprehensive list of risks that could impact its market entry. This exercise helps the startup develop a risk management plan that addresses key challenges and positions the company for success in the competitive mobile app market.

Risk Assessment Methodologies

After identifying potential risks, the next crucial step in the risk management process is risk assessment. Risk assessment involves evaluating the likelihood of each risk occurring and the potential impact it could have on the organization. This process helps prioritize risks and informs the development of mitigation strategies. By effectively assessing risks, organizations can allocate resources more efficiently and take proactive measures to mitigate those that pose the greatest threat.

Key Methodologies for Risk Assessment

5x5 RISK MATRIX

LIKELIHOOD ↓ / SEVERITY →	1	2	3	4	5
1	LOW 1	LOW 2	LOW 3	MEDIUM 4	MEDIUM 5
2	LOW 2	MEDIUM 4	MEDIUM 6	HIGH 8	HIGH 10
3	LOW 3	MEDIUM 6	HIGH 9	HIGH 12	EXTREME 15
4	MEDIUM 4	HIGH 8	HIGH 12	HIGH 16	EXTREME 20
5	MEDIUM 5	HIGH 10	EXTREME 15	EXTREME 20	EXTREME 25

Risk Matrix

A Risk Matrix is a visual tool that helps prioritize risks based on their likelihood and impact. It is typically represented as a grid where one axis indicates the likelihood of a risk occurring, and the other axis represents the potential impact. Risks are then plotted on the matrix to determine their severity and prioritize them accordingly.

Steps

- **Identify Risks:** List all identified risks that need to be assessed.
- **Evaluate Likelihood:** Determine the probability of each risk occurring, often on a scale from 1 (low likelihood) to 5 (high likelihood).
- **Evaluate Impact:** Assess the potential impact of each risk if it were to occur, often on a scale from 1 (low impact) to 5 (high impact).
- **Plot Risks:** Place each risk on the matrix according to its likelihood and impact scores.
- **Prioritize Risks:** Use the matrix to prioritize risks, focusing on those with high likelihood and high impact.

Practical Example

A financial services company uses a Risk Matrix to assess the risks associated with launching a new online banking platform. The team identifies the following risks:

- Cybersecurity Breach: Likelihood = 4, Impact = 5
- Regulatory Compliance Issues: Likelihood = 3, Impact = 4
- Technical Glitches: Likelihood = 5, Impact = 3
- Customer Adoption Lag: Likelihood = 3, Impact = 2

Step 1: Plot the risks on the Risk Matrix.

Step 2: Identify the risk scores

- Cybersecurity Breach: (4, 5)
- Regulatory Compliance Issues: (3, 4)
- Technical Glitches: (5, 3)
- Customer Adoption Lag: (3, 2)

Step 3: Prioritize the risks.

- **High Priority:** Cybersecurity Breach (High likelihood, High impact)
- **Medium Priority:** Regulatory Compliance Issues, Technical Glitches
- **Low Priority:** Customer Adoption Lag

Analysis

The Risk Matrix shows that a cybersecurity breach is the highest priority risk due to its combination of high likelihood and high impact. The company should focus its mitigation efforts on enhancing cybersecurity measures.

Exercise

- Create a Risk Matrix for a hypothetical manufacturing company planning to automate its production line.
- Assess the risks related to equipment failure, employee resistance, cybersecurity, and supply chain disruptions.
- Prioritize these risks based on their likelihood and impact.

Failure Modes and Effects Analysis (FMEA)

Failure Modes and Effects Analysis (FMEA) is a structured approach to identifying and assessing potential failure points in a process, product, or system. FMEA evaluates the severity, occurrence, and detection of each failure mode to determine its risk priority number (RPN).

FMEA

Process/Product Name: ____________ Prepared By: ____________

Responsible: ____________ FMEA Date (Orig.): ____________ (Rev.): ____________

Process Step/Input	Potential Failure Mode	Potential Failure Effects	SEVERITY (1 - 10)	Potential Causes	OCCURRENCE (1 - 10)	Current Controls	DETECTION (1 - 10)	RPN	Action Recommended	Resp.	Actions Taken	SEVERITY (1 - 10)	OCCURRENCE (1 - 10)	DETECTION (1 - 10)
What is the process step or feature under investigation?	In what ways could the step or feature go wrong?	What is the impact on the customer if this failure is not prevented or corrected?		What causes the step or feature to go wrong? (how could it occur?)		What controls exist that either prevent or detect the failure?			What are the recommended actions for reducing the occurrence of the cause or improving detection?	Who is responsible for making sure the actions are completed?	What actions were completed (and when) with respect to the RPN?			

Steps

- **Identify Failure Modes:** List all potential failure modes in the process or system.
- **Assess Severity:** Evaluate the impact of each failure mode on a scale from 1 (low severity) to 10 (high severity).
- **Assess Occurrence:** Estimate the likelihood of each failure mode occurring on a scale from 1 (low likelihood) to 10 (high likelihood).
- **Assess Detection:** Evaluate the ability to detect each failure mode before it causes harm, on a scale from 1 (high detection capability) to 10 (low detection capability).
- **Calculate RPN:** Multiply the severity, occurrence, and detection scores for each failure mode:

$$\text{RPN} = \text{Severity} \times \text{Occurrence} \times \text{Detection}$$

- **Prioritize Risks:** Focus on failure modes with the highest RPNs for mitigation.

Practical Example

A healthcare organization conducts an FMEA to assess risks associated with a new patient management system. The team identifies the following failure modes:

- **Data Entry Errors:** Severity = 8, Occurrence = 6, Detection = 5
- **System Downtime:** Severity = 7, Occurrence = 4, Detection = 3
- **Patient Record Mismatch:** Severity = 9, Occurrence = 5, Detection = 6

Step 1: Calculate the RPN for each failure mode

- **Data Entry Errors:**

  $8 \times 6 \times 5 = 240$

- **System Downtime:**

  $7 \times 4 \times 3 = 84$

- **Patient Record Mismatch:**

  $9 \times 5 \times 6 = 270$

Step 2: Prioritize the failure modes based on their RPNs.

Analysis

The FMEA reveals that "Patient Record Mismatch" has the highest RPN, indicating it poses the greatest risk. The organization should prioritize implementing measures to mitigate this risk, such as improving record-keeping protocols and enhancing verification processes.

Exercise

- Conduct an FMEA for a hypothetical automotive company introducing a new vehicle model.
- Identify potential failure modes in the production process, assess their severity, occurrence, and detection, and calculate the RPNs.
- Prioritize the top three risks for immediate action.

Root Cause Analysis (RCA)

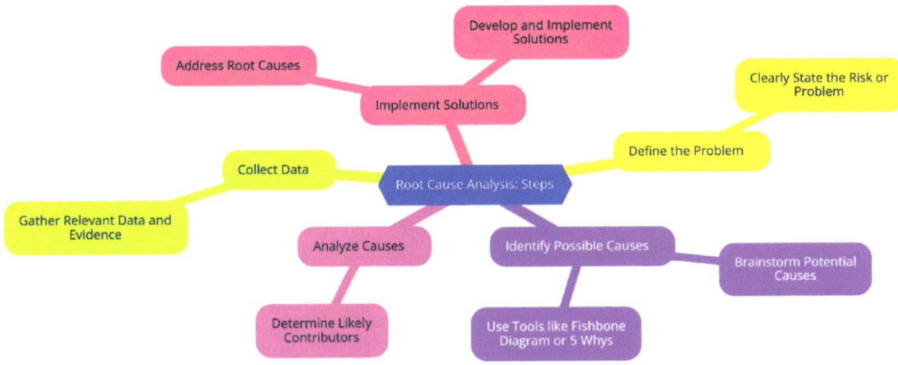

Root Cause Analysis (RCA) is a method used to identify the underlying causes of risks or problems, rather than just addressing their symptoms. By understanding the root causes, organizations can develop more effective and sustainable solutions to mitigate risks.

Steps

- **Define the Problem:** Clearly state the risk or problem that needs to be analyzed.
- **Collect Data:** Gather relevant data and evidence related to the problem.
- **Identify Possible Causes:** Brainstorm potential causes of the problem, often using tools like the Fishbone Diagram or the "5 Whys" technique.
- **Analyze Causes:** Determine which causes are the most likely contributors to the problem.
- **Implement Solutions:** Develop and implement solutions that address the root causes.

Practical Example

An IT company experiences frequent system outages and decides to conduct an RCA to identify the root causes. The analysis reveals that the outages are primarily due to outdated hardware, inadequate network infrastructure, and poor maintenance practices.

Step 1: Use the "5 Whys" technique to drill down into the causes of system outages

- Why are there frequent system outages? – Because the servers are failing.
- Why are the servers failing? – Because they are outdated.
- Why are the servers outdated? – Because the company has not invested in new hardware.
- Why has the company not invested in new hardware? – Because of budget constraints.
- Why are there budget constraints? – Because the IT budget has been cut in recent years.

Step 2: Implement solutions such as upgrading hardware, improving network infrastructure, and revising the IT budget to prevent future outages.

Analysis

The RCA reveals that outdated hardware and inadequate investment in IT infrastructure are the root causes of the system outages. By addressing these root causes, the company can reduce the frequency of outages and improve system reliability.

Exercise

Conduct an RCA for a hypothetical logistics company experiencing delays in deliveries. Use the "5 Whys" technique to identify the root causes of the delays and propose solutions to address them.

Delphi Method

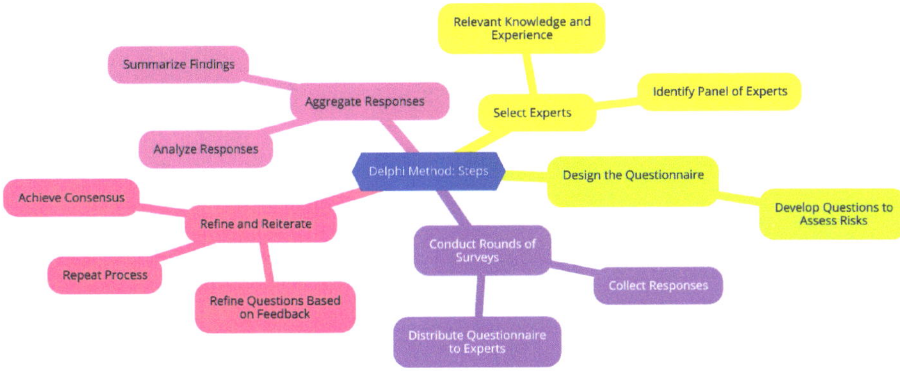

The Delphi Method is a structured communication technique used to gather expert opinions on a specific risk or problem. Experts provide their assessments independently, and their responses are aggregated to reach a consensus. The Delphi Method is particularly useful for assessing complex or uncertain risks where expert judgment is critical.

Steps

- **Select Experts:** Identify a panel of experts with relevant knowledge and experience.
- **Design the Questionnaire:** Develop a set of questions to assess the risks.
- **Conduct Rounds of Surveys:** Distribute the questionnaire to the experts and collect their responses.
- **Aggregate Responses:** Analyze the responses and summarize the findings.
- **Refine and Reiterate:** Repeat the process, refining the questions based on the feedback, until a consensus is reached.

Practical Example

A company planning to launch an online retail platform uses the Delphi Method to assess the risks associated with the project. The panel of experts includes professionals in e-commerce, cybersecurity, and supply chain management. The company conducts multiple rounds of surveys, asking the experts to assess the likelihood and impact of various risks, such as data breaches, supply chain disruptions, and customer acquisition challenges.

Step 1: Distribute the initial questionnaire to the experts.

Step 2: Aggregate the responses to identify the top risks

- **Data Breaches:** High likelihood, High impact
- **Supply Chain Disruptions:** Medium likelihood, High impact
- **Customer Acquisition Challenges:** High likelihood, Medium impact

Step 3: Conduct a second round of surveys to refine the assessments and reach a consensus.

Analysis

The Delphi Method allows the company to leverage the collective expertise of professionals in different fields, leading to a more informed and balanced risk assessment. The consensus reached through this method helps prioritize the most significant risks for mitigation.

Exercise

Using the Delphi Method, assess the risks associated with developing a new mobile app for a hypothetical technology startup. Gather input from experts in app development, cybersecurity, and user experience design, and use their assessments to prioritize the top three risks.

Practical Example: Risk Assessment for a Healthcare Organization

Scenario

A healthcare organization is implementing a new patient management system and needs to assess the associated risks. The organization decides to use multiple risk assessment methodologies to ensure a comprehensive evaluation.

Step 1: Risk Matrix

The team creates a Risk Matrix to assess the likelihood and impact of risks such as data entry errors, system downtime, and patient record mismatches. The matrix helps prioritize the risks that require immediate attention.

Step 2: Failure mode and effects analysis (FMEA)

The organization conducts an FMEA to assess the severity, occurrence, and detection of potential failure modes in the patient management system. The FMEA reveals that patient record mismatches have the highest A risk priority number (RPN), prompting the organization to focus on improving verification processes.

Step 3: Root Cause Analysis (RCA)

To address the root causes of frequent system downtimes, the organization conducts an RCA. The analysis identifies outdated hardware and inadequate maintenance practices as the primary causes, leading to the implementation of an IT infrastructure upgrade.

Step 4: Delphi Method

The organization uses the Delphi Method to gather expert opinions on the potential impact of cybersecurity breaches on the new system. The consensus reached through the Delphi Method highlights cybersecurity as a top priority, leading to the development of a comprehensive cybersecurity strategy.

Analysis

By using a combination of risk assessment methodologies, the healthcare organization gains a thorough understanding of the risks associated with the new patient management system. This multi-faceted approach allows the organization to prioritize and address the most critical risks effectively.

Exercise 2: Assessing Risks for an Online Retail Platform Using the Delphi Method

Scenario

A hypothetical company is planning to launch an online retail platform and wants to assess the associated risks using the Delphi Method. The company assembles a panel of experts in e-commerce, cybersecurity, and supply chain management to participate in the assessment.

Instructions

- **Select Experts:** Identify a panel of experts with relevant experience in online retail, cybersecurity, and supply chain management.
- **Design the Questionnaire:** Develop a set of questions to assess the likelihood and impact of potential risks, such as data breaches, supply chain disruptions, and customer acquisition challenges.
- **Conduct Rounds of Surveys:** Distribute the questionnaire to the experts and collect their responses. Aggregate the responses to identify the top risks.
- **Refine and Reiterate:** Conduct a second round of surveys to refine the assessments and reach a consensus on the top three risks.

Expected Outcome

The top three risks identified by the experts might include:

- **Data Breaches:** High likelihood, High impact
- **Supply Chain Disruptions:** Medium likelihood, High impact
- **Customer Acquisition Challenges:** High likelihood, Medium impact

Answer and Explanation

By using the Delphi Method, the company can leverage the collective expertise of professionals in different fields to assess the risks associated with launching the online retail platform. The consensus reached through this process helps the company prioritize the most significant risks and develop appropriate mitigation strategies.

Quantitative vs. Qualitative Risk Assessment

Risk assessment is a critical component of the risk management process and can be conducted using two primary approaches: quantitative and qualitative. Quantitative risk assessment relies on numerical data and statistical models to estimate risks, while qualitative risk assessment uses subjective judgment and descriptive analysis to evaluate risks. Both approaches have their strengths and weaknesses, and understanding how to leverage them effectively is essential for making informed decisions.

Quantitative Risk Assessment

Key Concepts

- **Probability:** The likelihood of a risk event occurring, often expressed as a percentage or a probability value between 0 and 1.
- **Impact:** The potential financial or operational consequences of a risk event if it occurs.
- **Risk Exposure:** The combination of probability and impact, representing the potential loss or negative outcome associated with a risk.
- **Statistical Models:** Mathematical models used to estimate the probability and impact of risks based on historical data and other relevant factors.

Steps

- **Data Collection:** Gather relevant data on historical events, market conditions, financial metrics, etc.
- **Probability Estimation:** Use statistical techniques to estimate the probability of each risk event occurring.
- **Impact Calculation:** Estimate the potential financial or operational impact of each risk event.
- **Risk Quantification:** Combine probability and impact to quantify the overall risk exposure.

Example

A bank uses quantitative models to assess the risk of loan defaults within its mortgage portfolio. The bank analyzes historical data on borrower credit scores, income levels, and past default rates to estimate the probability of default (PD) and the potential loss given default (LGD).

Step 1: Assume the following

- Average probability of default (PD): 5% (0.05)
- Average loss given default (LGD): 60% (0.60)
- Total mortgage portfolio value: $100 million

Step 2: Calculate the Expected Loss (EL)

- EL = PD × LGD × Portfolio Value
- EL = 0.05 × 0.60 × $100,000,000 = $3,000,000

Answer and Explanation

The bank's expected loss due to loan defaults is $3 million. This calculation helps the bank understand its potential exposure to credit risk and informs its decision-making regarding capital reserves and risk mitigation strategies.

Qualitative Risk Assessment

Key Concepts

- **Expert Judgment:** Leveraging the experience and knowledge of individuals to assess risks based on their subjective understanding.
- **Risk Categorization:** Grouping risks into categories such as high, medium, and low based on their perceived likelihood and impact.
- **Descriptive Analysis:** Using descriptive methods to explain the nature of risks and their potential consequences.

Steps

- **Risk Identification:** Identify risks based on expert knowledge, industry best practices, or brainstorming sessions.
- **Risk Categorization:** Categorize risks based on their perceived likelihood and impact.
- **Descriptive Analysis:** Analyze risks qualitatively by describing their potential effects on the organization.

Example

A project management team uses qualitative risk assessment to evaluate the risks associated with a large construction project. The team categorizes the risks into high, medium, and low based on their likelihood and potential impact on project timelines, costs, and quality.

Step 1: Identify risks, such as

- **Weather Delays:** High likelihood, high impact
- **Material Shortages:** Medium likelihood, medium impact
- **Labor Strikes:** Low likelihood, high impact

Step 2: Categorize risks into high, medium, and low

- **High:** Weather Delays

- **Medium:** Material Shortages
- **Low:** Labor Strikes

Step 3: Describe the potential effects of each risk

- **Weather Delays:** Could extend the project timeline, leading to increased costs.
- **Material Shortages:** May cause delays and increase procurement costs.
- **Labor Strikes:** Could halt the project entirely, leading to significant financial losses.

Answer and Explanation

The qualitative assessment provides a broad understanding of the risks and their potential impact on the construction project. This information allows the project team to focus on managing the most critical risks, such as weather delays, and to develop contingency plans for potential disruptions.

Comparison: Quantitative vs. Qualitative Risk Assessment

Aspect	Quantitative Risk Assessment	Qualitative Risk Assessment
Data Requirement	Requires extensive historical data and numerical inputs.	Relies on subjective judgment and expert opinion.
Precision	Provides precise, data-driven insights; useful for financial and operational risks.	Offers broad, descriptive insights; useful for strategic, reputational, and complex risks.
Application	Best suited for risks with measurable data, such as credit risk or market risk.	Best suited for risks that are difficult to quantify, such as strategic or reputational risks.

Decision-Making	Supports quantitative decision-making, such as capital allocation and risk pricing.	Supports qualitative decision-making, such as strategy development and risk prioritization.
Limitations	May overlook qualitative factors and relies heavily on the accuracy of data and models.	May lack precision and can be influenced by biases or subjective opinions.

Exercise 3

Compare and contrast the benefits and limitations of quantitative and qualitative risk assessments in the context of a global expansion strategy for a manufacturing company. Develop a hybrid approach that leverages both methods.

Practical Example: Global Expansion Strategy for a Manufacturing Company

Scenario

A manufacturing company is planning to expand its operations into new international markets. The company needs to assess the risks associated with this global expansion strategy. To ensure a comprehensive evaluation, the company decides to use both quantitative and qualitative risk assessment methods.

Quantitative Risk Assessment

The company analyzes historical market data, currency exchange rates, and economic indicators to assess financial risks associated with the expansion. It calculates the potential impact of currency fluctuations on revenue and estimates the probability of economic downturns in the target markets.

Step 1: Assume the following data

- Projected revenue in the new market: $50 million
- Expected currency fluctuation: +/- 10%
- Probability of an economic downturn: 20% (0.20)

Step 2: Calculate the potential impact of currency fluctuations

- Impact = 0.10 × $50,000,000 = $5,000,000

Step 3: Calculate the Expected Loss due to an economic downturn

- Expected Loss = 0.20 × $50,000,000 = $10,000,000

Answer and Explanation

The quantitative assessment reveals that currency fluctuations could lead to a $5 million impact on revenue, while an economic downturn could result in an expected loss of $10 million. This information helps the company understand its financial exposure and consider strategies like hedging or market diversification.

Qualitative Risk Assessment

The company also conducts a qualitative assessment to evaluate strategic risks, such as cultural differences, regulatory challenges, and potential reputational issues. The management team categorizes these risks based on their perceived impact on the company's brand and long-term success.

Step 1: Identify qualitative risks, such as:

- **Cultural Misalignment:** High impact, high likelihood
- **Regulatory Barriers:** Medium impact, medium likelihood
- **Reputational Damage:** High impact, low likelihood

Step 2: Describe the potential effects of each risk

- **Cultural Misalignment:** Could lead to poor market acceptance and hinder brand reputation.
- **Regulatory Barriers:** May delay market entry and increase compliance costs.
- **Reputational Damage:** Could result in long-term loss of customer trust and market share.

Answer and Explanation

The qualitative assessment highlights strategic risks that are not easily quantifiable but could significantly impact the company's long-term success in the new markets. These insights guide the company in developing strategies to address cultural differences and navigate regulatory environments.

Hybrid Approach: Leveraging Both Methods

To achieve a comprehensive risk assessment for its global expansion strategy, the manufacturing company adopts a hybrid approach that combines quantitative and qualitative methods. This approach allows the company to quantify financial risks while also addressing strategic and reputational risks through qualitative analysis.

Steps

- **Quantitative Analysis:** Use quantitative models to assess financial risks, such as currency fluctuations, economic downturns, and supply chain disruptions.
- **Qualitative Analysis:** Conduct qualitative assessments to evaluate strategic, cultural, and regulatory risks that could impact the company's long-term success.
- **Integration:** Combine the results of both assessments to prioritize risks and develop a holistic risk management plan.

- **Decision-Making:** Use quantitative data to inform financial decisions, such as pricing and capital allocation, while using qualitative insights to shape strategic decisions, such as market entry and brand positioning.

Example

The manufacturing company uses quantitative analysis to assess the financial impact of currency fluctuations and economic downturns, while qualitative analysis helps identify potential cultural and regulatory challenges. By integrating both methods, the company can make data-driven financial decisions and strategically plan its market entry to mitigate cultural and regulatory risks.

Exercise 3

- Develop a hybrid risk assessment plan for a hypothetical manufacturing company planning to expand into three international markets.
- Use quantitative methods to assess financial risks and qualitative methods to evaluate strategic and reputational risks.
- Integrate the findings into a comprehensive risk management strategy.

Scenario Analysis and Stress Testing

Scenario analysis and stress testing are advanced techniques used to evaluate how different scenarios and extreme conditions might impact an organization. These methods are critical for understanding the potential consequences of adverse events, preparing for unexpected challenges, and ensuring organizational resilience.

While scenario analysis explores a range of possible future events, stress testing focuses on simulating extreme but plausible events to evaluate an organization's ability to withstand financial shocks.

Scenario Analysis

Scenario analysis involves developing detailed narratives about possible future events and assessing their impact on the organization. These scenarios can range from best-case to worst-case situations and typically include variations in key external factors such as economic conditions, market trends, or regulatory environments. Scenario analysis helps organizations anticipate potential risks and opportunities, allowing them to devise strategies to navigate different outcomes.

Steps

- **Identify Key Variables:** Determine the external and internal factors that could significantly impact the organization, such as economic indicators, market conditions, regulatory changes, or technological advancements.
- **Develop Scenarios:** Create a range of scenarios, including best-case, worst-case, and base-case scenarios. Each scenario should detail how the identified variables could evolve over time.
- **Assess Impact:** Evaluate the potential impact of each scenario on the organization's operations, financial performance, and strategic objectives.
- **Formulate Strategies:** Develop strategies to mitigate risks or capitalize on opportunities identified in each scenario

Example

A financial institution conducts scenario analysis to assess the impact of various economic conditions on its operations. The institution considers the following scenarios:

Scenario 1: Economic Boom (Best-Case)

- GDP growth of 4%
- Interest rates remain stable
- Increased consumer spending boosts asset values

Scenario 2: Mild Recession (Base-Case)

- GDP growth slows to 1%
- Interest rates rise by 0.5%
- Consumer spending declines moderately, impacting profitability

Scenario 3: Severe Recession (Worst-Case)

- GDP contracts by 2%
- Interest rates spike by 2%
- Asset values decline sharply, leading to reduced liquidity and profitability

Step 1: Identify Key Variables

- GDP growth, interest rates, consumer spending, asset values

Step 2: Develop Scenarios

- Scenario 1: Economic Boom
- Scenario 2: Mild Recession
- Scenario 3: Severe Recession

Step 3: Assess Impact

- Scenario 1 Impact: The institution's asset values increase, liquidity remains strong, and profitability improves due to higher consumer spending.
- Scenario 2 Impact: Moderate decline in profitability due to higher interest rates and reduced consumer spending. Liquidity remains stable.

- Scenario 3 Impact: Significant decline in asset values, leading to reduced liquidity and a sharp drop in profitability. The institution may need to adjust its capital reserves.

Step 4: Formulate Strategies

- Scenario 1 Strategy: Expand lending operations and investment portfolios to capitalize on favorable economic conditions.
- Scenario 2 Strategy: Implement cost-saving measures and tighten credit standards to mitigate the impact of rising interest rates.
- Scenario 3 Strategy: Increase capital reserves and reduce exposure to high-risk assets to enhance financial resilience.

Answer and Explanation

The scenario analysis provides the financial institution with insights into how different economic conditions could impact its operations. By developing strategies tailored to each scenario, the institution can better navigate potential risks and capitalize on opportunities.

Stress Testing

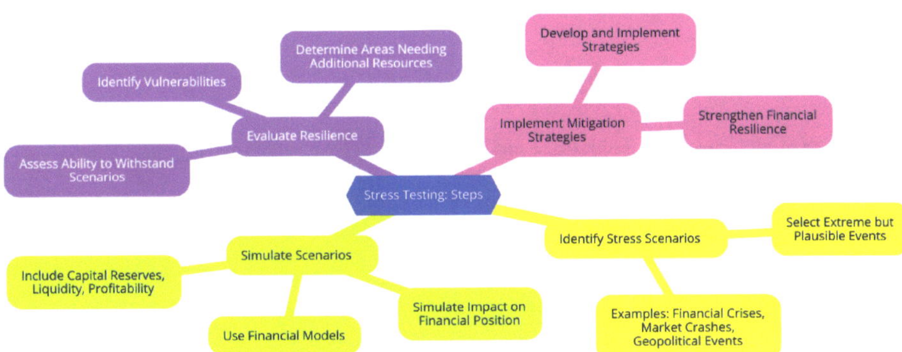

Stress testing involves simulating extreme but plausible events to evaluate the resilience of an organization's financial position or business model. Stress tests typically focus on financial stability, liquidity, and capital adequacy, helping organizations determine whether they have sufficient resources to survive adverse conditions.

Steps

- **Identify Stress Scenarios:** Select extreme but plausible events that could significantly impact the organization, such as financial crises, market crashes, or geopolitical events.
- **Simulate Scenarios:** Use financial models to simulate the impact of each stress scenario on the organization's financial position, including capital reserves, liquidity, and profitability.
- **Evaluate Resilience:** Assess the organization's ability to withstand the simulated stress scenarios. Identify potential vulnerabilities and areas where additional resources or strategies may be needed.
- **Implement Mitigation Strategies:** Develop and implement strategies to strengthen the organization's financial resilience based on the stress test results.

Example

A bank conducts stress tests to assess its ability to withstand a financial crisis. The bank considers the following stress scenarios:

Scenario 1: Sharp Decline in Asset Prices

- Stock market crashes, leading to a 30% decline in asset values
- Impact: Significant reduction in the value of the bank's investment portfolio

Scenario 2: Spike in Loan Defaults

- Unemployment rises sharply, leading to a 10% increase in loan defaults
- Impact: Increased credit losses and reduced profitability

Scenario 3: Liquidity Crunch

- A sudden withdrawal of deposits leads to a liquidity crisis
- Impact: The bank struggles to meet its short-term obligations

Step 1: Identify Stress Scenarios

Decline in asset prices, spike in loan defaults, liquidity crunch

Step 2: Simulate Scenarios

Scenario 1 Simulation

- Portfolio value before crash: $1 billion
- Portfolio value after 30% decline

  $\$1{,}000{,}000{,}000 \times (1-0.30) = \$700{,}000{,}000$

- Impact: Loss of $300 million in asset value

Scenario 2 Simulation

- Loan portfolio value: $500 million
- Increase in defaults: 10%
- Expected loss: $0.10 \times \$500{,}000{,}000 = \$50{,}000{,}000$
- Impact: $50 million in credit losses

Scenario 3 Simulation

- Current liquidity reserves: $200 million
- Required liquidity: $300 million
- Shortfall: $\$300{,}000{,}000 - \$200{,}000{,}000 = \$100{,}000{,}000$
- Impact: $100 million shortfall in liquidity

Step 3: Evaluate Resilience

- Scenario 1 Resilience: The bank's capital reserves are sufficient to absorb the loss, but the decline in asset value significantly reduces profitability.

- Scenario 2 Resilience: The bank's profitability is impacted by the increased credit losses, but it remains solvent.
- Scenario 3 Resilience: The bank faces a liquidity shortfall and may need to access emergency funding.

Step 4: Implement Mitigation Strategies

- Scenario 1 Strategy: Diversify the investment portfolio to reduce exposure to market crashes.
- Scenario 2 Strategy: Strengthen credit risk management practices and increase loan loss provisions.
- Scenario 3 Strategy: Increase liquidity reserves and establish contingency funding arrangements.

Answer and Explanation

The stress tests reveal that the bank is vulnerable to a liquidity crunch and a sharp decline in asset values. By implementing the recommended mitigation strategies, the bank can enhance its financial resilience and better withstand future crises.

Exercise 4: Scenario Analysis and Stress Testing for a Hypothetical Airline

Scenario

A hypothetical airline is facing several risks as it navigates an increasingly volatile global environment. The airline must conduct a scenario analysis and stress testing to evaluate its financial resilience under various adverse conditions.

Step 1: Scenario Analysis

Identify Key Variables

- **Fuel Price Volatility:** Changes in fuel prices can significantly impact operating costs.

- **Geopolitical Instability:** Political tensions or conflicts could disrupt flight routes and reduce demand.
- **Global Pandemic:** A pandemic could drastically reduce passenger numbers and revenue.

Develop Scenarios

Scenario 1: Fuel Price Spike

- Fuel prices increase by 50%
- Impact: Operating costs rise, reducing profitability

Scenario 2: Geopolitical Conflict

- A major geopolitical conflict disrupts key flight routes
- Impact: Decreased demand and increased operational costs due to rerouting

Scenario 3: Global Pandemic

- A global pandemic leads to a 70% drop in passenger numbers
- Impact: Severe reduction in revenue and potential liquidity crisis

Assess Impact

- Scenario 1 Impact: Increased operating costs by $200 million annually, reducing net profit.
- Scenario 2 Impact: A 20% decrease in revenue due to route disruptions, leading to a $100 million revenue shortfall.
- Scenario 3 Impact: A $500 million loss in revenue, putting the airline at risk of insolvency.

Formulate Strategies

- Scenario 1 Strategy: Implement fuel hedging strategies to lock in fuel prices and reduce exposure to price volatility.
- Scenario 2 Strategy: Diversify flight routes to minimize reliance on conflict-prone regions.

- Scenario 3 Strategy: Reduce operational costs, delay non-essential capital expenditures, and explore government aid to survive the revenue shortfall.

Step 2: Stress Testing

Identify Stress Scenarios

Scenario 1: Fuel Price Spike

- Fuel cost per barrel before spike: $50
- Fuel cost per barrel after 50% increase: $50 × (1+0.50) = $75
- Additional cost impact: $25 × Annual Fuel Consumption in Barrels

Scenario 2: Geopolitical Conflict

- Revenue before conflict: $1 billion
- Revenue reduction due to conflict: 20%
- Revenue after conflict: $1,000,000,000 × (1−0.20) = $800,000,000
- Impact: $200 million revenue loss

Scenario 3: Global Pandemic

- Revenue before pandemic: $1 billion
- Revenue reduction due to pandemic: 70%
- Revenue after pandemic: $1,000,000,000 × (1−0.70) = $300,000,000
- Impact: $700 million revenue loss

Evaluate Resilience

- **Scenario 1 Resilience:** The airline's cost structure is severely impacted, requiring immediate fuel hedging strategies to stabilize costs.
- **Scenario 2 Resilience:** The airline can survive the geopolitical conflict with reduced profitability but needs to explore new markets to offset revenue losses.

- **Scenario 3 Resilience:** The airline faces a severe liquidity crisis and may need to access emergency funding, government support, or reduce operations to survive.

Implement Mitigation Strategies

- **Fuel Price Spike:** Hedge against fuel price increases and explore fuel-efficient technologies.
- **Geopolitical Conflict:** Expand operations in less volatile regions and establish contingency plans for route disruptions.
- **Global Pandemic:** Reduce fleet size temporarily, renegotiate lease agreements, and seek government assistance to maintain operations.

Answer and Explanation

The scenario analysis and stress testing reveal significant risks associated with fuel price volatility, geopolitical instability, and global pandemics. The airline's financial resilience is tested under each scenario, highlighting the need for robust mitigation strategies to manage costs, maintain liquidity, and ensure operational continuity during crises.

Strategic Implications of Risk Assessment

Risk assessment is more than a technical exercise; it plays a crucial role in shaping an organization's strategic direction. By integrating risk assessment into strategic decision-making, organizations can align their risk management practices with long-term goals, enhance competitive positioning, and ensure sustainable growth. This chapter explores how organizations can leverage risk assessment to inform strategic decisions, proactively manage emerging risks, and align risk management with their overall strategy.

Key Concepts in Strategic Risk Assessment

Alignment with Strategy

Aligning risk assessment with an organization's strategy ensures that the risks identified and managed are those that could significantly impact the achievement of strategic objectives. This alignment allows organizations to focus their risk management efforts on areas that are critical to their long-term success.

Steps

- **Identify Strategic Objectives:** Clearly define the organization's long-term goals, such as market expansion, innovation, or cost leadership.
- **Assess Risks:** Conduct risk assessments that focus on identifying risks that could hinder the achievement of these objectives.
- **Prioritize Strategic Risks:** Use the results of the risk assessment to prioritize risks that have the most significant impact on strategic objectives.
- **Integrate with Strategic Planning:** Ensure that risk management practices are embedded in the strategic planning process to address prioritized risks effectively.

Example

A technology company aiming to become a leader in artificial intelligence (AI) identifies key strategic objectives such as developing cutting-edge AI technologies and expanding into new markets. The company conducts a risk assessment to identify potential risks, including rapid technological changes, regulatory challenges, and intellectual property issues.

Step 1: Identify Strategic Objectives

- Objective 1: Lead in AI technology development.
- Objective 2: Expand AI applications into new industries.

Step 2: Assess Risks

- Risk 1: Rapid technological advancements could render current AI technologies obsolete.
- Risk 2: Regulatory hurdles could delay market entry.
- Risk 3: Intellectual property disputes could arise, threatening innovation.

Step 3: Prioritize Strategic Risks

- Priority 1: Rapid technological changes (high impact, high likelihood).
- Priority 2: Regulatory challenges (medium impact, medium likelihood).
- Priority 3: Intellectual property issues (medium impact, low likelihood).

Step 4: Integrate with Strategic Planning

- The company prioritizes investments in R&D to stay ahead of technological advancements and engages with regulators early to navigate potential hurdles. It also strengthens its IP portfolio to protect innovations.

Answer and Explanation

By aligning risk assessment with its strategic objectives, the technology company ensures that its risk management efforts directly support its goal of becoming a leader in AI. This alignment helps the company proactively address critical risks and capitalize on opportunities in the AI sector.

Risk-Informed Decision-Making

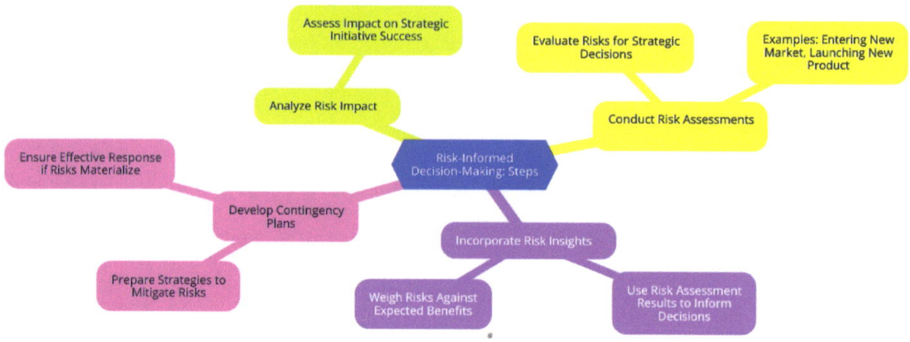

Risk-informed decision-making involves using insights gained from risk assessments to guide strategic decisions. This approach ensures that decisions regarding market entry, mergers and acquisitions, product development, and resource allocation are made with a clear understanding of the associated risks.

Steps

- **Conduct Risk Assessments:** Evaluate the risks associated with key strategic decisions, such as entering a new market or launching a new product.
- **Analyze Risk Impact:** Assess how identified risks could impact the success of the strategic initiative.
- **Incorporate Risk Insights:** Use the risk assessment results to inform decision-making, weighing the potential risks against the expected benefits.
- **Develop Contingency Plans:** Prepare strategies to mitigate identified risks, ensuring that the organization can respond effectively if risks materialize.

Example

A multinational corporation is considering expanding its operations into emerging markets. The company conducts risk assessments to evaluate the potential impact of political instability, currency fluctuations, and regulatory changes in the target markets.

Step 1: Conduct Risk Assessments

- **Political Risk:** Assess the likelihood of political instability and its potential impact on operations.
- **Currency Risk:** Analyze the potential for currency fluctuations and their effect on revenue.
- **Regulatory Risk:** Evaluate the likelihood of changes in local regulations that could affect market entry.

Step 2: Analyze Risk Impact

- **Political Instability:** Could lead to operational disruptions and increased costs.
- **Currency Fluctuations:** Could erode profit margins and affect financial stability.
- **Regulatory Changes:** Could delay market entry or increase compliance costs.

Step 3: Incorporate Risk Insights

- The corporation decides to enter markets with lower political risk and implements currency hedging strategies to mitigate currency risk.

Step 4: Develop Contingency Plans

- Develop plans to exit or reduce operations in high-risk markets if political instability escalates and engage with local regulators to stay informed about potential regulatory changes.

Answer and Explanation

By incorporating risk assessment insights into its decision-making process, the corporation makes informed choices about market entry, balancing the potential risks against the strategic benefits. This approach helps the company minimize exposure to adverse outcomes while pursuing growth opportunities in emerging markets.

Proactive Risk Management

Proactive risk management involves identifying emerging risks early and developing strategies to mitigate them before they escalate. By staying ahead of potential risks, organizations can avoid disruptions and ensure that their strategic objectives remain on track.

Steps

- **Monitor Emerging Risks:** Continuously monitor the external environment for signs of emerging risks, such as changes in market trends, technological advancements, or regulatory shifts.
- **Conduct Regular Risk Assessments:** Perform risk assessments regularly to identify new risks and reassess existing ones.
- **Develop Early Warning Systems:** Implement systems to detect early signs of risk, such as market indicators or changes in consumer behavior.
- **Implement Mitigation Strategies:** Develop and implement strategies to mitigate identified risks, ensuring that the organization can respond quickly to changes in the risk landscape.

Example

A pharmaceutical company is planning to enter the biotechnology sector, which is characterized by rapid technological advancements and regulatory complexities. The company proactively monitors the industry for emerging risks, such as new regulations, advances in gene therapy, and shifts in market demand.

Step 1: Monitor Emerging Risks

- **Technological Risks:** Monitor advancements in gene therapy that could impact the company's biotechnology products.

- **Regulatory Risks:** Stay informed about potential changes in regulations affecting biotechnology.
- **Market Risks:** Track shifts in market demand for biotechnology products.

Step 2: Conduct Regular Risk Assessments

- Assess the impact of emerging technologies on the company's product pipeline.
- Evaluate the potential impact of new regulations on product development timelines.
- Analyze the likelihood of market shifts affecting product demand.

Step 3: Develop Early Warning Systems

- Implement monitoring tools to track technological advancements and regulatory developments.
- Establish key performance indicators (KPIs) to detect changes in market demand.

Step 4: Implement Mitigation Strategies

- Invest in R&D to stay ahead of technological advancements.
- Engage with regulators to influence the development of new regulations.
- Diversify the product portfolio to reduce reliance on any single market segment.

Answer and Explanation

By proactively managing emerging risks, the pharmaceutical company can navigate the complexities of the biotechnology sector and ensure that its strategic objectives are not derailed by unforeseen challenges. This approach positions the company to capitalize on new opportunities while mitigating potential threats.

Exercise 5: Strategic Risk Assessment Plan for a Hypothetical Pharmaceutical Company

Scenario

A hypothetical pharmaceutical company is planning to enter the biotechnology sector, focusing on the development of gene therapies. The company needs to create a strategic risk assessment plan to identify and manage the risks associated with this expansion.

Step 1: Identify Key Risks

- **Technological Risk:** The rapid pace of technological advancements in gene therapy could render the company's products obsolete before they reach the market.
- **Regulatory Risk:** The biotechnology sector is heavily regulated, and changes in regulations could delay product approval or increase compliance costs.
- **Market Risk:** The demand for gene therapies could fluctuate based on healthcare trends, reimbursement policies, and public perception.
- **Intellectual Property (IP) Risk:** There is a risk of IP disputes over gene therapy technologies, which could lead to legal challenges and delays.

Step 2: Use Scenario Analysis

Scenario 1: Technological Leap (Best-Case)

A breakthrough in gene therapy technology accelerates product development, leading to early market entry and high demand.

- Impact: Increased revenue and market share.
- Strategy: Increase investment in R&D to capitalize on technological advancements.

Scenario 2: Regulatory Tightening (Base-Case)

New regulations are introduced, requiring additional clinical trials and increasing compliance costs.

- Impact: Delays in product approval and higher development costs.
- Strategy: Engage with regulators early to influence policy development and allocate resources for additional trials.

Scenario 3: Market Backlash (Worst-Case)

Public concern over the safety and ethics of gene therapies leads to reduced demand and negative media coverage.

- Impact: Decline in sales and reputational damage.
- Strategy: Launch a public awareness campaign to educate the public about the benefits of gene therapy and address ethical concerns.

Step 3: Align Risk Management with Strategic Objectives

Objective 1: Lead in the development of innovative gene therapies.

- Risk: Technological Risk
- Strategy: Invest in cutting-edge R&D and partner with leading research institutions to stay at the forefront of gene therapy advancements.

Objective 2: Successfully navigate the regulatory environment to achieve timely product approvals.

- Risk: Regulatory Risk
- Strategy: Build a strong regulatory affairs team and engage with policymakers to influence the regulatory landscape.

Objective 3: Establish a strong market presence and build trust with stakeholders.

- Risk: Market and Reputational Risk

- Strategy: Develop a comprehensive marketing and communications strategy that emphasizes the safety, efficacy, and ethical considerations of gene therapies.

Answer and Explanation

The strategic risk assessment plan enables the pharmaceutical company to align its risk management efforts with its strategic objectives in the biotechnology sector. By identifying key risks and using scenario analysis, the company can develop targeted strategies to mitigate potential threats and capitalize on opportunities. This approach ensures that the company is well-positioned to succeed in the rapidly evolving field of gene therapy.

Chapter

05

Measuring and Quantifying Risk

Effective risk management hinges on the ability to measure and quantify risk accurately. By employing various methodologies and models, organizations can better understand their exposure to different types of risks and develop strategies to mitigate them. This chapter explores key concepts and techniques for measuring and quantifying risk, with practical examples and exercises to solidify understanding.

Value at Risk (VaR) and its Variants

Value at Risk (VaR) is a widely used risk measure that estimates the potential loss in value of a portfolio over a specified period, given a certain confidence level. VaR provides a single number summarizing the maximum expected loss over a given time horizon with a specified probability. It is an essential tool for financial institutions, investment managers, and risk professionals to quantify the risk of loss in their portfolios and make informed decisions.

Key Concepts in VaR

Confidence Level

The confidence level represents the probability that the loss will not exceed the VaR estimate. Common confidence levels are 95% and 99%. For example, a 95% confidence level implies that there is a 5% chance that the loss will exceed the VaR estimate.

Time Horizon

The time horizon is the period over which the VaR is calculated, typically one day, one week, or one month. The choice of time horizon depends on the context and the specific needs of the organization.

Formula for VaR

The basic formula for VaR, assuming normally distributed returns, is:

$$VaR = Z\alpha \times \sigma \times \sqrt{T} \times \text{Portfolio Value}$$

Where:

- $Z\alpha$ is the Z-score corresponding to the confidence level.
- σ is the standard deviation of portfolio returns.
- T is the time horizon.

Example Calculation: 1-Day VaR at 95% Confidence Level

Scenario

Assume a portfolio worth $10 million with a daily standard deviation (volatility) of 2%. Calculate the 1-day VaR at a 95% confidence level.

Step 1: Identify the Z-score

- The Z-score for a 95% confidence level is 1.65.

Step 2: Apply the VaR formula

- $\text{VaR} = 1.65 \times 0.02 \times \sqrt{1} \times \$10{,}000{,}000 = \$330{,}000$

Answer and Explanation

The 1-day VaR at a 95% confidence level is $330,000. This means there is a 95% probability that the portfolio will not lose more than $330,000 in one day. Conversely, there is a 5% probability that the loss could exceed $330,000 in one day.

Variants of VaR

Historical VaR

Historical VaR uses actual historical returns to calculate potential losses. The method reorders past returns to determine the loss at the desired confidence level.

Steps

- Collect historical return data for the portfolio.
- Order the returns from worst to best.
- Identify the return corresponding to the desired confidence level.

- Calculate VaR as the negative of this return multiplied by the portfolio value.

Example Calculation

Assume a portfolio with the following five daily returns: -2.5%, -1.8%, -1.2%, 0.5%, and 1.0%. For a 95% confidence level, the worst 5% of outcomes corresponds to the -1.8% return.

VaR = −(−1.8%) × \$10,000,000 = 1.8% × \$10,000,000 = \$180,000

Answer and Explanation

The Historical VaR at a 95% confidence level is \$180,000, meaning there is a 95% probability that the portfolio will not lose more than \$180,000 in one day based on historical data.

Monte Carlo VaR

Monte Carlo VaR uses simulations to model a wide range of possible outcomes based on random sampling from a probability distribution. It provides a more comprehensive view of potential losses by considering a large number of simulated scenarios.

Steps

- Define the probability distribution of returns (e.g., normal distribution).
- Simulate a large number of potential future returns based on this distribution.
- Calculate the portfolio value under each simulated return.
- Identify the loss corresponding to the desired confidence level.

Example Calculation

Suppose we simulate 10,000 daily returns for a portfolio with a mean return of 0% and a standard deviation of 2%. After running the simulations, we find that the 95th percentile loss is \$350,000.

VaR = $350,000

Answer and Explanation

The Monte Carlo VaR at a 95% confidence level is $350,000, indicating that there is a 95% probability that the portfolio will not lose more than $350,000 in one day under the simulated scenarios.

Exercise 1: Calculate 10-Day VaR at 99% Confidence Level

Scenario

Calculate the 10-day VaR at a 99% confidence level for a portfolio with a value of $5 million and a daily standard deviation of 1.5%. Use both the parametric and historical methods.

Parametric VaR Calculation

Step 1: Identify the Z-score

- The Z-score for a 99% confidence level is 2.33.

Step 2: Apply the VaR formula

- VaR = 2.33 × 0.015 × √10 × $5,000,000
- VaR = 2.33 × 0.015 × 3.16 × $5,000,000
- VaR = 2.33 × 0.0474 × $5,000,000 = $553,710

Answer and Explanation

The 10-day VaR at a 99% confidence level using the parametric method is $553,710. This means there is a 99% probability that the portfolio will not lose more than $553,710 over 10 days.

Historical VaR Calculation

Step 1: Gather historical return data

- Assume we have 100 days of historical returns for the portfolio, and the worst 1% of returns corresponds to a -4% return.

Step 2: Calculate Historical VaR

- Historical VaR = –(–4%) × \$5,000,000 = 4% × \$5,000,000 = \$200,000

Answer and Explanation

The Historical VaR at a 99% confidence level for a 10-day period is \$200,000, based on the worst 1% of historical returns. This indicates there is a 99% probability that the portfolio will not lose more than \$200,000 over 10 days based on past performance.

Expected Shortfall (ES) and Tail Risk

Expected Shortfall (ES), also known as Conditional Value at Risk (CVaR), is a risk measure that provides insights into the tail end of the loss distribution. While Value at Risk (VaR) indicates the maximum loss at a specified confidence level, ES estimates the average loss if the actual loss exceeds the VaR threshold. This makes ES particularly useful for understanding the potential impact of extreme events, also known as tail risks, which are not fully captured by traditional risk measures like VaR.

Key Concepts in Expected Shortfall and Tail Risk

Tail Risk

Tail risk refers to the risk of extreme loss events that occur at the far ends (tails) of the probability distribution. These risks are rare but can have severe financial consequences. Traditional measures like VaR may not fully capture tail risks because they focus only on the maximum expected loss at a given confidence level, without considering what happens beyond that point.

Expected Shortfall (ES)

Expected Shortfall is a measure that estimates the average loss beyond the VaR threshold. It provides a more comprehensive view of risk by considering the severity of losses in the tail of the distribution, offering valuable insights for managing extreme risks.

Formula for Expected Shortfall (ES): For normally distributed returns, ES can be approximated as: ES = 1 / 1 – α [$\int\alpha$ VaR$\beta d\beta$]

However, in practical applications, ES is often estimated by adding an expected mean excess loss beyond VaR to the VaR itself: ES ≈ VaR + mean excess loss beyond VaR

Example Calculation: Expected Shortfall (ES) at 99% Confidence Level

Scenario

Assume a portfolio has a 1-day VaR at a 99% confidence level of $400,000. Calculate the Expected Shortfall (ES), assuming normally distributed returns and an additional expected mean excess loss of $50,000 beyond the VaR threshold.

Step 1: Identify the VaR

- The 1-day VaR at a 99% confidence level is given as $400,000.

Step 2: Estimate the Expected Shortfall (ES)

- ES can be approximated by adding the mean excess loss beyond VaR to the VaR:
- ES = VaR + mean excess loss beyond VaR
- ES = $400,000 + $50,000 = $450,000

Answer and Explanation

The Expected Shortfall (ES) at a 99% confidence level is \$450,000. This means that if losses exceed the VaR threshold of \$400,000, the average loss would be \$450,000. ES provides a more complete picture of the potential severity of losses by accounting for extreme events beyond the VaR threshold.

Exercise 2: Estimating Expected Shortfall (ES) for a 5-Day VaR

Scenario

A portfolio has a 5-day VaR of \$200,000 at a 95% confidence level. Estimate the Expected Shortfall (ES), assuming an average excess loss of 10% beyond the VaR. How does this compare to the VaR?

Step 1: Identify the 5-Day VaR

- The 5-day VaR at a 95% confidence level is given as \$200,000.

Step 2: Calculate the Mean Excess Loss Beyond VaR

- Assume the mean excess loss beyond the VaR is 10% of the VaR

  $\text{Mean Excess Loss} = 0.10 \times \$200,000 = \$20,000$

Step 3: Estimate the Expected Shortfall (ES)

- Use the formula to estimate ES

  $\text{ES} = \text{VaR} + \text{Mean Excess Loss}$

  $\text{ES} = \$200,000 + \$20,000 = \$220,000$

Answer and Explanation

The Expected Shortfall (ES) for the portfolio is \$220,000. This means that if losses exceed the 5-day VaR of \$200,000, the average loss is expected to be \$220,000. Compared to the VaR, the ES provides a more comprehensive measure of risk by considering the potential severity of losses beyond the VaR threshold.

Comparison of VaR and Expected Shortfall

VaR (Value at Risk)

- Provides a threshold value that losses are not expected to exceed within a given confidence level.
- Does not account for the magnitude of losses beyond the VaR threshold.

ES (Expected Shortfall)

- Measures the average loss beyond the VaR threshold, offering a more complete view of tail risk.
- Provides valuable insights for managing extreme risks that are not captured by VaR alone.

Key Takeaway

While VaR is useful for determining the maximum expected loss within a certain confidence level, Expected Shortfall (ES) provides a more comprehensive understanding of potential risks by considering the severity of losses beyond the VaR threshold. ES is particularly valuable for organizations that need to manage tail risks and prepare for extreme loss events.

Conclusion

Expected Shortfall (ES) and tail risk measures are critical tools for understanding the potential impact of extreme events on a portfolio. By focusing on losses beyond the VaR threshold, ES provides a more complete picture of risk, helping organizations better manage the potential severity of losses. The examples and exercises in this chapter demonstrate how ES can be calculated and compared to VaR, offering valuable insights for managing extreme risks in various financial contexts.

Credit Scoring Models and Credit Risk Measurement

Credit risk measurement is a fundamental aspect of risk management in financial institutions, involving the assessment of the likelihood that a borrower will default on their obligations. Credit scoring models, such as the FICO score, play a crucial role in quantifying credit risk and informing lending decisions. These models help lenders evaluate the creditworthiness of borrowers by predicting the probability of default (PD), assessing the potential loss given default (LGD), and determining the exposure at default (EAD).

Key Concepts in Credit Risk Measurement

Probability of Default (PD)

PD is the likelihood that a borrower will default on their loan within a specified period, typically one year. It is expressed as a percentage and is a key component in calculating the expected credit loss (ECL).

Calculation

PD is often derived from credit scoring models or historical data on borrower defaults.

Loss Given Default (LGD)

LGD represents the portion of the loan that is lost if the borrower defaults, after accounting for recoveries such as collateral liquidation or guarantor payments. It is also expressed as a percentage.

Calculation

LGD is calculated by subtracting the recovery rate from 100%. For example, if the recovery rate is 40%, then LGD is 60%.

Exposure at Default (EAD)

EAD is the total value exposed to loss at the time of default. It represents the outstanding loan balance at the time of default, including any accrued interest or fees.

Calculation

EAD is typically the outstanding loan balance, but it may also include undrawn credit lines or other contingent exposures.

Credit Risk Formula

The ECL is the expected amount of loss due to credit risk and is calculated using the following formula: ECL = PD × LGD × EAD

This formula quantifies the average loss that a lender expects to incur due to borrower default.

Example Calculation: Expected Credit Loss (ECL)

Scenario

A bank lends $1 million to a borrower with the following credit risk parameters:

- Probability of Default (PD): 5% (0.05)
- Loss Given Default (LGD): 60% (0.60)
- Exposure at Default (EAD): $1,000,000

Step 1: Apply the ECL Formula

- ECL = PD × LGD × EAD

  ECL = 0.05 × 0.60 × \$1,000,000

  ECL = 0.03 × \$1,000,000 = \$30,000

Answer and Explanation

The Expected Credit Loss for this loan is \$30,000. This means that, on average, the bank expects to lose \$30,000 from this loan due to the potential default of the borrower. This calculation helps the bank determine how much capital it needs to set aside to cover potential losses from this loan.

Application of Credit Scoring Models
FICO Score

The FICO score is a commonly used credit scoring model that assesses a borrower's creditworthiness based on factors such as payment history, amounts owed, length of credit history, new credit, and types of credit used. Higher FICO scores indicate lower credit risk and a lower probability of default.

Custom Credit Scoring Models

Financial institutions often develop custom credit scoring models tailored to their specific portfolios and risk preferences. These models may incorporate additional factors, such as income, employment history, and industry-specific risks.

Use of PD in Credit Scoring

The probability of default is a direct output of credit scoring models. For example, a borrower with a FICO score of 720 may have an estimated PD of 2%, while a borrower with a score of 600 may have a PD of 8%.

Exercise 3: Calculate the Expected Credit Loss (ECL) for a Loan Portfolio

Scenario

A bank has a loan portfolio worth $10 million, consisting of various borrowers with different credit risk profiles. The bank uses the following average credit risk parameters across the portfolio:

- Average Probability of Default (PD): 4% (0.04)
- Average Loss Given Default (LGD): 50% (0.50)
- Exposure at Default (EAD): $10,000,000

Step 1: Apply the ECL Formula

- ECL = PD × LGD × EAD

  ECL = 0.04 × 0.50 × $10,000,000

  ECL = 0.02 × $10,000,000 = $200,000

Answer and Explanation

The Expected Credit Loss for the entire loan portfolio is $200,000. This calculation indicates that the bank expects to lose $200,000 on average from its $10 million loan portfolio due to borrower defaults. This figure helps the bank in determining the necessary provisions for potential credit losses and informs its capital allocation strategies.

Strategic Implications of Credit Risk Measurement

Risk-Based Pricing

By accurately measuring credit risk, financial institutions can implement risk-based pricing, where higher-risk borrowers are charged higher interest rates to compensate for the increased risk of default. This approach ensures that the lender is adequately compensated for the risk it assumes.

Capital Allocation

Credit risk measurement informs the amount of capital that a bank must set aside to cover potential losses. Institutions with higher credit risk exposures may need to hold more capital to absorb potential losses, which can impact their profitability and lending capacity.

Portfolio Management

Understanding the credit risk profile of a loan portfolio allows financial institutions to optimize their portfolio by diversifying their exposures and avoiding excessive concentration in high-risk segments. This can lead to more stable returns and reduced volatility.

Regulatory Compliance

Accurate credit risk measurement is essential for regulatory compliance, particularly under frameworks such as Basel III, which require banks to maintain adequate capital based on their risk-weighted assets. Failure to accurately measure and manage credit risk can result in regulatory penalties and increased capital requirements.

Conclusion

Credit scoring models and credit risk measurement are vital tools for managing the risk of borrower defaults. By calculating key metrics such as Probability of Default (PD), Loss Given Default (LGD), and Exposure at Default (EAD), financial institutions can estimate the Expected Credit Loss (ECL) and make informed decisions about lending, pricing, and capital allocation. The examples and exercises provided in this chapter demonstrate how these concepts can be applied to assess and manage credit risk effectively, ensuring that financial institutions remain resilient in the face of potential defaults.

Measuring Operational and Liquidity Risks

Operational and liquidity risks are two critical aspects of risk management that organizations must address to ensure stability and resilience. Operational risk arises from failures in internal processes, systems, people, or external events, while liquidity risk pertains to the organization's ability to meet its short-term financial obligations. This guide explores the key concepts, formulas, and practical examples for quantifying and managing these risks.

Operational Risk

Operational risk is the risk of loss resulting from inadequate or failed internal processes, people, systems, or external events. This type of risk can be quantified by assessing the frequency of loss events and the severity of their financial impact.

Key Concepts in Operational Risk

- **Frequency:** The expected number of operational loss events within a given time period, typically measured annually.
- **Severity:** The potential financial impact of a single loss event, often expressed as an average loss amount.
- **Operational Risk Formula:** The expected operational risk loss can be calculated using the formula: Operational Risk Loss = Frequency × Severity

Example Calculation: Operational Risk Loss

Scenario

A bank expects to experience 5 operational loss events per year, with each event resulting in an average loss of $100,000.

Step 1: Apply the Operational Risk Formula

- Operational Risk Loss = Frequency × Severity

  Operational Risk Loss = 5 × $100,000 = $500,000

Answer and Explanation

The bank's expected operational risk loss is $500,000 annually. This figure represents the potential financial impact of operational risks that the bank might face over the course of a year. By quantifying this risk, the bank can allocate resources to mitigate these risks and reduce potential losses.

Liquidity Risk

Liquidity risk refers to the risk that an organization will not be able to meet its short-term financial obligations due to the inability to quickly convert assets into cash without incurring significant losses. This risk is critical for financial institutions, as it can lead to insolvency if not properly managed.

Key Concepts in Liquidity Risk

- **Liquidity Coverage Ratio (LCR):** The Liquidity Coverage Ratio is a regulatory standard that ensures a financial institution has enough high-quality liquid assets (HQLA) to cover its net cash outflows over a 30-day stress period.

LCR Formula

- The LCR is calculated using the following formula

  LCR = High-Quality Liquid Assets (HQLA) / Net Cash Outflows over 30 Days × 100

A higher LCR indicates better liquidity coverage and a stronger ability to meet short-term obligations.

Example Calculation: Liquidity Coverage Ratio (LCR)

Scenario

Assume a financial institution has high-quality liquid assets (HQLA) worth $500 million and expected net cash outflows of $400 million over a 30-day stress period.

Step 1: Calculate the LCR

- LCR = $500,000,000 / $400,000,000 × 100 = 125%

Answer and Explanation

The institution's LCR is 125%, indicating that it has sufficient liquid assets to cover its short-term obligations during a stress scenario. A ratio above 100% suggests that the institution is well-prepared to handle short-term liquidity needs, while a lower ratio might indicate potential liquidity risk.

Exercise 4: Calculating the Liquidity Coverage Ratio (LCR)

Scenario

A financial institution has high-quality liquid assets (HQLA) worth $800 million and expected net cash outflows of $1 billion over a 30-day stress period. Calculate the LCR and discuss the implications of the result.

Step 1: Calculate the LCR

- LCR = $800,000,000 / $1,000,000,000 × 100 = 80%

Answer and Explanation

The LCR for this institution is 80%. This indicates that the institution only has enough high-quality liquid assets to cover 80% of its expected net cash outflows over a 30-day period. An LCR below 100% suggests that the institution may face difficulties in meeting its short-term obligations during a stress scenario, potentially leading to liquidity shortages or the need to liquidate assets at unfavorable prices. This could impact the institution's financial stability and necessitate immediate action to bolster liquidity reserves.

Implications

- **Liquidity Shortfall:** An LCR of 80% highlights a potential liquidity shortfall, meaning the institution may not be able to cover all its short-term liabilities if faced with a stress scenario.
- **Regulatory Compliance:** Financial institutions are typically required to maintain an LCR of at least 100% under regulatory standards (e.g., Basel III). Falling below this threshold could result in regulatory penalties or the need for corrective action.
- **Risk Mitigation:** To address this risk, the institution may need to increase its holdings of high-quality liquid assets, reduce its net cash outflows, or explore other liquidity management strategies such as securing additional lines of credit or raising capital.

Strategic Implications of Operational and Liquidity Risk Measurement

Operational Risk Management

By quantifying operational risk, organizations can identify areas of vulnerability and implement controls to reduce the frequency and severity of loss events. This could include strengthening internal processes, investing in technology to improve system reliability, and enhancing employee training programs.

Liquidity Management

Monitoring and maintaining a strong Liquidity Coverage Ratio (LCR) is critical for ensuring that financial institutions can withstand periods of financial stress. Institutions must regularly assess their liquidity positions and adjust their asset-liability management strategies to avoid liquidity crises.

Regulatory Compliance

Both operational and liquidity risk measures are essential for meeting regulatory requirements. Financial institutions must demonstrate that they have adequate risk management frameworks in place to address these risks, ensuring compliance with standards such as Basel III.

Strategic Decision-Making

Understanding operational and liquidity risks allows organizations to make informed strategic decisions, such as expanding operations, launching new products, or entering new markets. Effective risk management ensures that these decisions are made with a clear understanding of the potential risks and the measures needed to mitigate them.

Conclusion

Measuring operational and liquidity risks is essential for the stability and resilience of financial institutions and other organizations. By quantifying operational risks through frequency and severity assessments and managing liquidity risks using metrics like the Liquidity Coverage Ratio (LCR), organizations can proactively address potential challenges and maintain financial stability. The examples and exercises provided in this chapter illustrate how these risks can be measured and managed effectively, ensuring that organizations are well-prepared to navigate periods of uncertainty and financial stress.

Strategic Considerations in Risk Measurement

Strategic risk measurement is the process of aligning risk measurement practices with an organization's strategic goals. This approach ensures that risk management activities support long-term success by identifying, quantifying, and mitigating risks that could hinder the achievement of strategic objectives. A well-integrated risk measurement framework considers the interdependencies between different types of risks and provides insights into how these risks collectively impact the organization.

Key Concepts in Strategic Risk Measurement

Alignment with Strategy

Risk measurement should be directly aligned with the organization's strategic priorities. This means focusing on risks that could impede the achievement of long-term goals and ensuring that risk metrics are relevant to strategic decision-making.

Holistic Approach

A holistic approach to risk measurement involves considering the interdependencies between different types of risks, such as market risk, credit risk, operational risk, and liquidity risk. Understanding how these risks interact and affect each other allows for more comprehensive risk management.

Integration of Risk Metrics

Strategic risk measurement requires the integration of various risk metrics, such as Value at Risk (VaR), Expected Shortfall (ES), and credit scoring models, to provide a comprehensive view of potential threats and opportunities.

Example: Strategic Risk Measurement for Market Expansion

Scenario

A multinational corporation is planning to expand into emerging markets. The company's strategic goal is to capture a significant market share in these regions while managing potential risks such as political instability, economic volatility, and currency fluctuations. To achieve this, the corporation aligns its risk measurement practices with its expansion strategy.

Step 1: Align Risk Measurement with Strategy

- **Strategic Objective:** Expand into emerging markets with a focus on long-term growth.
- **Risk Measurement Focus:** Identify and quantify risks related to market entry, political stability, economic conditions, and currency fluctuations.

Step 2: Use VaR to Measure Market Risk

- **Objective:** Assess the potential impact of market volatility on the company's financial performance.
- **Application:** Calculate the 1-year VaR for investments in emerging market currencies and equities to estimate potential losses due to market fluctuations.

Example Calculation

Assume the company's investment in an emerging market currency is $10 million with a daily standard deviation (volatility) of 2.5% and a 1-year VaR at a 95% confidence level.

Step 1 Identify the Z-score for a 95% confidence level (Z = 1.65).

Step 2 Apply the VaR formula

- $\text{VaR} = Z\alpha \times \sigma \times \sqrt{T} \times \text{Portfolio Value}$
  $\text{VaR} = 1.65 \times 0.025 \times \sqrt{252} \times \$10{,}000{,}000$
  $\text{VaR} = 1.65 \times 0.025 \times 15.87 \times \$10{,}000{,}000 = \$6{,}560{,}175$

Answer and Explanation

The 1-year VaR at a 95% confidence level is approximately $6.56 million. This indicates that there is a 95% probability that the company will not lose more than $6.56 million due to currency fluctuations in the emerging market over one year.

Step 3: Use Expected Shortfall to Assess Tail Risk

- **Objective:** Estimate the average loss beyond the VaR threshold in extreme market conditions.
- **Application:** Calculate the Expected Shortfall (ES) to understand the potential impact of severe market events.
- **Example Calculation:** Assume the Expected Shortfall for the same investment is calculated with an additional expected loss beyond VaR of $1 million.
  ES ≈ VaR + Mean Excess Loss
  ES = $6,560,175 + $1,000,000 = $7,560,175

Answer and Explanation

The Expected Shortfall (ES) is approximately $7.56 million. This indicates that if losses exceed the VaR threshold, the average loss is expected to be $7.56 million, providing a more comprehensive view of potential extreme losses.

Step 4: Use Credit Scoring Models to Assess Credit Risk

- **Objective:** Evaluate the creditworthiness of potential business partners and counterparties in emerging markets.
- **Application:** Implement credit scoring models to assess the Probability of Default (PD) and calculate the Expected Credit Loss (ECL) for loans or receivables associated with market expansion.
- **Example Calculation:** Assume the company extends $5 million in credit to a partner in an emerging market with a PD of 6% and an LGD of 50%.

  Apply the ECL formula
  ECL = PD × LGD × EAD
  ECL = 0.06 × 0.50 × $5,000,000 = $150,000

Answer and Explanation

The Expected Credit Loss (ECL) is $150,000. This calculation helps the company understand the potential credit risk associated with extending credit to a partner in the emerging market.

Step 5: Develop a Holistic Risk Management Strategy

- **Objective:** Ensure that the company's risk management practices support its strategic goals by considering all relevant risks.
- **Application:** Integrate the results of VaR, ES, and credit risk assessments into a comprehensive risk management plan that addresses the key risks of market entry.

Strategic Considerations

- **Risk Mitigation:** Develop strategies to mitigate identified risks, such as using currency hedging to manage market risk, diversifying investments to reduce exposure, and requiring collateral to lower credit risk.
- **Scenario Analysis:** Conduct scenario analysis to explore potential future outcomes and their impact on the company's strategy. Consider best-case, base-case, and worst-case scenarios for market entry.
- **Continuous Monitoring**: Establish a framework for ongoing monitoring of risks, with regular updates to risk assessments as market conditions change.

Exercise 5: Strategic Risk Measurement Plan for a Renewable Energy Company

Scenario

A hypothetical company is planning to enter the renewable energy sector, focusing on solar and wind energy projects. The company needs to develop a strategic risk measurement plan to assess the risks associated with this initiative, including market risk, credit risk, and tail risk.

Step 1: Align Risk Measurement with Strategic Goals

- **Strategic Objective:** Become a leader in renewable energy by developing large-scale solar and wind projects.
- **Risk Measurement Focus:** Identify and quantify risks related to market volatility, creditworthiness of partners, and extreme events.

Step 2: Use VaR to Measure Market Risk

- **Objective:** Assess the potential impact of fluctuations in energy prices on project profitability.
- **Application:** Calculate the 1-year VaR for the company's investment in solar and wind projects.
- **Example Calculation:** Assume the company's investment in renewable energy is $20 million with a daily standard deviation (volatility) of 3% and a 1-year VaR at a 99% confidence level.

  Step 1: Identify the Z-score for a 99% confidence level (Z = 2.33).
  Step 2: Apply the VaR formula
  $\text{VaR} = 2.33 \times 0.03 \times \sqrt{252} \times \$20{,}000{,}000$
  $\text{VaR} = 2.33 \times 0.03 \times 15.87 \times \$20{,}000{,}000 = \$22{,}130{,}334$

Answer and Explanation

The 1-year VaR at a 99% confidence level is approximately $22.13 million, indicating that there is a 99% probability that the company will not lose more than $22.13 million due to fluctuations in energy prices over one year.

Step 3: Use Expected Shortfall to Assess Tail Risk

- **Objective:** Estimate the average loss beyond the VaR threshold in extreme market conditions.

- **Application:** Calculate the Expected Shortfall (ES) for the same investment in renewable energy projects.
- **Example Calculation:** Assume an additional expected loss beyond VaR of $2 million.

$$ES \approx VaR + \text{Mean Excess Loss}$$
$$ES = \$22,130,334 + \$2,000,000 = \$24,130,334$$

Answer and Explanation

The Expected Shortfall (ES) is approximately $24.13 million, providing a more comprehensive view of potential extreme losses in the renewable energy sector.

Step 4: Use Credit Scoring Models to Assess Credit Risk

- **Objective:** Evaluate the creditworthiness of suppliers, contractors, and partners involved in the renewable energy projects.
- **Application:** Implement credit scoring models to assess the Probability of Default (PD) and calculate the Expected Credit Loss (ECL).
- **Example Calculation:** Assume the company extends $10 million in credit to a contractor with a PD of 4% and an LGD of 40%.

Apply the ECL formula

$$ECL = PD \times LGD \times EAD$$
$$ECL = 0.04 \times 0.40 \times \$10,000,000 = \$160,000$$

Answer and Explanation

The Expected Credit Loss (ECL) is $160,000, helping the company understand the potential credit risk associated with its contractors.

Step 5: Develop a Holistic Risk Management Strategy

- **Objective:** Ensure that the company's risk management practices support its strategic goals in the renewable energy sector.

- **Application:** Integrate the results of VaR, ES, and credit risk assessments into a comprehensive risk management plan.

Strategic Considerations

- **Risk Mitigation:** Implement hedging strategies to manage energy price volatility, diversify projects across different locations to reduce exposure to localized risks, and require strong contractual protections with suppliers and contractors to mitigate credit risk.
- **Scenario Analysis:** Conduct scenario analysis to explore different outcomes for renewable energy projects, considering factors such as regulatory changes, technological advancements, and market demand.
- **Continuous Monitoring:** Establish a risk monitoring framework to track changes in market conditions, creditworthiness, and project performance, with regular updates to the risk measurement plan.

Conclusion

Strategic risk measurement is essential for aligning risk management practices with an organization's long-term goals. By integrating risk metrics such as Value at Risk (VaR), Expected Shortfall (ES), and credit scoring models into a comprehensive risk management plan, organizations can better understand and mitigate the risks associated with their strategic initiatives. The examples and exercises in this chapter demonstrate how to apply these concepts in various contexts, ensuring that risk measurement supports informed decision-making and sustainable growth.

Chapter

06

Risk Mitigation Strategies

Risk mitigation is the process of developing and implementing strategies to reduce or manage the impact of potential risks on an organization. Effective risk mitigation not only helps in safeguarding assets and revenues but also ensures that the organization can achieve its strategic objectives even in the face of uncertainty. This chapter explores various risk mitigation strategies, including hedging, diversification, derivatives, insurance, and strategic measures, supplemented with practical examples and exercises to reinforce the concepts.

Hedging and Diversification

Hedging and diversification are two essential strategies in financial risk management, each playing a critical role in protecting against potential losses and managing risk exposure. Hedging involves taking offsetting positions in related assets to reduce the impact of adverse price movements, while diversification spreads investments across various assets to reduce exposure to any single risk. This chapter explores these strategies in detail, providing extended explanations, calculations, and practical examples, along with exercises designed to reinforce the concepts.

Hedging

Hedging is a financial strategy designed to reduce the risk of adverse price movements in an asset by taking an opposing position in a related asset. The primary goal of hedging is to reduce uncertainty and protect against potential losses. While hedging can effectively reduce risk, it often comes with a cost and may limit potential gains.

Key Concepts

- **Hedging Instruments:** Common instruments used for hedging include forward contracts, futures contracts, options, and swaps.
- **Hedging Cost:** The cost of implementing a hedge, such as the premium paid for an option or the opportunity cost of locking in a forward rate, must be considered when deciding whether to hedge.
- **Perfect vs. Imperfect Hedging:** A perfect hedge completely eliminates risk, whereas an imperfect hedge reduces risk but does not eliminate it entirely.

- **Example:** Consider a U.S.-based company that imports raw materials from Europe. The company is concerned about the risk of the euro appreciating against the U.S. dollar, which would increase the cost of imports in dollar terms. To hedge this currency risk, the company enters into a forward contract to purchase euros at the current exchange rate, locking in the rate and eliminating the uncertainty of future exchange rate fluctuations.

Detailed Example with Calculations

Scenario

A U.S.-based company expects to receive €1 million in six months from a European customer. The current exchange rate is 1.10 USD/EUR. The company is concerned that the euro might depreciate against the dollar, reducing the dollar value of the payment.

Task

Design a hedging strategy using forward contracts to protect against this currency risk. What will be the outcome if the exchange rate falls to 1.05 USD/EUR?

Step-by-Step Solution

- **Identify the Exposure**
  - The company is exposed to the risk of the euro depreciating against the U.S. dollar. If the euro's value decreases, the company will receive fewer dollars when converting the payment.
- **Hedging Strategy**
  - The company can enter into a forward contract to sell €1 million in six months at the current exchange rate of 1.10 USD/EUR. This locks in the rate and guarantees that the company

will receive $1.1 million, regardless of future exchange rate movements.

- **Forward Contract Details**
    - Amount: €1,000,000
    - Forward Rate: 1.10 USD/EUR
    - Settlement Date: Six months from now

- **Outcome if the Exchange Rate Falls to 1.05 USD/EUR**
    - Without the hedge: If the exchange rate falls to 1.05 USD/EUR, the company would receive €1,000,000 × 1.05 = $1,050,000.
    - With the hedge: The forward contract ensures that the company receives €1,000,000 × 1.10 = $1,100,000, regardless of the exchange rate at the time of settlement.

- **Comparison**
    - By hedging, the company secures an additional $50,000 compared to not hedging, effectively mitigating the currency risk.

Exercise 1

Scenario: Assume a U.S.-based company expects to pay €500,000 for imported goods in three months. The current exchange rate is 1.15 USD/EUR, and the company fears that the euro might appreciate against the dollar.

Task: Design a hedging strategy using forward contracts to protect against the risk of the euro appreciating. What will be the outcome if the exchange rate rises to 1.20 USD/EUR?

Answer and Explanation

- **Hedging Strategy:** The company can enter into a forward contract to buy €500,000 at the current exchange rate of 1.15 USD/EUR.

This locks in the rate and guarantees that the company will pay \$575,000 for the euros in three months.

- **Outcome:** If the exchange rate rises to 1.20 USD/EUR, the company would have had to pay €500,000 × 1.20 = \$600,000 without the hedge. With the hedge, the company only pays \$575,000, saving \$25,000 by hedging.

Diversification

Diversification is a risk management strategy that involves spreading investments across various assets, sectors, or geographic regions to reduce exposure to any single risk. The core idea is that the poor performance of one asset or sector can be offset by the strong performance of another, thereby reducing overall portfolio risk.

Key Concepts

- **Asset Allocation:** Diversifying investments across different asset classes, such as equities, bonds, and commodities, helps reduce the risk of significant losses.
- **Sector Diversification:** Investing in stocks from different industries reduces the impact of sector-specific risks.
- **Geographic Diversification:** Investing in assets from different geographic regions reduces the risk associated with country-specific events, such as political instability or economic downturns.
- **Example:** An investment portfolio that includes a mix of stocks from different industries, bonds, and commodities is diversified. For instance, if the technology sector underperforms, the negative impact may be mitigated by gains in other sectors like healthcare or energy, as well as the stability provided by bonds and commodities.

Detailed Example with Calculations

Scenario

You have $100,000 to invest and want to create a diversified portfolio. You decide to allocate your funds across equities, bonds, and commodities. Your goal is to minimize risk while aiming for steady returns.

Task

Construct a diversified investment portfolio, allocate funds to different asset classes, and justify your allocation choices.

Step-by-Step Solution

- **Asset Allocation**
    - Equities: $50,000 (50% of the portfolio)
    - Bonds: $30,000 (30% of the portfolio)
    - Commodities: $20,000 (20% of the portfolio)
- **Justification of Allocation**
    - Equities (50%): Equities typically offer higher potential returns, but they also come with higher risk. By spreading investments across different industries (e.g., technology, healthcare, consumer goods), the portfolio reduces sector-specific risks.
    - Bonds (30%): Bonds are generally considered safer investments with lower returns. They provide stability and income through interest payments, reducing overall portfolio volatility.
    - Commodities (20%): Commodities, such as gold or oil, often behave differently from stocks and bonds, providing diversification benefits. They can act as a hedge against inflation and economic uncertainty.

- **Expected Portfolio Behavior**
    - In a bull market, equities may drive portfolio growth, while bonds and commodities provide stability.
    - In a bear market, bonds may help cushion losses, while commodities could act as a safe haven.

Exercise 2

Scenario: Assume you are managing a portfolio with $200,000 to invest. Your client prefers a balanced approach, seeking moderate growth with minimal risk. Construct a diversified investment portfolio, allocate funds across equities, bonds, and alternative investments (e.g., real estate, commodities), and explain your allocation decisions.

Answer and Explanation

- Equities (40%): $80,000 invested in a mix of large-cap and mid-cap stocks across various sectors, such as technology, healthcare, and consumer goods. This allocation provides growth potential while managing risk through sector diversification.
- Bonds (40%): $80,000 invested in a mix of government and corporate bonds with varying maturities. This allocation offers income stability and reduces portfolio volatility.
- Alternative Investments (20%): $40,000 invested in real estate investment trusts (REITs) and commodities like gold. This allocation provides additional diversification and acts as a hedge against inflation and market downturns.

Outcome

The portfolio is well-diversified across different asset classes, sectors, and investment types. It is designed to achieve steady returns while minimizing exposure to any single risk.

Derivatives as Risk Management Tools

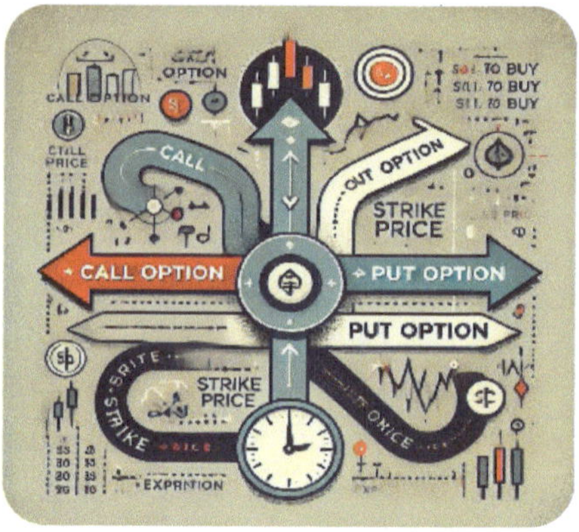

Derivatives are financial instruments whose value is derived from an underlying asset, such as stocks, bonds, commodities, or currencies. They are widely used as risk management tools to hedge against price fluctuations and other financial risks. This chapter explores three common types of derivatives—options, futures, and swaps—and demonstrates how they can be used to manage various financial risks. Through extended examples, calculations, and exercises, readers will gain a deeper understanding of how to effectively use derivatives in risk management.

Options

Options are contracts that give the holder the right, but not the obligation, to buy (call option) or sell (put option) an underlying asset at a predetermined price (strike price) before or at the expiration date. Options are commonly used to hedge against adverse price movements in the underlying asset.

Key Concepts

- **Call Option:** Gives the holder the right to buy the underlying asset at the strike price.
- **Put Option:** Gives the holder the right to sell the underlying asset at the strike price.
- **Premium:** The cost of purchasing the option, paid upfront.
- **Strike Price:** The price at which the option holder can buy or sell the underlying asset.
- **Expiration Date:** The date by which the option must be exercised or allowed to expire.

- **Example:** A farmer expects to harvest wheat in six months and is concerned that wheat prices might drop. To hedge against this risk, the farmer buys a put option to sell wheat at a specified strike price. If market prices fall, the option ensures that the farmer can sell the wheat at the agreed price, offsetting the potential loss.

Detailed Example with Calculations

Scenario

A company holds 1,000 shares of a stock currently priced at $50 per share. The company is concerned about a potential price drop in the next three months and wants to hedge against this risk by purchasing put options.

Task

Describe how buying put options can help mitigate this risk. Assume a put option allows the company to sell the shares at $48 each and costs $2 per option.

Step-by-Step Solution

Identify the Exposure

The company is exposed to the risk of the stock price falling below $50 per share. A significant price drop will result in a capital loss if the company sells the shares at a lower price.

Hedging Strategy

The company buys 10 put options (each option typically covers 100 shares) to protect its 1,000 shares. The put options give the company the right to sell the shares at $48 per share, regardless of how much the market price drops.

Cost of the Hedge

The premium paid for each option is $2. Since the company buys 10 options, the total cost of the hedge is 10 options × $2 × 100 shares = $2,000.

Outcome if the Stock Price Falls

- Stock Price Drops to $45: Without the hedge, the company would sell the shares at $45, resulting in a loss of $5 per share (total loss = $5 × 1,000 shares = $5,000).
- With the hedge, the company exercises the put options and sells the shares at $48 per share, limiting the loss to $2 per share (strike price - current price). The total loss is $2,000, plus the $2,000 premium paid for the options, for a total cost of $4,000.

Outcome if the Stock Price Stays Above $48

If the stock price remains above $48, the company may choose not to exercise the options. The only cost incurred is the $2,000 premium paid for the options.

Exercise 3

Scenario

A company holds 1,000 shares of a stock currently priced at $60 per share. The company is concerned that the stock price might drop in the next three months. Put options with a strike price of $58 are available for $1.50 per option.

Task

Calculate the cost of buying put options to hedge the stock position and the financial outcome if the stock price falls to $55 per share.

Answer and Explanation

- **Hedging Strategy:** The company buys 10 put options (covering 1,000 shares) at a cost of $1,500 (10 options × $1.50 × 100 shares).
- **Outcome:** If the stock price falls to $55, the company can exercise the put options to sell the shares at $58 per share, limiting the loss to $3 per share. The total loss would be $3,000, plus the $1,500 premium, for a total cost of $4,500. Without the hedge, the loss would have been $5,000.

Futures

Futures contracts are agreements to buy or sell an asset at a predetermined price on a specific future date. Unlike options, futures contracts obligate the parties to execute the transaction. Futures are commonly used to hedge against price fluctuations in commodities, interest rates, currencies, and other assets.

Key Concepts

- **Long Position:** The buyer of the futures contract agrees to purchase the asset at the future date.
- **Short Position:** The seller of the futures contract agrees to sell the asset at the future date.
- **Margin:** A deposit required to enter into a futures contract, ensuring that both parties can fulfill their obligations.
- **Mark-to-Market:** The daily adjustment of the futures contract's value based on market prices.
- **Example:** An airline company expects fuel prices to rise and enters into a futures contract to buy fuel at the current price for delivery in six months. If fuel prices increase, the airline saves money by

purchasing at the lower, pre-agreed price, thereby hedging against the risk of rising fuel costs.

Detailed Example with Calculations

Scenario

A manufacturing company requires 1,000 barrels of oil in three months and wants to hedge against potential price increases. The current price of oil is $70 per barrel, and the company enters into a futures contract at this price.

Task

Calculate the financial impact of the futures contract if the market price of oil rises to $75 per barrel.

Step-by-Step Solution

Identify the Exposure

- The company is exposed to the risk of oil prices increasing, which would raise the cost of production.

Hedging Strategy

- The company enters into a futures contract to purchase 1,000 barrels of oil at $70 per barrel, locking in the price for future delivery.

Financial Outcome if Oil Prices Rise

- Market Price Rises to $75 per Barrel: Without the hedge, the company would have to pay $75,000 for 1,000 barrels of oil.
- With the hedge, the company pays $70,000 as per the futures contract, saving $5,000 ($5 per barrel × 1,000 barrels).

Comparison

- The futures contract effectively mitigates the risk of rising oil prices, ensuring that the company pays the lower, locked-in price.

Exercise 4

Scenario

A construction company expects to need 500 tons of steel in six months. The current price of steel is $500 per ton, and the company is concerned that prices may rise. The company enters into a futures contract to buy steel at the current price.

Task

Calculate the financial impact if the market price of steel rises to $550 per ton. How much does the company save by using the futures contract?

Answer and Explanation

- **Hedging Strategy:** The company enters into a futures contract to buy 500 tons of steel at $500 per ton, locking in the price.
- **Outcome:** If the market price rises to $550 per ton, the company will have had to pay $275,000 without the hedge. With the hedge, the company pays $250,000, saving $25,000 ($50 per ton × 500 tons).

Swaps

Swaps are financial agreements in which two parties exchange cash flows or liabilities to manage specific risks, such as interest rate, currency, or credit risks. The most common types of swaps include interest rate swaps, currency swaps, and credit default swaps.

Key Concepts

- **Interest Rate Swap:** Involves exchanging fixed-rate interest payments for floating-rate payments (or vice versa) to manage interest rate risk.
- **Currency Swap:** Involves exchanging cash flows in different currencies to manage exchange rate risk.
- **Credit Default Swap (CDS):** A contract that provides protection against the default of a borrower, where the seller of the CDS compensates the buyer in case of default.
- **Example:** A company with a floating-rate loan fears rising interest rates and enters into an interest rate swap to exchange its floating-rate payments for fixed-rate payments. This strategy stabilizes the company's interest expenses, protecting against the risk of increasing interest rates.

Detailed Example with Calculations

Scenario

A company has a $10 million floating-rate loan with an interest rate of London InterBank Offered Rate (LIBOR) + 2%. The company fears that LIBOR will rise and wants to stabilize its interest payments. To mitigate this risk, the company enters into an interest rate swap, agreeing to pay a fixed rate of 4% while receiving LIBOR from the swap counterparty.

Task

Calculate the financial impact of the swap if LIBOR rises to 3%.

Step-by-Step Solution

Identify the Exposure

- The company is exposed to the risk of rising LIBOR, which would increase its interest payments on the floating-rate loan.

Hedging Strategy

- The company enters into an interest rate swap where it agrees to pay a fixed rate of 4% and receives LIBOR from the counterparty.

Financial Outcome if LIBOR Rises

- **Without the Swap:** The company would pay an interest rate of 5% (LIBOR + 2%) on the $10 million loan, resulting in $500,000 in annual interest payments.
- **With the Swap:** The company pays a fixed rate of 4%, resulting in $400,000 in annual interest payments. The company receives LIBOR (3%) from the counterparty, offsetting the floating-rate payments.
- The total net payment with the swap is $400,000, saving the company $100,000 compared to the floating-rate scenario.

Exercise 5

Scenario

A company has a $20 million floating-rate loan with an interest rate of LIBOR + 1.5%. To mitigate the risk of rising interest rates, the company enters into an interest rate swap, agreeing to pay a fixed rate of 3.5% while receiving LIBOR. If LIBOR rises to 4%, calculate the financial impact of the swap.

Answer and Explanation

- **Hedging Strategy:** The company swaps its floating-rate payments for a fixed rate of 3.5%.
- **Outcome:** Without the swap, the company would pay 5.5% interest on the loan, totaling $1.1 million annually. With the swap, the company pays a fixed rate of 3.5%, totaling $700,000 annually, saving $400,000.

Insurance and Reinsurance

Insurance and reinsurance are fundamental components of risk management, providing mechanisms for transferring risk from one party to another. Insurance allows businesses and individuals to protect against specific losses by paying premiums, while reinsurance enables insurance companies to manage their risk exposure by sharing it with other insurers. This chapter delves into the principles of insurance and reinsurance, offering detailed examples, calculations, and practical exercises to illustrate their application in risk management.

Insurance

Insurance is a contract in which an organization or individual (the insured) pays premiums to an insurance company (the insurer) in exchange for protection against specific financial losses. If a covered event occurs, such as property damage, liability, or business interruption, the insurer compensates the insured for the loss, subject to the terms and limits of the policy.

Key Concepts

- **Premium:** The amount paid by the insured to the insurer for coverage, typically on an annual or monthly basis.
- **Policy Limit:** The maximum amount the insurer will pay for a covered loss.
- **Deductible:** The amount the insured must pay out of pocket before the insurer covers the remaining loss.

- **Coverage:** The specific risks or perils that the insurance policy protects against.
- **Example:** A manufacturing company insures its factory against fire damage with a policy limit of $10 million and a $100,000 deductible. If a fire causes $2 million in damage, the insurance policy covers $1.9 million, after the company pays the deductible.

Detailed Example with Calculations

Scenario

A retail chain insures its inventory for $2 million against theft and natural disasters, paying an annual premium of $50,000. If a natural disaster causes $500,000 in damage, calculate the net financial impact after insurance coverage.

Step-by-Step Solution

Identify the Insurance Coverage

- The retail chain has a $2 million insurance policy covering inventory losses due to theft and natural disasters.

Determine the Damage and Coverage

- A natural disaster causes $500,000 in damage to the inventory.

Calculate the Insurance Payout

- The insurance policy covers the full $500,000 loss since it is within the policy limit of $2 million.

Calculate the Net Financial Impact

- The retail chain pays an annual premium of $50,000 for the insurance coverage.
- The insurance payout of $500,000 covers the damage, leaving the company with a net cost of $50,000 (the premium paid).

Conclusion

The net financial benefit from the insurance coverage is $450,000 ($500,000 - $50,000), as the insurance policy fully covers the loss minus the premium.

Exercise 6

Scenario

A logistics company insures its fleet of trucks for a total value of $5 million against accidents and theft, with a deductible of $100,000 per incident. The annual premium is $75,000. One of the trucks is stolen, resulting in a loss of $150,000. Calculate the net financial impact after insurance coverage.

Answer and Explanation

- **Insurance Coverage:** The insurance policy covers the loss of $150,000, minus the $100,000 deductible.
- **Insurance Payout:** The insurer pays $50,000 ($150,000 - $100,000).
- **Net Financial Impact:** The company's total cost is $125,000 ($75,000 premium + $100,000 deductible - $50,000 payout), resulting in a net financial impact of $125,000.

Reinsurance

Reinsurance is a risk management strategy used by insurance companies to transfer portions of their risk portfolios to other insurers (reinsurers). By doing so, the original insurer reduces its exposure to large claims, helping to maintain financial stability and solvency. Reinsurance allows insurers to underwrite more policies and manage the risks associated with catastrophic events.

Key Concepts

- **Ceding Company:** The original insurer that transfers risk to the reinsurer.
- **Reinsurer:** The insurance company that assumes the risk from the ceding company.
- **Retention Limit:** The amount of risk the ceding company retains before the reinsurer's coverage begins.
- **Quota Share Reinsurance:** A type of reinsurance where the reinsurer covers a fixed percentage of all claims.
- **Excess of Loss Reinsurance:** A type of reinsurance where the reinsurer covers losses exceeding a specified amount.
- **Example:** An insurance company provides flood coverage for multiple regions. To manage its risk, the insurer purchases reinsurance from another company, transferring a portion of the potential losses in case of a major flood. If a flood causes extensive damage, the reinsurer shares the burden of paying out claims, reducing the financial impact on the original insurer.

Detailed Example with Calculations

Scenario

An insurance company covers $100 million in policies across a region prone to hurricanes. To manage its risk, it buys reinsurance that covers 60% of any claims exceeding $10 million. If a hurricane causes $40 million in claims, calculate the amount covered by reinsurance and the amount the original insurer must pay.

Step-by-Step Solution
Identify the Coverage Structure

- The insurance company retains the first $10 million of any claim (retention limit).
- The reinsurer covers 60% of claims that exceed the $10 million retention limit.

Calculate the Total Claim

- A hurricane causes $40 million in claims.

Determine the Reinsurance Payout

- The original insurer pays the first $10 million.
- The remaining $30 million ($40 million - $10 million) is subject to reinsurance coverage.
- The reinsurer covers 60% of the $30 million, which is $18 million.

Calculate the Amount the Original Insurer Must Pay

- The original insurer pays the $10 million retention limit plus the remaining 40% of the $30 million, which is $12 million.
- Total payment by the original insurer = $10 million + $12 million = $22 million.

Conclusion

The reinsurer pays $18 million, while the original insurer pays $22 million.

Exercise 7

Scenario

An insurance company covers $200 million in earthquake policies and purchases reinsurance that covers 75% of any claims exceeding $50 million. If an earthquake causes $120 million in claims, calculate the amount covered by reinsurance and the amount the original insurer must pay.

Answer and Explanation

- Reinsurance Coverage: The reinsurer covers 75% of claims exceeding the $50 million retention limit.

- Reinsurance Payout: The total claim is $120 million, so the reinsurer covers 75% of the $70 million ($120 million - $50 million), which is $52.5 million.
- Amount Paid by the Original Insurer: The original insurer pays the first $50 million plus the remaining 25% of the $70 million ($17.5 million), for a total of $67.5 million.

Implementing Strategic Risk Mitigation Measures

Strategic risk mitigation is a critical aspect of risk management that involves aligning risk management practices with an organization's long-term strategic goals. By proactively identifying and addressing potential risks, organizations can enhance their resilience and increase the likelihood of achieving their objectives. This chapter explores the principles of strategic risk mitigation, providing detailed examples, calculations, and a comprehensive exercise to illustrate how these measures can be implemented effectively.

Strategic Risk Mitigation

Strategic risk mitigation involves integrating risk management into the overall strategy of an organization. This process ensures that potential risks are identified, assessed, and managed in a way that supports the organization's long-term objectives. The goal is to proactively address risks that could hinder the achievement of strategic goals, thereby enhancing the organization's ability to navigate uncertainties and capitalize on opportunities.

Key Concepts

- **Risk Identification:** Identifying risks that could impact the organization's strategy, such as regulatory changes, market competition, operational risks, and geopolitical events.
- **Risk Assessment:** Evaluating the likelihood and potential impact of identified risks on the organization's strategic goals.
- **Risk Mitigation Strategies:** Developing and implementing measures to reduce the likelihood or impact of risks. This could include hedging, diversification, insurance, and process improvements.
- **Continuous Monitoring:** Regularly reviewing and updating the risk mitigation plan to ensure it remains aligned with the organization's evolving strategy and external environment.

Example: A technology company plans to expand its operations globally. To support this strategic initiative, the company develops a strategic risk mitigation plan that includes:

- **Currency Hedging:** To protect against adverse currency fluctuations, the company enters into forward contracts to lock in exchange rates for its foreign revenues.
- **Geopolitical Risk Analysis:** The company conducts thorough geopolitical risk assessments to identify potential risks in target markets, such as political instability or regulatory challenges.
- **Supply Chain Insurance:** To mitigate the risk of supply chain disruptions, the company purchases insurance coverage that protects against delays or losses due to natural disasters, transportation issues, or supplier insolvency.

Detailed Example with Calculations

Scenario

A pharmaceutical company is entering the biotechnology sector, which involves significant risks such as regulatory changes, intellectual property disputes, and intense market competition. The company aims to develop a strategic risk mitigation plan to manage these risks effectively.

Task

Develop a strategic risk mitigation plan for the pharmaceutical company, outlining key strategies to address regulatory risks, intellectual property risks, and market competition.

Step-by-Step Solution

Identify Key Risks

- **Regulatory Risks:** The biotechnology sector is heavily regulated, with strict requirements for drug approval, safety testing, and marketing.
- **Intellectual Property Risks:** The sector is characterized by extensive research and development (R&D) efforts, making intellectual property (IP) protection crucial. There is a risk of patent disputes and challenges to IP rights.
- **Market Competition:** The biotechnology sector is highly competitive, with many companies vying for market share. The company faces the risk of being outpaced by competitors in terms of innovation and market presence.

Develop Mitigation Strategies

- **Regulatory Risks**
- **Engage with Regulatory Bodies:** The company should establish strong relationships with regulatory agencies in key markets. This includes participating in industry forums, staying informed about regulatory changes, and seeking early guidance on compliance requirements.
- **Invest in Compliance:** Allocate resources to ensure that all products and processes meet regulatory standards. This could involve hiring

compliance experts, conducting regular audits, and implementing robust quality control systems.

- **Scenario Planning:** Develop scenarios to assess the potential impact of regulatory changes on the company's operations and plan contingency measures.

Intellectual Property Risks

- **Secure Patents:** The company should secure patents for its biotechnology innovations as early as possible. This includes filing for patents in multiple jurisdictions to protect against global IP theft.
- **Monitor IP Landscape:** Regularly monitor the IP landscape for potential infringement or disputes. This involves tracking competitor patents and engaging legal experts to address any challenges.
- **Develop Contingency Plans:** In the event of an IP dispute, the company should have contingency plans in place, such as alternative R&D paths, cross-licensing agreements, or legal strategies.

Market Competition

- **Diversify Product Offerings:** To reduce dependence on a single product, the company should invest in a diversified portfolio of biotechnology products. This strategy helps mitigate the risk of market competition by spreading risk across multiple revenue streams.
- **Invest in R&D:** Continuous investment in R&D is essential to maintain a competitive edge. The company should allocate a significant portion of its budget to innovation, focusing on developing cutting-edge treatments and technologies.
- **Strategic Partnerships:** Form partnerships with other biotech firms, research institutions, or healthcare providers to leverage complementary strengths and enhance market presence.

Calculate Potential Impacts

- **Regulatory Compliance Costs:** Estimate the cost of compliance efforts, including hiring experts, conducting audits, and implementing quality control measures. For example, if the company allocates $5 million annually to compliance, this represents a strategic investment in mitigating regulatory risks.
- **IP Protection Costs:** Calculate the costs associated with securing patents and legal fees for monitoring and defending IP rights. If the company files patents in multiple countries, the costs could total $2 million annually, ensuring robust IP protection.
- **R&D and Diversification Costs:** Estimate the investment required to diversify product offerings and sustain R&D efforts. For example, if the company invests $50 million annually in R&D and new product development, this strategy helps mitigate the risk of market competition.

Monitor and Review

The company should regularly monitor the effectiveness of its risk mitigation strategies. This involves tracking key performance indicators (KPIs), conducting regular reviews of the risk landscape, and adjusting the plan as needed to address emerging risks or changes in the external environment.

Conclusion

By implementing a comprehensive strategic risk mitigation plan, the pharmaceutical company can proactively manage the risks associated with entering the biotechnology sector. This plan enhances the company's ability to navigate regulatory challenges, protect its intellectual property, and maintain a competitive edge in the market.

Exercise 8: Strategic Risk Mitigation Plan

Scenario

You are the Chief Risk Officer of a hypothetical pharmaceutical company planning to enter the biotechnology sector. Develop a strategic risk mitigation plan addressing the following risks: regulatory changes, intellectual property disputes, and market competition. Outline key mitigation strategies for each risk.

Answer and Explanation

- **Regulatory Risks**
    - **Engage with Regulatory Bodies:** Establish ongoing communication with regulatory agencies and participate in industry groups to stay informed about potential regulatory changes.
    - **Invest in Compliance:** Allocate resources for compliance efforts, including hiring experts and conducting regular audits to ensure all products meet regulatory standards.
    - **Scenario Planning:** Develop contingency plans for different regulatory scenarios, such as delays in drug approvals or changes in safety requirements.
- **Intellectual Property Risks**
    - **Secure Patents:** File patents early and in multiple jurisdictions to protect biotechnology innovations from infringement.
    - **Monitor Competitor Patents:** Continuously monitor the IP landscape and engage legal experts to address potential disputes or challenges to the company's patents.
    - **Develop Contingency Plans:** Prepare alternative strategies in case of IP disputes, such as pursuing different R&D paths or negotiating cross-licensing agreements.

- **Market Competition**
  - **Diversify Product Offerings:** Invest in a broad portfolio of biotechnology products to reduce dependence on any single product and spread market risk.
  - **Invest in R&D:** Allocate significant resources to ongoing research and development to stay ahead of competitors in innovation and product development.
  - **Strategic Partnerships:** Form alliances with other companies, research institutions, or healthcare providers to enhance market presence and leverage complementary strengths.

Case Studies on Effective Risk Mitigation

Effective risk mitigation is critical for organizations operating in industries where exposure to volatile markets, catastrophic events, or other significant risks is common. This chapter presents detailed case studies illustrating successful risk mitigation strategies in the airline and insurance industries. By examining these real-world examples, we can better understand how hedging, reinsurance, and other risk management techniques can protect organizations from financial instability and enhance long-term profitability.

Case Study 1: The Airline Industry and Fuel Hedging

The airline industry is highly sensitive to fluctuations in fuel prices, which can significantly impact profitability. Airlines typically spend a large portion of their operating expenses on fuel, making them vulnerable to price volatility in the global oil market. To manage this risk, many airlines employ fuel hedging strategies, using financial derivatives such as futures contracts to lock in fuel prices and stabilize costs.

Key Concepts

- **Fuel Hedging:** A risk management strategy used by airlines to protect against fuel price volatility by locking in prices through futures contracts or options.

- **Futures Contracts:** Agreements to buy or sell a specific quantity of fuel at a predetermined price on a future date, regardless of market prices at that time.
- **Price Volatility:** The degree of variation in fuel prices over time, which can create financial uncertainty for airlines.

Detailed Example with Calculations

Scenario

An airline company, XYZ Airlines, is concerned about the volatility of jet fuel prices, which have fluctuated between $1.50 and $3.00 per gallon over the past year. To manage this risk, XYZ Airlines decides to hedge its fuel costs by entering into futures contracts. The airline locks in a price of $2.00 per gallon for 10 million gallons of jet fuel, which it expects to use over the next year.

Step-by-Step Solution

Identify the Risk

- XYZ Airlines is exposed to the risk of rising fuel prices, which could increase operating costs and reduce profitability.

Hedging Strategy

- XYZ Airlines enters into futures contracts to purchase 10 million gallons of jet fuel at $2.00 per gallon. This locks in the price, ensuring that the airline will not pay more than $2.00 per gallon, regardless of future price movements.

Calculate the Cost without Hedging

- Suppose the market price of jet fuel rises to $2.50 per gallon over the next year. Without hedging, XYZ Airlines would pay $2.50 × 10 million gallons = $25 million for fuel.

Calculate the Cost with Hedging

- With the futures contracts, XYZ Airlines pays $2.00 × 10 million gallons = $20 million for fuel, regardless of the market price.

Financial Impact

- The hedging strategy saves XYZ Airlines $5 million ($25 million - $20 million) by locking in the lower price of $2.00 per gallon. This strategy protects the airline from rising fuel costs, stabilizes its expenses, and contributes to higher profitability.

Outcome

- During a period of rising fuel prices, XYZ Airlines benefits from its hedging strategy, which ensures predictable fuel costs and helps maintain profitability.

Key Takeaways

- **Hedging can effectively manage price volatility:** By using futures contracts, XYZ Airlines successfully mitigates the risk of rising fuel prices, ensuring cost stability.
- **Long-term planning and consistent monitoring are crucial for successful risk mitigation:** Regularly reviewing and adjusting hedging strategies based on market conditions is essential to maximize the benefits of risk management.

Case Study 2: Reinsurance in the Insurance Industry

The insurance industry faces significant risks from natural disasters, such as hurricanes, earthquakes, and floods. These events can result in substantial claims, threatening the financial stability of insurance companies. Reinsurance is a key strategy used by insurers to manage catastrophic risks by transferring a portion of their exposure to other insurers, thereby protecting their balance sheets and ensuring they can continue operations even after major events.

Key Concepts

- **Reinsurance:** A risk management strategy where an insurance company transfers a portion of its risk to another insurer (the reinsurer) to reduce its exposure to large claims.
- **Catastrophic Risk:** The risk of significant financial loss resulting from a major event, such as a natural disaster, that affects a large number of policyholders.
- **Retention Limit:** The maximum amount of risk the original insurer retains before reinsurance coverage begins.

Detailed Example with Calculations
Scenario

An insurance company, ABC Insurance, has significant exposure to natural disasters in a coastal region prone to hurricanes. To manage this risk, ABC Insurance purchases reinsurance that covers 70% of any claims exceeding $20 million. A major hurricane strikes the region, resulting in $100 million in claims.

Step-by-Step Solution

- Identify the Risk
    - ABC Insurance faces the risk of large claims from natural disasters, which could deplete its financial reserves and threaten its solvency.
- Reinsurance Strategy
    - ABC Insurance buys reinsurance that covers 70% of claims exceeding $20 million. This strategy limits ABC Insurance's exposure to catastrophic losses.

- Calculate the Total Claim
  - The hurricane causes $100 million in claims.
  - Determine the Reinsurance Payout:
  - ABC Insurance retains the first $20 million of the claims (retention limit).
  - The remaining $80 million ($100 million - $20 million) is subject to reinsurance coverage.
  - The reinsurer covers 70% of the $80 million, which is $56 million.
- Calculate the Amount the Original Insurer Must Pay
  - ABC Insurance pays the $20 million retention limit plus 30% of the $80 million ($24 million).
  - Total payment by ABC Insurance = $20 million + $24 million = $44 million.
- Financial Impact
  - The reinsurer pays $56 million, while ABC Insurance pays $44 million.
- Outcome
  - Despite the $100 million in claims, ABC Insurance manages to maintain financial stability, thanks to its reinsurance policy. The reinsurer absorbs a significant portion of the losses, allowing ABC Insurance to continue operations without significant financial strain.

Key Takeaways

- **Reinsurance helps manage catastrophic risks:** By transferring a portion of its exposure to a reinsurer, ABC Insurance effectively mitigates the financial impact of a major hurricane.

- **Diversifying risk across multiple insurers can enhance financial resilience:** Reinsurance enables insurers to spread risk and protect their balance sheets from large, unexpected claims.

Chapter

07

Risk Governance and Organizational Structure

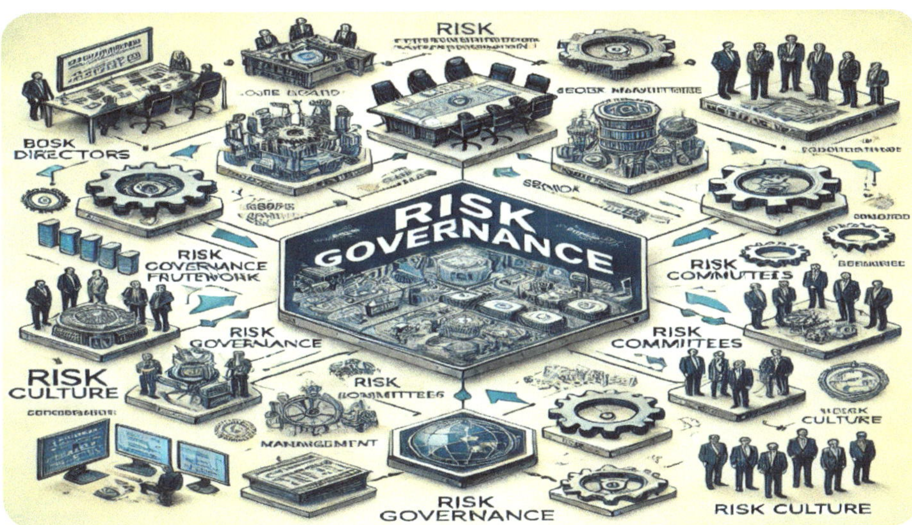

Risk governance is the framework through which an organization manages and oversees its risks, ensuring that they are aligned with the company's strategic objectives. Effective risk governance involves the roles of the board, senior management, and specialized risk committees, all of which work together to create a risk-aware culture. This chapter explores the key components of risk governance, the roles and responsibilities of various stakeholders, and how to align risk governance with business strategy. It also delves into the strategic importance of risk culture, with practical examples and exercises to reinforce the concepts.

Role of the Board and Senior Management in Risk Management

Effective risk management is critical to the success and sustainability of any organization. The board of directors and senior management play pivotal roles in establishing and maintaining a robust risk management framework. The board is responsible for overseeing risk management at the highest level, ensuring alignment with the organization's strategic goals, while senior management is tasked with implementing the framework and managing risks in day-to-day operations. This chapter explores these roles in detail, providing examples, calculations, and practical exercises to illustrate how both the board and senior management contribute to effective risk management.

Role of the Board of Directors

The board of directors holds the ultimate responsibility for risk oversight within an organization. The board ensures that the risk management framework is comprehensive, effective, and aligned with the company's strategic goals. This oversight includes defining the organization's risk appetite, approving risk management policies, and regularly reviewing the organization's risk profile.

Key Responsibilities

- **Risk Oversight:** The board oversees the organization's risk management activities, ensuring that all significant risks are identified, assessed, and managed appropriately. This involves reviewing risk reports, understanding key risks, and challenging management on the effectiveness of risk mitigation strategies.
- **Approval of Risk Appetite:** The board defines and approves the organization's risk appetite, which is the level of risk the company is

willing to accept in pursuit of its objectives. This sets the boundaries for risk-taking and guides decision-making across the organization.

- **Strategic Alignment:** The board ensures that risk management is integrated into the strategic planning process. This means aligning risk-taking with the company's long-term goals and ensuring that strategic initiatives are pursued within the defined risk appetite.
- **Example:** A multinational corporation's board of directors establishes a risk committee to focus on key risks associated with its global operations. This committee regularly reviews the company's risk profile, including geopolitical risks, currency risks, and operational risks. The committee ensures that the management's risk mitigation strategies are aligned with the board-approved risk appetite. For instance, before entering a new market, the board requires a thorough risk assessment and mitigation plan to be presented by senior management, ensuring that the risks of the expansion are in line with the company's risk appetite and strategic objectives.

Case Example with Practical Questions

Scenario

You are a member of the board of directors for a technology company considering expanding into a new market with significant political and economic risks. The potential market offers substantial growth opportunities, but the risks could impact the company's operations and financial performance.

Exercise 1: Key Questions for the Board

Task

Identify key questions the board should ask to ensure that the expansion aligns with the company's risk appetite and strategic objectives.

Answer and Explanation

- What is the potential impact of political and economic risks on the company's operations in the new market?
  - This question helps the board assess the magnitude of the risks and their potential effect on the company's operations, revenues, and overall performance. The board should consider the likelihood of these risks materializing and their possible consequences.
- How does the expansion align with the company's overall risk appetite?
  - The board must ensure that the risks associated with the expansion are within the company's risk appetite. If the risks exceed the defined appetite, the board may require additional mitigation strategies or reconsider the expansion.
- What risk mitigation strategies are in place to manage these risks?
  - The board should evaluate the effectiveness of the proposed risk mitigation strategies, such as currency hedging, political risk insurance, or partnerships with local entities. These strategies should be robust enough to address the identified risks.
- How will the board monitor the ongoing risks associated with this expansion?
  - Continuous monitoring is crucial for managing risks over time. The board should establish a process for regular updates on the risk environment and the effectiveness of the mitigation strategies. This might include setting up key risk indicators (KRIs) and requiring periodic reports from senior management.

Conclusion

By asking these key questions, the board ensures that the expansion is thoroughly evaluated and that the associated risks are managed within the company's strategic and risk management frameworks.

Role of Senior Management

Senior management is responsible for implementing the risk management framework and ensuring that it is effectively integrated into the organization's daily operations. This includes identifying and assessing risks, developing and executing risk mitigation strategies, and reporting on the organization's risk profile to the board.

Key Responsibilities

- **Risk Identification and Assessment:** Senior management is tasked with identifying risks that could impact the organization's objectives. This involves conducting risk assessments to evaluate the likelihood and potential impact of these risks.
- **Risk Mitigation:** Management develops and implements strategies to mitigate identified risks. This might include operational adjustments, financial hedging, process improvements, or other actions designed to reduce the likelihood or impact of risks.
- **Reporting to the Board:** Senior management regularly reports on the organization's risk profile, providing the board with the information needed to perform its oversight function. This includes updates on emerging risks, the effectiveness of mitigation strategies, and alignment with the organization's risk appetite.

- **Example:** The CEO of a financial institution leads the development of a comprehensive risk management strategy that includes scenario analysis, stress testing, and regular risk assessments. This strategy is reviewed and approved by the board, ensuring alignment with the institution's risk appetite. The CEO also ensures that risk management is integrated into the company's strategic planning and operational processes, with regular reports provided to the board on key risks and the effectiveness of the mitigation strategies.

Case Example with Practical Steps

Scenario

You are a senior manager at a manufacturing company facing supply chain disruptions due to geopolitical tensions. These disruptions are affecting production schedules and delivery timelines, posing a significant risk to the company's operations and financial performance.

Exercise 2: Developing a Risk Management Plan

Task

Outline a risk management plan that you will present to the board to address these supply chain disruptions.

Answer and Explanation

- **Risk Identification**
    - Identify specific geopolitical risks affecting the supply chain. This could include trade restrictions, political instability, or regulatory changes in key supplier countries. For example, if the company sources raw materials from a region experiencing political unrest, the risk could be a delay or complete halt in the supply of these materials.

- **Risk Assessment**
  - Evaluate the potential impact of these risks on production and delivery schedules. This involves estimating the likelihood of disruptions and their potential financial impact on the company. For instance, calculate the cost of production delays, missed deadlines, and the potential loss of revenue due to these disruptions.
- **Risk Mitigation**
  - Develop strategies to mitigate the identified risks. These strategies might include:
    - **Diversifying Suppliers:** Identify and engage alternative suppliers in different geographic regions to reduce reliance on a single source.
    - **Increasing Inventory Levels:** Build up inventory levels of critical materials to buffer against supply disruptions.
    - **Relocating Production Facilities:** Consider relocating production facilities to regions with lower geopolitical risks or establishing additional production sites to diversify risk.
- **Monitoring and Reporting**
  - Implement a monitoring system to track geopolitical developments and assess their impact on the supply chain. This could involve setting up a dedicated risk monitoring team and using data analytics to predict potential disruptions. Regularly report to the board on the status of these risks and the effectiveness of the mitigation strategies. Provide updates on key risk indicators (KRIs) and recommend adjustments to the plan as needed.
- **Conclusion**

By developing and presenting this risk management plan, senior management can demonstrate a proactive approach to managing supply chain disruptions and ensuring that the company's operations continue to run smoothly despite geopolitical challenges.

Risk Committees and Risk Officers

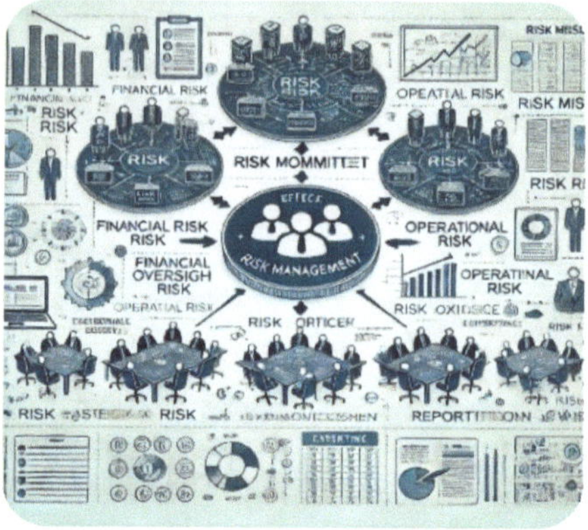

Effective risk management requires specialized oversight and expertise to ensure that risks are identified, assessed, and managed appropriately across the organization. Risk committees and risk officers play a crucial role in this process, with risk committees providing detailed oversight of specific risk areas and risk officers managing day-to-day risk activities. This chapter explores the functions and responsibilities of both risk committees and risk officers, offering extended examples, calculations, and practical exercises to illustrate their roles in risk governance.

Risk Committees

Risk committees are specialized groups within an organization that focus on specific risk areas. They provide detailed oversight and governance of the organization's risk management activities, ensuring that risks are effectively managed in alignment with the organization's strategic objectives and regulatory requirements. Different types of risk committees focus on various aspects of risk, from enterprise-wide risks to specific risks like credit or compliance.

Types of Risk Committees

- **Enterprise Risk Committee:** This committee oversees the organization's overall risk management framework, ensuring that risk management practices are consistent across the enterprise. It focuses on identifying, assessing, and mitigating risks that could impact the organization's strategic objectives.

- **Audit and Compliance Committee:** This committee focuses on financial reporting risks, compliance with laws and regulations, and the effectiveness of internal controls. It ensures that the organization adheres to regulatory requirements and that financial statements are accurate and transparent.
- **Credit Risk Committee:** This committee manages credit risk, including the approval of credit policies, monitoring credit exposures, and ensuring adequate provisioning for potential losses. It plays a key role in maintaining the organization's credit risk profile within acceptable limits.
- **Example:** A large bank has an enterprise risk committee that meets quarterly to review the bank's risk profile, assess emerging risks, and ensure that the risk management framework is aligned with regulatory requirements. The committee reviews reports from various departments, including credit, market, and operational risk, and makes recommendations to the board on risk mitigation strategies.

Case Example with Practical Application

Scenario

You are the chair of the enterprise risk committee for a global retail company. The company is planning to launch an e-commerce platform, which introduces new risks related to cybersecurity, data privacy, technology implementation, supply chain management, and market competition.

Exercise 3: Identifying and Prioritizing Risks

Task

As the chair of the enterprise risk committee, identify the specific risks associated with launching the e-commerce platform and explain how you would prioritize them.

Answer and Explanation

- **Cybersecurity Risks**
    - **Risk:** The e-commerce platform is vulnerable to cyber-attacks, which could lead to data breaches, financial losses, and reputational damage.
    - **Prioritization:** High priority due to the potential for significant financial and reputational impact. Cybersecurity risks should be addressed with robust security measures, such as encryption, firewalls, and regular security audits.
- **Data Privacy Risks**
    - **Risk:** The platform will handle sensitive customer data, including payment information, which must be protected to comply with data protection regulations.
    - **Prioritization:** High priority due to the regulatory and reputational risks associated with data breaches. Compliance with data protection laws, such as GDPR, should be ensured through stringent data handling and storage practices.
- **Technology Implementation Risks**
    - **Risk:** The successful launch of the platform depends on the seamless integration of technology, which may face challenges such as system downtime, bugs, or compatibility issues.
    - **Prioritization:** Medium priority, as technology failures could delay the launch and affect user experience. Mitigation strategies could include thorough testing, phased rollouts, and contingency planning.
- **Supply Chain Management Risks**
    - **Risk:** The platform's success relies on efficient supply chain management to fulfill customer orders. Disruptions in the supply chain could lead to delays and dissatisfied customers.

    - **Prioritization:** Medium priority, with a focus on diversifying suppliers, improving logistics, and implementing real-time tracking systems to manage supply chain risks.

- **Market Competition Risks**
    - **Risk:** The e-commerce market is highly competitive, and the company must differentiate itself to attract and retain customers.
    - **Prioritization:** Medium to low priority, as this risk can be mitigated through marketing strategies, competitive pricing, and customer service excellence.

- **Conclusion**

  The enterprise risk committee should prioritize cybersecurity and data privacy risks due to their potential to cause significant financial and reputational damage. Technology implementation, supply chain management, and market competition should also be addressed, with appropriate mitigation strategies developed for each.

Risk Officers

Chief Risk Officers (CROs) and other risk officers are responsible for the day-to-day management of the organization's risk management activities. They act as a bridge between senior management and the board, ensuring that risk management practices are effectively implemented and communicated. Risk officers are key players in developing risk policies, monitoring risk exposures, and reporting to the board and risk committees on the organization's risk profile.

Key Responsibilities

- **Risk Policy Development:** Risk officers develop and implement risk management policies and procedures that align with the organization's risk appetite. They ensure that these policies are communicated across the organization and are adhered to by all departments.

- **Risk Monitoring:** They continuously monitor the organization's risk profile, identifying emerging risks and ensuring that existing risks are being managed effectively. This includes using data analytics and risk assessment tools to track key risk indicators (KRIs).
- **Risk Reporting:** Risk officers prepare regular reports for the board and risk committees, highlighting key risks, the effectiveness of risk management strategies, and any areas of concern. These reports provide the board with the information needed to perform its oversight function.
- **Example:** The CRO of an energy company oversees the development of risk management policies related to environmental risks, regulatory compliance, and operational safety. The CRO regularly reports to the board on the company's risk exposure, including potential environmental liabilities, regulatory changes, and safety incidents. The CRO also ensures that risk mitigation strategies, such as environmental monitoring and safety training, are implemented effectively.

Case Example with Practical Steps

Scenario

You are the Chief Risk Officer (CRO) for a healthcare organization that is considering adopting new medical technologies. These technologies have the potential to improve patient outcomes but also introduce risks related to technology implementation, patient safety, regulatory compliance, and data security.

Exercise 4: Developing a Risk Management Plan

Task

Outline the steps you would take to assess the risks associated with these new technologies and explain how you would communicate your findings to the board.

Answer and Explanation

- **Risk Identification**
  - **Technology Implementation Risks:** Identify potential challenges in implementing the new technologies, such as system integration issues, user errors, and technology failures.
  - **Patient Safety Risks:** Assess the potential impact of the new technologies on patient safety, including the risk of adverse outcomes, incorrect diagnoses, or treatment errors.
  - **Regulatory Compliance Risks:** Ensure that the new technologies comply with healthcare regulations and standards, such as those set by the FDA or other regulatory bodies.
  - **Data Security Risks:** Identify risks related to the storage, transmission, and protection of patient data, particularly with regard to compliance with data protection laws such as HIPAA.
- **Risk Assessment**
  - **Likelihood and Impact:** Evaluate the likelihood of each identified risk occurring and the potential impact on the organization. For example, assess the probability of technology failure and its potential impact on patient care.
  - **Cost-Benefit Analysis:** Conduct a cost-benefit analysis to weigh the potential benefits of adopting the new technologies against the risks and costs of implementation. This might include calculating the potential return on investment (ROI) from improved patient outcomes and operational efficiencies.
- **Risk Mitigation**
  - **Pilot Testing:** Implement a pilot program to test the new technologies in a controlled environment, allowing for the identification and resolution of issues before full deployment.

- **Training:** Develop comprehensive training programs for healthcare staff to ensure they are proficient in using the new technologies and understand the associated risks.
- **Data Security Measures:** Implement robust data security measures, such as encryption, access controls, and regular audits, to protect patient data and ensure compliance with regulations.

- **Communication with the Board**

  - **Risk Report Preparation:** Prepare a detailed report for the board that outlines the identified risks, the results of the risk assessment, and the proposed mitigation strategies. Include quantitative data, such as the likelihood and impact of each risk, and the results of the cost-benefit analysis.
  - **Board Presentation:** Present the findings to the board during a meeting, providing a clear overview of the risks and the steps being taken to mitigate them. Be prepared to answer questions and provide additional information as needed.
  - **Ongoing Monitoring:** Recommend a plan for ongoing monitoring of the risks associated with the new technologies, including regular updates to the board on the effectiveness of the mitigation strategies and any emerging risks.

- **Conclusion**

  As the CRO, your role is to ensure that the adoption of new medical technologies is carefully managed, with a clear understanding of the risks involved and the strategies in place to mitigate them. By effectively communicating your findings to the board, you help ensure that the organization's risk management practices are aligned with its strategic objectives and regulatory requirements.

Aligning Risk Governance with Business Strategy

Aligning risk governance with business strategy is essential for ensuring that risk management practices support an organization's strategic objectives. This alignment enables organizations to manage risks proactively, avoiding excessive or inappropriate risks that could threaten long-term success. By embedding risk management into the strategic planning process, organizations can better navigate uncertainties and capitalize on opportunities. This chapter explores the importance of aligning risk governance with business strategy, offering extended examples, calculations, and practical exercises to illustrate the concept.

Importance of Alignment

Aligning risk governance with business strategy involves ensuring that risk management practices are integrated into the strategic decision-making process. This alignment helps organizations manage risks that could impact their strategic goals and ensures that the level of risk taken is consistent with the organization's risk appetite.

Key Principles

- **Strategic Risk Assessment:** Regularly assess risks that could impact the organization's strategic goals. This includes identifying potential risks during the strategic planning process and continuously monitoring them as the strategy is implemented.
- **Risk Appetite:** Clearly define the organization's risk appetite and ensure that it aligns with strategic objectives. The risk appetite

should reflect the level of risk the organization is willing to accept in pursuit of its goals.

- **Integrated Risk Management:** Embed risk management practices into the strategic planning process, ensuring that risks are considered at every stage of decision-making. This includes evaluating the potential risks of strategic initiatives and developing mitigation strategies as part of the planning process.
- **Example:** A pharmaceutical company aligns its risk governance framework with its strategy to innovate and bring new drugs to market. The company's risk appetite allows for high levels of research and development (R&D) risk, recognizing that innovation is critical to its competitive advantage. However, the company maintains strict controls over regulatory compliance and product safety to protect its reputation and ensure long-term success. This alignment ensures that while the company pursues ambitious R&D projects, it does so within a framework that mitigates risks that could have catastrophic consequences.

Case Example with Practical Application

Scenario

You are part of the strategic planning team for a renewable energy company that is planning to expand its wind energy projects into new markets. This strategic initiative introduces various risks related to market entry, regulatory compliance, and operational challenges.

Exercise 5: Developing a Risk Governance Plan

Task

Develop a risk governance plan that aligns with the company's strategic initiative to expand its wind energy projects into new markets, focusing on market entry risks, regulatory compliance risks, and operational risks.

Answer and Explanation

- **Market Entry Risks**
    - **Risk Identification:** Assess the political, economic, and competitive landscape in the new markets. Consider risks such as political instability, economic fluctuations, and competition from local or established energy providers.
    - **Risk Mitigation Strategy:** Implement market-specific risk management strategies to address these risks. For example:
    - **Political Risk Insurance:** Obtain insurance coverage to protect against losses due to political instability, such as expropriation or civil unrest.
    - **Local Partnerships:** Form strategic partnerships with local companies or governments to gain market insights and build local support, reducing the risk of market entry.
    - **Market Analysis:** Conduct thorough market analysis to understand the competitive landscape and identify potential barriers to entry, such as regulatory hurdles or market saturation.
- **Calculation Example**
    - **Political Risk Insurance Premium:** Suppose the cost of political risk insurance is 1.5% of the total investment in a new market, and the company plans to invest $50 million. The premium would be $750,000.
    - **Impact:** This insurance mitigates potential losses due to political instability, protecting the company's investment and ensuring financial stability.
- **Regulatory Compliance Risks**
    - **Risk Identification:** Identify and comply with all relevant regulations in each new market, including environmental regulations, land use laws, and energy production standards.

- **Risk Mitigation Strategy:** Engage with local regulators early in the project planning process to ensure compliance and build relationships. Develop a compliance monitoring system to track adherence to regulations and quickly address any issues.
- **Regulatory Engagement:** Establish a regulatory affairs team to manage interactions with local authorities and ensure that all permits and approvals are obtained in a timely manner.
- **Compliance Monitoring System:** Implement software tools to monitor compliance with local regulations continuously, ensuring that any changes in the regulatory environment are promptly addressed.

- **Calculation Example**

  - Cost of Compliance Monitoring System: Suppose the implementation of a compliance monitoring system costs $200,000 annually. This system helps the company avoid potential fines and delays due to regulatory non-compliance, ensuring smooth project execution.
  - Impact: By ensuring regulatory compliance, the company avoids legal penalties and project delays, contributing to the successful execution of its strategic goals.

- **Operational Risks**

  - **Risk Identification:** Evaluate the risks associated with constructing and operating wind energy facilities in new environments. Consider factors such as supply chain disruptions, adverse weather conditions, and equipment failure.
  - **Risk Mitigation Strategy:** Develop contingency plans for potential operational disruptions. This could include:
  - **Diversifying Suppliers:** Identify multiple suppliers for critical components to reduce the risk of supply chain disruptions.
  - **Weather Contingency Planning:** Develop plans to manage the impact of adverse weather conditions, such as severe storms or extreme temperatures, on construction and operations.

- **Maintenance and Monitoring:** Implement a robust maintenance and monitoring program to ensure that wind turbines and other equipment operate efficiently and that any issues are detected early.

- **Calculation Example**
  - **Cost of Diversifying Suppliers:** Suppose diversifying suppliers increases procurement costs by 5%, and the total procurement budget is $20 million. The additional cost would be $1 million.
  - **Impact:** This investment in supplier diversification reduces the risk of supply chain disruptions, ensuring that the project remains on schedule and within budget.

- **Conclusion:**

  The risk governance plan aligns with the company's strategic initiative to expand its wind energy projects into new markets by addressing key risks related to market entry, regulatory compliance, and operational challenges. By implementing these risk management strategies, the company can mitigate potential risks and increase the likelihood of successful expansion.

Risk Culture and Its Strategic Importance

Risk culture is a critical component of an organization's overall risk management framework. It encompasses the shared values, beliefs, and attitudes toward risk that influence how an organization identifies, assesses, and manages risks. A strong risk culture ensures that risk management practices are embedded in every aspect of the organization, promoting proactive risk management and enhancing the organization's ability to achieve its strategic objectives. This chapter delves into the concept of risk culture, its key elements, and its strategic importance, providing extended examples, calculations, and practical exercises to illustrate how to build and sustain a strong risk culture.

Defining Risk Culture

Risk culture refers to the collective mindset and behaviors within an organization that shape how risks are perceived, communicated, and managed. A positive risk culture encourages employees at all levels to take ownership of risk management, ensuring that risks are identified and addressed before they escalate into significant issues. Conversely, a weak risk culture can lead to complacency, poor decision-making, and a higher likelihood of adverse outcomes.

Key Elements

- **Tone at the Top:** The board of directors and senior management set the tone for the organization's risk culture by demonstrating a commitment to risk management and leading by example. Their actions and attitudes toward risk heavily influence the behavior of employees throughout the organization.
- **Risk Awareness:** Employees at all levels should be aware of the risks associated with their roles and understand the importance of managing these risks effectively. This awareness is fostered through training, communication, and a clear understanding of risk management policies and procedures.
- **Open Communication:** An open communication environment is essential for a strong risk culture. Employees should feel comfortable discussing risks, reporting concerns, and sharing insights without fear of retaliation. This openness encourages transparency and helps the organization identify and mitigate risks more effectively.
- **Example:** A financial services firm fosters a strong risk culture by implementing several key initiatives:

- **Regular Risk Training Programs:** The firm conducts mandatory risk management training for all employees, tailored to the specific risks associated with different roles. This training ensures that employees understand the importance of risk management and are equipped with the knowledge to identify and manage risks in their daily activities.
- **Encouraging Open Communication:** The firm establishes multiple channels for employees to report risks, including anonymous hotlines, regular risk meetings, and a dedicated risk management platform. Employees are encouraged to speak up about potential risks without fear of retribution, fostering a culture of transparency and accountability.
- **Integration into Performance Evaluations:** The firm integrates risk management into its performance evaluation process. Employees are assessed not only on their job performance but also on their contribution to identifying and mitigating risks. This approach incentivizes proactive risk management and reinforces the importance of risk culture.

Case Example with Practical Application

Scenario

You are responsible for enhancing the risk culture at a manufacturing company that has recently experienced several operational disruptions due to a lack of proactive risk management. The company's leadership recognizes the need to foster a stronger risk culture to prevent future disruptions and improve overall operational resilience.

Exercise 6: Promoting Risk Awareness and Encouraging Participation

Task

Outline the steps you would take to promote risk awareness and encourage employees to actively participate in risk management.

Answer and Explanation

- **Develop and Implement Regular Risk Management Training Programs**
    - **Risk Training for All Employees:** Design and deliver risk management training programs tailored to the specific risks associated with different roles within the manufacturing company. For example, production line workers should receive training on identifying and mitigating safety risks, while supply chain managers should focus on risks related to supplier reliability and logistics.
    - **Interactive Learning:** Use interactive methods such as workshops, case studies, and scenario analysis to engage employees and reinforce the importance of risk management. For example, a workshop on supply chain disruptions could include a scenario where employees must identify potential risks and develop mitigation strategies.
- **Calculation Example**
    - **Training Costs:** Assume the cost of developing and delivering a risk management training program is $100,000 annually. If the program reduces the frequency of operational disruptions by 20%, and each disruption typically costs the company $500,000, the savings would be $100,000 per disruption avoided. With five disruptions avoided annually, the total savings would be $500,000, resulting in a net benefit of $400,000.
- **Establish Clear Communication Channels for Reporting Risks**
    - **Anonymous Hotlines:** Implement an anonymous hotline where employees can report risks or concerns without fear of retaliation. This hotline should be easily accessible and widely communicated throughout the organization.

- **Regular Risk Meetings:** Schedule regular risk meetings at the departmental level to discuss potential risks, share insights, and develop mitigation strategies. These meetings should be inclusive, encouraging participation from employees at all levels.
- **Risk Management Platform:** Develop a digital platform where employees can report risks, track risk mitigation efforts, and access risk management resources. This platform should provide real-time updates on the organization's risk profile and allow employees to contribute to risk management initiatives.
- **Calculation Example**
  - **Cost of Communication Channels:** Assume the cost of implementing these communication channels (hotlines, meetings, platform) is $50,000 annually. If these channels lead to the early identification of risks that prevent one major operational disruption, the savings could be $500,000, resulting in a net benefit of $450,000.

- **Link Risk Management Practices to Performance Evaluations and Provide Incentives**
  - **Performance Metrics:** Incorporate risk management metrics into employee performance evaluations. For example, managers could be evaluated on their ability to identify and mitigate risks within their teams, while frontline workers could be assessed on their adherence to safety protocols.
  - **Incentives for Proactive Risk Management:** Develop an incentive program that rewards employees who actively contribute to risk management. For example, employees who identify significant risks that lead to cost savings or operational improvements could receive bonuses or recognition awards.
  - **Leadership Engagement:** Encourage senior leaders to actively participate in risk management discussions and demonstrate their commitment to a strong risk culture. Leaders should regularly communicate the importance of risk management

and recognize employees who contribute to the organization's risk management efforts.

- **Calculation Example**
    - **Cost of Incentive Program:** Assume the cost of the incentive program is $25,000 annually. If the program encourages the identification of risks that prevent three minor disruptions, each costing $100,000, the total savings would be $300,000, resulting in a net benefit of $275,000.

- **Conclusion**

  By implementing these steps, the manufacturing company can enhance its risk culture, promoting greater risk awareness and encouraging employees to actively participate in risk management. This approach not only helps prevent future operational disruptions but also aligns the organization's risk culture with its strategic goals, improving overall operational resilience and long-term success.

Strategic Importance of Risk Culture

A strong risk culture is essential for ensuring that risk management practices are not just formalities but are embedded in the day-to-day operations of the organization. When employees at all levels understand and embrace the importance of risk management, the organization is better equipped to identify and respond to risks in a timely manner. This proactive approach reduces the likelihood of negative outcomes, supports the achievement of strategic objectives, and enhances the organization's reputation and resilience.

Examples and Strategic Considerations

Example

Consider a global technology company that emphasizes innovation as a key component of its strategy. The company's risk culture is critical in balancing the pursuit of innovative projects with the need to manage the risks associated with rapid technological change, intellectual property protection, and market competition. The company's risk culture encourages employees to take calculated risks in innovation while maintaining rigorous processes for risk assessment and mitigation. This balance ensures that the company remains competitive and innovative without exposing itself to excessive risk.

Strategic Considerations

- **Alignment with Business Strategy:** Risk culture should align with the organization's overall business strategy. For example, a company pursuing aggressive growth through mergers and acquisitions must foster a risk culture that emphasizes thorough due diligence, integration planning, and post-merger risk management.
- **Supporting Innovation:** In industries where innovation is key to competitive advantage, a strong risk culture can support the pursuit of new opportunities while managing the risks associated with innovation. This includes fostering an environment where employees are encouraged to explore new ideas but are also mindful of the potential risks.
- **Enhancing Resilience:** A strong risk culture enhances organizational resilience by ensuring that risks are identified, assessed, and managed before they escalate into significant issues. This proactive approach helps the organization navigate uncertainties and recover quickly from setbacks.

Strategic Example with Calculation

Scenario

A pharmaceutical company is developing a new drug that has the potential to be a blockbuster product. However, the development process is fraught with risks, including regulatory approval challenges, clinical trial failures, and potential safety concerns.

Task

Calculate the potential impact of a strong risk culture on the success of the drug development process.

Answer and Explanation

- **Risk Identification and Mitigation**
    - **Risk Culture Impact:** A strong risk culture ensures that risks related to regulatory approval, clinical trials, and safety are identified early and managed effectively. This includes conducting rigorous clinical trials, engaging with regulatory bodies early, and continuously monitoring for safety issues.
    - **Calculation Example:** Assume the potential revenue from the drug is $1 billion annually, but the probability of success is only 50% due to the risks involved. If a strong risk culture increases the probability of success to 70% by effectively managing these risks, the expected value of the project increases from $500 million (50% of $1 billion) to $700 million (70% of $1 billion).
- **Cost-Benefit Analysis**
    - **Cost of Enhancing Risk Culture:** Suppose the cost of enhancing the risk culture through training, communication, and incentives is $5 million annually.
    - **Benefit:** The increase in the expected value of the project by $200 million ($700 million - $500 million) far outweighs the cost of enhancing the risk culture, resulting in a net benefit of $195 million.
- **Conclusion**

  A strong risk culture significantly increases the likelihood of success in high-risk, high-reward projects like drug development.

By embedding risk management into every aspect of the process, the pharmaceutical company can enhance its ability to bring innovative products to market while managing the associated risks, ultimately supporting its long-term strategic goals.

Chapter

08

Strategic Risk Management in Practice

Strategic risk management is the process of identifying, assessing, and managing risks that could impact an organization's ability to achieve its long-term goals. By integrating risk management into the strategic planning process, organizations can make informed decisions that balance risk and opportunity. This chapter explores the practical aspects of strategic risk management, including developing a strategic risk management plan, integrating risk management into strategic planning, and applying these concepts to mergers and acquisitions (M&A). The chapter also presents real-world examples of strategic risk management failures and successes, along with exercises to reinforce the concepts.

Developing a Strategic Risk Management Plan

A strategic risk management plan is essential for organizations to proactively identify, assess, and manage risks that could hinder the achievement of their strategic objectives. This plan provides a structured approach to aligning risk management practices with the organization's goals, ensuring that risks are managed effectively and strategically. This chapter outlines the steps to develop a strategic risk management plan, provides a detailed example, and includes a practical exercise with calculations and answers to illustrate the process.

Importance of a Strategic Risk Management Plan

A strategic risk management plan helps organizations systematically identify and manage risks that could impact their strategic goals. The plan outlines the organization's risk appetite, identifies key risks, and establishes strategies to mitigate those risks. By aligning risk management with strategic planning, organizations can make informed decisions that balance risk and reward, enhance resilience, and support long-term success.

Key Benefits

- **Proactive Risk Management:** Anticipate and address risks before they become significant issues.
- **Alignment with Strategy:** Ensure that risk management practices support the achievement of strategic objectives.
- **Improved Decision-Making:** Provide a framework for making informed decisions that consider both risks and opportunities.
- **Enhanced Resilience:** Strengthen the organization's ability to adapt to changes in the external environment.

Steps to Develop a Strategic Risk Management Plan

- **Identify Strategic Objectives**
  - **Define Long-Term Goals:** Clearly define the organization's long-term goals and objectives. This step involves understanding what the organization aims to achieve, such as market expansion, product innovation, or revenue growth.
- **Identify Key Risks**
  - **Risk Identification:** Identify risks that could affect the achievement of strategic objectives. These might include market risks (e.g., competitive pressure), operational risks (e.g., supply chain disruptions), regulatory risks (e.g., compliance issues), and reputational risks (e.g., brand damage).
- **Assess and Prioritize Risks**
  - **Evaluate Likelihood and Impact:** Evaluate the likelihood (probability) and impact (consequences) of each identified risk. Use a risk matrix to categorize risks into high, medium, or low priority based on their potential to disrupt strategic objectives.

- **Develop Risk Mitigation Strategies**
  - **Mitigation Strategies:** Create strategies to mitigate prioritized risks. This could include:
  - **Risk Avoidance:** Eliminate the risk by avoiding the risky activity.
  - **Risk Reduction:** Reduce the likelihood or impact of the risk through preventive measures.
  - **Risk Transfer:** Transfer the risk to another party (e.g., through insurance or outsourcing).
  - **Risk Acceptance:** Accept the risk and prepare contingency plans.
- **Assign Responsibilities**
  - **Responsibility Assignment:** Assign responsibility for managing each risk to specific individuals or teams within the organization. This ensures accountability and effective risk management.
- **Monitor and Review**
  - **Continuous Monitoring:** Continuously monitor risks and the effectiveness of mitigation strategies. Regularly review and update the risk management plan to reflect changes in the external environment or organizational objectives.
  - **Example:** A retail company is planning to expand into international markets. The strategic risk management plan identifies key risks such as currency fluctuations, supply chain disruptions, and regulatory compliance. The company develops strategies such as currency hedging (to manage currency risks), diversifying suppliers (to mitigate supply chain risks), and establishing a compliance team (to address regulatory risks).

Practical Example: Strategic Risk Management Plan for a Technology Company

Scenario

A technology company is planning to launch a new product line in a highly competitive market. The company's strategic objectives include capturing a significant market share, achieving rapid growth, and maintaining technological leadership. However, the company faces several risks related to competition, technological changes, supply chain management, and regulatory compliance.

Exercise 1: Developing a Strategic Risk Management Plan

Task

Develop a strategic risk management plan for the technology company. Identify the key risks, assess their likelihood and impact, and outline risk mitigation strategies.

Answer and Explanation

- **Identify Strategic Objectives**
  - Objective 1: Capture a 15% market share within the first year of the product launch.
  - Objective 2: Achieve a 20% annual growth rate in sales.
  - Objective 3: Maintain a leadership position in technology innovation.

- **Identify Key Risks**
  - **Competitive Pressure:** Risk of losing market share due to aggressive competitors with established products.
  - **Rapid Technological Changes:** Risk of technological obsolescence or failure to keep up with emerging trends.
  - **Supply Chain Issues:** Risk of delays or disruptions in the supply chain, affecting the timely delivery of the product.

- **Regulatory Compliance:** Risk of non-compliance with regulations in different markets, leading to fines or legal challenges.

- **Assess and Prioritize Risks**

Risk	Likelihood (1-5)	Impact (1-5)	Risk Score (Likelihood x Impact)	Priority
Competitive Pressure	5	4	20	High
Rapid Technological Changes	4	5	20	High
Supply Chain Issues	3	3	9	Medium
Regulatory Compliance	2	4	8	Medium

- **Risk Score Calculation**
  - Competitive Pressure: Likelihood = 5, Impact = 4, Risk Score = 5 × 4 = 20 (High Priority)
  - Rapid Technological Changes: Likelihood = 4, Impact = 5, Risk Score = 4 × 5 = 20 (High Priority)
  - Supply Chain Issues: Likelihood = 3, Impact = 3, Risk Score = 3 × 3 = 9 (Medium Priority)
  - Regulatory Compliance: Likelihood = 2, Impact = 4, Risk Score = 2 × 4 = 8 (Medium Priority)

- **Develop Risk Mitigation Strategies**
  - **Competitive Pressure**
    - Mitigation Strategy: Invest in Research & Development (R&D) to stay ahead of competitors and develop innovative products. Allocate 15% of annual revenue to R&D to fund innovation.

- **Rapid Technological Changes**
  - Mitigation Strategy: Form strategic alliances with technology partners to leverage new technologies and trends. Monitor industry developments and adapt product designs accordingly.
- **Supply Chain Issues**
  - Mitigation Strategy: Diversify suppliers to reduce dependence on a single source. Maintain a buffer stock of critical components to ensure continuity in case of delays.
- **Regulatory Compliance**
  - Mitigation Strategy: Engage with regulators early in the product development process to understand compliance requirements. Establish a compliance team to monitor and ensure adherence to regulations.

- **Assign Responsibilities**
  - **Competitive Pressure:** Chief Technology Officer (CTO) is responsible for driving R&D and innovation.
  - **Rapid Technological Changes:** Chief Strategy Officer (CSO) is responsible for forming alliances and monitoring technological trends.
  - **Supply Chain Issues:** Supply Chain Manager is responsible for supplier diversification and inventory management.
  - **Regulatory Compliance:** Legal and Compliance Team is responsible for monitoring regulations and ensuring compliance.

- **Monitor and Review**
  - **Continuous Monitoring:** Implement a monthly review process to assess the effectiveness of mitigation strategies and make adjustments as needed. Use key risk indicators (KRIs)

to track changes in the risk environment and take corrective actions promptly.

Example Calculations for Risk Mitigation Costs and Benefits

Scenario: The technology company decides to invest in R&D to mitigate competitive pressure and technological changes. The company allocates 15% of its annual revenue of $100 million to R&D.

Calculation:

- **R&D Investment:** 15% of $100 million = $15 million.
- **Expected Benefit:** The investment is expected to increase market share by 5%, resulting in an additional $5 million in annual revenue.
- **Net Benefit:** Additional revenue ($5 million) - R&D Investment ($15 million) = -$10 million in the first year. However, the company expects to achieve long-term benefits through sustained competitive advantage.

The strategic risk management plan outlines the key risks, assesses their likelihood and impact, and develops mitigation strategies to address them. By aligning risk management practices with strategic objectives, the technology company can better navigate uncertainties, capitalize on opportunities, and achieve its long-term goals.

Integrating Risk Management into Strategic Planning

Integrating risk management into strategic planning is critical for ensuring that risks are considered at every stage of decision-making. This approach helps organizations proactively identify potential obstacles to their strategic goals, assess their impact, and develop strategies to manage them effectively. By aligning risk management with strategic planning, organizations can better navigate uncertainties, make informed decisions, and enhance their resilience to changing external conditions. This chapter outlines the role of risk management in strategic planning, provides extended examples, and includes a practical exercise with calculations and answers to illustrate the integration process.

The Role of Risk Management in Strategic Planning

Integrating risk management into strategic planning means embedding risk assessment and mitigation practices into the process of setting strategic goals, formulating strategies, and making key business decisions. This integration ensures that risks are identified and managed in alignment with the organization's objectives, risk appetite, and external environment.

Key Concepts

- **Risk-Informed Decision-Making:** Strategic decisions should be informed by a thorough understanding of the risks involved. This requires assessing the potential impact of different strategic options and selecting the one that aligns with the organization's risk appetite.
- **Scenario Analysis:** Scenario analysis involves exploring different future scenarios to understand how they might impact the organization's strategy. This helps in preparing for uncertainties and developing contingency plans.
- **Continuous Monitoring:** Strategic risks should be continuously monitored, and the strategic plan should be adjusted as necessary to respond to changes in the external environment.
- **Example:** A financial services company integrates risk management into its strategic planning by conducting scenario analysis to assess the impact of potential economic downturns on its growth strategy. For example, the company considers scenarios where interest rates rise or fall significantly, impacting loan demand and investment returns. Based on this analysis, the company develops contingency plans, such as adjusting its investment portfolio to include more stable, low-risk assets and diversifying revenue streams by expanding into new markets or services.

Practical Example: Integrating Risk Management into Strategic Planning for a Healthcare Company

Scenario

You are part of the strategic planning team for a healthcare company considering entering the telemedicine market. The company's strategic objectives include capturing a significant share of the telemedicine market, leveraging technology to improve patient care, and achieving sustainable growth. However, several risks must be managed, including regulatory changes, technological challenges, cybersecurity threats, and market acceptance.

Exercise 2: Integrating Risk Management into Strategic Planning

Task

Outline how you would integrate risk management into the strategic planning process for entering the telemedicine market, considering potential risks such as regulatory changes, technological challenges, and market acceptance.

Answer and Explanation

- **Risk Identification**
  - **Regulatory Changes:** Identify risks related to changes in telemedicine regulations, such as licensing requirements, reimbursement policies, and privacy laws. For example, if regulations become more stringent, the company may face increased compliance costs or delays in market entry.
  - **Technological Challenges:** Identify risks related to the adoption and implementation of telemedicine technology, such as software glitches, integration issues, and data compatibility problems.
  - **Cybersecurity Risks:** Identify risks related to data breaches, cyber-attacks, and the loss of sensitive patient information.

These risks could lead to financial losses, reputational damage, and legal liabilities.

- **Market Acceptance:** Identify risks related to customer acceptance of telemedicine services, including concerns about data privacy, technology adoption barriers, and the perceived quality of remote care.

- **Scenario Analysis**

  Conduct scenario analysis to assess the impact of different regulatory environments and technological advancements on the telemedicine market. Consider the following scenarios:

  - Scenario 1: Favorable Regulatory Environment: Regulations become more supportive of telemedicine, with streamlined licensing and reimbursement policies.
  - Scenario 2: Adverse Regulatory Changes: Regulations become more restrictive, requiring additional compliance efforts and increasing entry costs.
  - Scenario 3: Rapid Technological Advancement: Technology evolves rapidly, enhancing the quality and efficiency of telemedicine services but requiring continuous investment in new technologies.
  - Scenario 4: Low Market Acceptance: Customers are slow to adopt telemedicine due to privacy concerns, lack of awareness, or preference for in-person consultations.

- **Calculate Impact**

  Assume the potential revenue from entering the telemedicine market is $100 million annually under a favorable regulatory environment, but only $50 million under an adverse environment due to increased compliance costs and delays. The expected revenue difference is $50 million ($100 million - $50 million).

  If the likelihood of a favorable regulatory environment is 60%, and an adverse environment is 40%, calculate the expected revenue:

Expected Revenue = $(0.6 \times 100M) + (0.4 \times 50M) = 60M + 20M = 80M$

This analysis helps the company understand the potential financial impact of different regulatory scenarios and informs strategic decision-making.

- **Risk Mitigation**
  - Regulatory Compliance: Engage with regulators early to understand requirements and advocate for favorable policies. Allocate $1 million annually for a regulatory affairs team to monitor changes and ensure compliance.
  - Technological Investment: Invest in secure, scalable technology platforms and establish partnerships with technology providers. Allocate $5 million for technology development and integration, and another $1 million for continuous updates and improvements.
  - Cybersecurity Measures: Develop a robust cybersecurity strategy, including encryption, multi-factor authentication, and regular audits. Allocate $2 million for cybersecurity infrastructure and training.
  - Market Research and Education: Conduct market research to understand customer needs and preferences. Develop marketing campaigns to educate customers about the benefits of telemedicine. Allocate $2 million for market research and outreach efforts.
- **Continuous Monitoring**
  - Key Risk Indicators (KRIs): Establish KRIs to monitor changes in the regulatory environment, technological landscape, and market trends. For example, track the number of new regulations impacting telemedicine, the rate of technology adoption, and customer feedback on telemedicine services.

- Review and Adjust: Set up quarterly review meetings to evaluate the effectiveness of mitigation strategies and adjust the strategic plan as needed. Use data analytics to identify emerging risks and opportunities.

Example Calculations for Risk Mitigation Costs and Benefits

Scenario

The healthcare company decides to invest in regulatory compliance and technology to mitigate the risks associated with entering the telemedicine market. The total budget for these initiatives is $9 million annually.

Calculation

- **Cost of Risk Mitigation**
  - **Regulatory Compliance:** $1 million annually for regulatory affairs.
  - **Technology Investment:** $5 million for technology development and integration, plus $1 million for updates.
  - **Cybersecurity:** $2 million for cybersecurity infrastructure and training.

  Total Cost: $1M + $5M + $1M + $2M = $9 million annually.

- **Expected Revenue with Risk Mitigation**

  Assume the risk mitigation efforts increase the likelihood of achieving the favorable regulatory environment from 60% to 80%.

  Calculate the new expected revenue:

  Expected Revenue = (0.8 × 100M) + (0.2 × 50M) = 80M + 10M = 90M

  The increase in expected revenue due to risk mitigation is $90 million - $80 million = $10 million.

- **Net Benefit**
  - **Net Benefit of Risk Mitigation Efforts:** $10 million (increased expected revenue) - $9 million (cost of risk mitigation) = $1 million.

  The net benefit indicates that integrating risk management into strategic planning and investing in mitigation strategies has a positive financial impact and supports the company's strategic objectives.

Strategic Risk Management in Mergers and Acquisitions

Mergers and acquisitions (M&A) are complex strategic transactions that offer significant growth opportunities but also carry substantial risks. Effective risk management is crucial to the success of M&A activities, as it helps organizations identify, assess, and mitigate risks that could threaten the transaction's success. This chapter explores the role of risk management in M&A, key considerations during the process, and provides a practical exercise with calculations, examples, and answers to illustrate strategic risk management in M&A.

The Role of Risk Management in Mergers and Acquisitions

Mergers and acquisitions involve various risks, including financial, operational, legal, and cultural challenges. Effective risk management helps organizations anticipate these risks, develop strategies to mitigate them, and increase the likelihood of a successful transaction.

Key Considerations

- **Due Diligence:** Conduct thorough due diligence to identify potential risks associated with the target company, including financial, legal, operational, and market risks. Due diligence involves analyzing the target's financial statements, legal liabilities, compliance status, intellectual property, and market position.

- **Cultural Integration:** Assess the cultural compatibility of the merging organizations. Cultural misalignment is a common source of failure in M&A transactions, leading to employee dissatisfaction, loss of key talent, and reduced productivity.
- **Synergy Realization:** Evaluate the likelihood of achieving anticipated synergies, such as cost savings, increased market share, or expanded capabilities. Develop strategies to realize these synergies while managing associated risks.
- **Post-Merger Integration:** Plan for post-merger integration, focusing on aligning systems, processes, and cultures to ensure a smooth transition. A well-defined integration plan reduces operational disruptions and facilitates a seamless merger.
- **Example:** A global pharmaceutical company acquires a smaller biotech firm to expand its product portfolio. The company conducts extensive due diligence to assess the biotech firm's financial health, regulatory compliance, and intellectual property risks. Key findings include potential patent disputes and compliance gaps in clinical trial documentation. A detailed integration plan is developed to align the two companies' cultures, streamline processes, and address identified risks, ensuring a successful merger.

Practical Example: Strategic Risk Management in M&A for a Manufacturing Company

Scenario

You are advising a manufacturing company that is considering acquiring a competitor to expand its market share and production capabilities. The strategic objectives of the acquisition include achieving cost synergies, gaining access to new markets, and increasing operational efficiencies. However, several risks must be managed to ensure a successful transaction.

Exercise 3: Identifying and Mitigating Key Risks in M&A

Task

Identify the key risks the company should consider during the due diligence process and outline strategies to mitigate these risks.

Answer and Explanation

- **Financial Risks**
    - **Risk Identification:** Assess the target company's financial statements, including debt levels, revenue projections, cash flow, and working capital. Identify potential financial risks such as overstated assets, understated liabilities, and aggressive revenue recognition practices.
    - **Risk Mitigation Strategy**
        - **Price Adjustments:** Negotiate price adjustments based on findings during the due diligence process. For example, if the target company's debt level is higher than initially disclosed, reduce the purchase price accordingly.
        - **Contingent Payments:** Structure the deal with contingent payments, such as earn-outs, that depend on the target company's future performance. This reduces the upfront payment risk and aligns incentives.
    - **Calculation Example**
        - **Adjustment for Overstated Revenue:** Assume the target company reported annual revenue of $50 million, but due diligence reveals that $5 million of this revenue is non-recurring. Adjust the valuation by reducing the purchase price proportionally to the revenue adjustment:

          Adjusted Revenue = 50M – 5M = 45M

If the original purchase price was $200 million based on a 4x revenue multiple, the new price should be:

New Price = 4 × 45M = 180M

The reduction in purchase price is $20 million, reflecting the overstatement of revenue.

- **Legal Risks**
  - **Risk Identification:** Identify potential legal issues, such as ongoing litigation, intellectual property disputes, compliance violations, or regulatory challenges. Review the target company's contracts, licenses, and any pending lawsuits or investigations.
  - **Risk Mitigation Strategy**
    - **Indemnities and Escrows:** Negotiate indemnities to protect against specific legal risks, such as litigation or environmental liabilities. Consider establishing an escrow account to cover potential legal claims.
    - **Adjusting Purchase Price:** Reduce the purchase price to reflect potential legal liabilities or secure warranties from the seller to cover undisclosed risks.
  - **Calculation Example**
    - **Potential Legal Liability:** If due diligence reveals a pending lawsuit with a potential cost of $10 million, negotiate a reduction in the purchase price or require the seller to set aside $10 million in escrow to cover the potential liability.
- **Operational Risks**
  - **Risk Identification:** Evaluate the compatibility of the two companies' operations, including supply chain management, production processes, technology systems, and organizational structures. Identify potential disruptions that could arise from integrating different systems and processes.

- **Risk Mitigation Strategy**
    - **Integration Planning:** Develop a detailed integration plan that outlines how operations will be combined, including aligning supply chain processes, standardizing technology platforms, and consolidating production facilities.
    - **Supply Chain Diversification:** Diversify suppliers to reduce dependence on a single source and ensure continuity during the integration process.
- **Calculation Example**
    - **Integration Costs:** Assume the cost of integrating technology systems and aligning supply chain processes is estimated at $5 million. Factor these costs into the overall acquisition budget to ensure sufficient resources are allocated for a smooth transition.

- **Cultural Risks**
    - **Risk Identification:** Assess cultural differences between the two organizations, including differences in management styles, corporate values, employee engagement practices, and communication approaches. Cultural misalignment can lead to employee turnover, loss of key talent, and reduced productivity.
    - **Risk Mitigation Strategy**
        - **Change Management Initiatives:** Implement change management programs to facilitate cultural integration. This could include workshops, team-building activities, and regular communication to align employees with the new organizational culture.
        - **Retention Plans:** Develop retention plans to retain key employees, such as offering retention bonuses, career development opportunities, and engagement programs.

- **Calculation Example**
  - **Retention Bonus Cost:** If the company identifies 20 key employees critical to post-merger success and offers a retention bonus of $50,000 each, the total cost would be:

    $$\text{Total Retention Bonus} = 20 \times 50{,}000 = 1{,}000{,}000$$

Example Calculation for Total M&A Costs and Benefits

Scenario

The manufacturing company decides to acquire the competitor, with an initial purchase price of $180 million. Due diligence reveals several risks, leading to additional costs for integration, legal indemnities, and retention bonuses.

Calculation

- **Total Acquisition Cost:**
  - Purchase Price: $180 million
  - Integration Costs: $5 million
  - Legal Escrow/Indemnity Costs: $10 million (escrow set aside for potential legal liabilities)
  - Retention Bonuses: $1 million

  $$\text{Total Cost} = 180M + 5M + 10M + 1M = 196M$$

- **Expected Benefits**
  - **Revenue Synergies:** The acquisition is expected to generate $50 million in additional annual revenue due to expanded market share and production capabilities.
  - **Cost Synergies:** Operational efficiencies and economies of scale are expected to save $10 million annually.

- **Net Present Value (NPV) of Expected Benefits**

  Assume the company uses a discount rate of 8% to evaluate the acquisition's NPV over 5 years. Calculate the NPV of the revenue and cost synergies:

  $$\text{NPV of Revenue Synergies} = \sum_{t=1}^{5} 50M/(1+0.08)^{t}$$

  $$\text{NPV of Cost Synergies} = \sum_{t=1}^{5} 50M/(1+0.08)^{t}$$

  After calculating these sums:

  NPV of Total Synergies ≈ 199.5M + 39.9M = 239.4M

- **Net Benefit**

  Net Benefit = NPV of Total Synergies – Total Cost

  Net Benefit = 239.4M – 196M = 43.4M

- **Conclusion**

  The net benefit of $43.4 million suggests that the acquisition, after considering the costs and risks, is a financially viable decision that aligns with the company's strategic objectives.

Real-world Examples of Strategic Risk Management Failures and Successes

Strategic risk management involves identifying, assessing, and addressing risks that could impact an organization's long-term objectives. Real-world examples of both failures and successes illustrate the critical importance of effective strategic risk management. This chapter provides detailed examples of companies that either failed or succeeded in managing strategic risks, highlighting the key lessons learned and the outcomes of their approaches. Additionally, an exercise is included to encourage further exploration of real-world cases.

Example of Strategic Risk Management Failure: Kodak

Kodak, once a dominant player in the photography industry, is a prime example of a company that failed to manage strategic risk effectively. Despite being a pioneer in digital photography (Kodak invented the first digital camera in 1975), the company hesitated to fully embrace digital technology due to its reliance on its profitable film business. As the market shifted rapidly towards digital photography in the 2000s, Kodak continued to prioritize its traditional film business, missing the opportunity to lead in the digital market. This strategic misstep led to a sharp decline in market share and ultimately, bankruptcy in 2012.

Key Lessons from Kodak's Failure

- **Adaptability:** Organizations must be willing to adapt their strategies in response to technological advancements and market changes. Kodak's reluctance to pivot away from film to digital photography shows how failing to adapt can lead to decline.
- **Proactive Risk Management:** Identifying and addressing strategic risks early can prevent long-term decline. Kodak identified the risk of digital disruption but failed to act on it decisively and in a timely manner.
- **Extended Analysis**

  Strategic Risk: Technological Disruption

  - **Risk Identification:** Kodak faced the risk of technological disruption as digital photography began to replace traditional film photography.
  - **Risk Management Approach:** Kodak's management believed that digital technology would cannibalize its lucrative film business. Therefore, it chose to focus on its core film products rather than invest aggressively in digital.
  - **Consequences of Failure:** By the time Kodak attempted to pivot to digital products, it had already lost its market

dominance to more agile competitors like Canon and Sony. The company's revenues fell sharply, and it filed for bankruptcy in 2012.

Calculation Example: Financial Impact of Strategic Missteps

- **Lost Market Share**

  Assume Kodak's market share in the photography industry was 60% in 2000, with annual revenues of $10 billion.

  By 2010, its market share fell to 10%, with annual revenues declining to $2 billion due to the shift to digital photography.

  Revenue Loss Calculation:

  Revenue Loss = 10B – 2B = 8B

  This represents an 80% decline in revenue over 10 years.

- **Missed Digital Market Opportunity**

  Assume the global digital camera market grew to $50 billion by 2010. If Kodak had maintained just a 10% market share, it could have generated $5 billion in revenue from digital products alone.

- **Potential Revenue from Digital Market**

  Potential Digital Revenue = 10% × 50B = 5B

  Combined with its actual revenue of $2 billion, Kodak could have had $7 billion in revenue instead of $2 billion, reducing its revenue loss significantly.

Example of Strategic Risk Management Success: Apple

Apple's decision to pivot from being primarily a computer company to a leader in consumer electronics is a textbook example of successful strategic risk management. In the early 2000s, Apple recognized the declining growth in the personal computer market and the potential for consumer electronics to drive future growth. Under Steve Jobs' leadership, Apple launched innovative products like the iPod in 2001, the iPhone in 2007, and the iPad in 2010, transforming itself into a diversified technology giant and one of the world's most valuable companies.

Key Lessons from Apple's Success

- **Strategic Vision:** Successful strategic risk management involves having a clear vision of where the market is headed and making bold decisions to capitalize on opportunities.
- **Innovation:** Investing in innovation can help mitigate risks associated with market saturation or decline in existing products. Apple's investment in product development enabled it to stay ahead of competitors and capture new market segments.
- **Extended Analysis:**

  Strategic Risk: Market Saturation and Technological Change

  - **Risk Identification:** Apple identified the risk of market saturation in the personal computer segment and the need to diversify its revenue streams.
  - **Risk Management Approach:** Apple made a strategic decision to invest in consumer electronics, leveraging its expertise in design and user experience to create groundbreaking products. The company focused on developing new product categories that would drive growth.
  - **Outcomes of Success:** Apple's strategic pivot paid off handsomely, leading to exponential growth. The iPhone, in particular, became a blockbuster product, driving a significant portion of Apple's revenue and profits.

Calculation Example: Financial Impact of Strategic Decisions

- **Revenue Growth from New Products**

  Assume Apple's revenue from computers was $5 billion annually in 2000. After the launch of the iPod, iPhone, and iPad, Apple's revenue grew to $156 billion by 2012.

  Revenue Growth Calculation:

  Revenue Growth = 156B – 5B = 151B

  This represents a 3020% increase in revenue over 12 years.

- **Contribution of iPhone to Revenue**

  Assume the iPhone contributed 60% of Apple's total revenue in 2012. Calculate the revenue from the iPhone:

  Revenue from iPhone = 60% × 156B = 93.6B

  The iPhone alone generated $93.6 billion, demonstrating the success of Apple's strategic pivot.

Exercise: Exploring Real-World Strategic Risk Management Cases Exercise 4: Researching a Recent Example of Strategic Risk Management

Task

Research a recent example of a company that successfully managed a strategic risk or failed to do so. Describe the risk, how the company addressed it, and the outcomes.

Answer and Explanation: Responses will vary depending on the chosen company, but the answer should include the following elements:

- **Description of the Strategic Risk**

  Provide a clear explanation of the risk the company faced. For example, was it a market risk, technological risk, regulatory risk, or a combination of factors?

- **Risk Management Approach**

  Detail how the company addressed the risk. Did it adopt a proactive strategy, such as investing in new technologies, entering new markets, or restructuring its operations? Or did it fail to recognize and manage the risk effectively?

- **Outcomes**

  Discuss the results of the company's risk management efforts. If the strategy was successful, describe the positive outcomes, such as increased market share, revenue growth, or enhanced reputation. If the strategy failed, explain the negative consequences, such as financial losses, market share decline, or reputational damage.

Example Solution: Company: Netflix

- **Description of the Strategic Risk:** In the early 2010s, Netflix faced the risk of losing market share due to increased competition from new streaming services and changing consumer preferences.
- **Risk Management Approach:** Netflix chose to invest heavily in original content production, recognizing that exclusive content could differentiate it from competitors and attract a loyal customer base. It also expanded internationally to tap into new markets.
- **Outcomes:** Netflix's strategy proved successful, leading to a significant increase in subscribers, revenue growth, and market valuation. The company's original content strategy paid off with hits like "Stranger Things" and "The Crown," helping it become a leader in the streaming industry.

- **Key Lessons**
  - **Differentiation:** Investing in unique value propositions, such as original content, can help mitigate competitive risks.
  - **Market Expansion:** Proactively expanding into new markets can offset risks in saturated or highly competitive domestic markets.

Strategic risk management is essential for ensuring that an organization's long-term goals are achieved in the face of uncertainty. By developing a strategic risk management plan, integrating risk management into strategic planning, and applying these concepts to mergers and acquisitions, organizations can navigate complex challenges and capitalize on opportunities. The real-world examples of strategic risk management failures and successes highlighted in this chapter provide valuable lessons for businesses aiming to enhance their strategic risk management practices. The exercises included in this chapter are designed to help readers apply these concepts in practical scenarios, reinforcing their understanding and skills in strategic risk management.

Chapter

09

Emerging Risks and Strategic Challenges

In today's rapidly evolving business environment, organizations face an array of emerging risks that can significantly impact their long-term strategies and success. These risks, including cybersecurity threats, climate change, and geopolitical instability, require proactive and strategic management. This chapter explores the nature of these emerging risks, their strategic implications, and how organizations can address them effectively. Practical examples and exercises are provided to help readers understand and apply the concepts discussed.

Cybersecurity and Technological Risks

In today's digital age, cybersecurity and technological risks have become critical strategic concerns for organizations across all sectors. The increasing reliance on digital systems, coupled with the growing sophistication of cyberattacks, necessitates a proactive approach to managing these risks. This chapter explores the various types of cybersecurity risks, their potential impacts, and effective strategies for managing them. A practical exercise is provided to illustrate the development of a comprehensive cybersecurity risk management plan.

Understanding Cybersecurity Risks

Cybersecurity risks involve the potential for unauthorized access, data breaches, and other cyber threats that can compromise an organization's information systems. These risks are particularly concerning as they can lead to significant financial losses, regulatory penalties, reputational damage, and operational disruptions.

Key Concepts

- **Data Breaches:** Unauthorized access to sensitive information, such as customer data, intellectual property, or financial records. Data breaches can result from hacking, insider threats, or inadequate security controls.
- **Ransomware Attacks:** Malicious software that encrypts files and locks users out of their systems until a ransom is paid. Ransomware can disrupt business operations, cause data loss, and lead to substantial financial costs.
- **Phishing:** Deceptive attempts to acquire sensitive information (e.g., passwords, credit card numbers) by masquerading as a trustworthy entity in electronic communications. Phishing attacks often target employees to gain access to the organization's internal systems.

- **Example:** A retail company experiences a data breach that exposes the personal information of millions of customers. The breach leads to financial losses due to legal fees, compensation to affected customers, and regulatory fines. Additionally, the company's reputation suffers, leading to a decline in customer trust and sales. In response, the company invests in advanced cybersecurity measures, including encryption, multi-factor authentication, and employee training, to prevent future incidents.

Financial Impact of Data Breach

- Assume the cost of the data breach is as follows:
  - Legal and Compensation Costs: $20 million
  - Regulatory Fines: $10 million
  - Loss of Sales Due to Reputational Damage: $30 million
- Total Financial Impact

  Total Impact = 20M + 10M + 30M = 60M

  By investing $5 million in advanced cybersecurity measures, the company aims to prevent future breaches, protecting its financial stability and reputation.

Practical Example: Developing a Cybersecurity Risk Management Plan for a Financial Institution

Scenario

You are the Chief Information Security Officer (CISO) of a financial institution. The institution is highly vulnerable to cybersecurity threats due to the sensitive nature of its operations and the valuable data it holds. Potential threats include phishing, ransomware, and data breaches. To safeguard the institution's assets, a comprehensive cybersecurity risk management plan is required.

Exercise 1: Creating a Cybersecurity Risk Management Plan

Task

Develop a cybersecurity risk management plan that addresses potential threats such as phishing, ransomware, and data breaches. Include preventive measures, detection strategies, and response protocols.

Answer and Explanation

- **Preventive Measures**
  - **Multi-Factor Authentication (MFA):** Implement MFA for all employees and customers to provide an additional layer of security. This reduces the likelihood of unauthorized access even if passwords are compromised.
    - **Cost Calculation:** Assume implementing MFA costs $1 million annually, including software licenses, maintenance, and user support.
  - **Regular Software Updates**: Ensure that all software, including operating systems and applications, is regularly updated to patch security vulnerabilities. Automate updates where possible to reduce manual intervention.
    - **Cost Calculation:** Assume the cost of automated software updates and patches is $200,000 annually.
  - **Encryption of Sensitive Data:** Encrypt all sensitive data, both in transit and at rest, to protect it from unauthorized access. Use strong encryption protocols such as AES-256.
    - **Cost Calculation:** Assume the cost of implementing encryption is $500,000, including software, hardware, and training.

- **Detection Strategies**
    - **Intrusion Detection Systems (IDS):** Deploy IDS to monitor network traffic for suspicious activity and potential intrusions. IDS tools can detect abnormal patterns and alert security teams in real-time.
        - **Cost Calculation:** Assume the cost of IDS implementation is $300,000 annually, including software and monitoring.
    - **Regular Vulnerability Assessments:** Conduct regular vulnerability assessments and penetration testing to identify potential weaknesses in the institution's cybersecurity defenses.
        - **Cost Calculation:** Assume vulnerability assessments cost $100,000 per quarter, totaling $400,000 annually.
    - **Network Traffic Monitoring:** Continuously monitor network traffic for anomalies that may indicate a cyberattack, such as unusual data transfers or unauthorized access attempts.
        - **Cost Calculation:** Assume network monitoring costs $200,000 annually.
- **Response Protocols**
    - **Incident Response Plan (IRP):** Develop a detailed IRP that outlines the steps to be taken in the event of a cybersecurity incident, including roles, responsibilities, communication protocols, and recovery procedures.
        - **Cost Calculation**: Assume developing and maintaining the IRP costs $150,000 annually, including staff training and regular updates.
    - **Cybersecurity Team:** Establish a dedicated cybersecurity team responsible for managing and responding to incidents. Ensure that team members are trained in the latest cybersecurity practices and incident response techniques.

- **Cost Calculation:** Assume the cost of a cybersecurity team (salaries, benefits, and training) is \$2 million annually.

- **Regular Drills:** Conduct regular cybersecurity drills and simulations to test the effectiveness of the IRP and ensure that all employees are prepared to respond to an incident.
  - **Cost Calculation:** Assume cybersecurity drills cost \$100,000 annually.

Total Annual Cost of Cybersecurity Plan:

Total Cost = 1M + 200K + 500K + 300K + 400K + 200K + 150K + 2M + 100K = 4.85M

Example Calculation: Cost-Benefit Analysis of Cybersecurity Investment

Scenario

The financial institution estimates that without the cybersecurity measures, the potential cost of a major data breach could be \$100 million, considering legal fees, regulatory fines, compensation to customers, and reputational damage. The probability of a major breach is estimated to be 10% annually.

Expected Cost Without Cybersecurity Measures

Expected Cost = 0.1 × 100M = 10M

Expected Cost with Cybersecurity Measures

Assume the cybersecurity measures reduce the probability of a breach to 1%.

Expected Cost with Measures = 0.01 × 100M = 1M

Net Benefit of Cybersecurity Investment

Cost of Cybersecurity Measures: \$4.85 million annually.

Reduction in Expected Cost

Cost Reduction = 10M - 1M = 9M

Net Benefit Calculation

Net Benefit = 9M - 4.85M = 4.15M

Conclusion

The net benefit of $4.15 million indicates that investing in cybersecurity measures is financially justified, reducing the potential cost of a data breach and aligning with the institution's strategic objective to safeguard its assets and maintain customer trust.

Climate Change and Environmental Risks

Climate change presents a wide array of risks that can significantly impact businesses across all industries. These risks include physical risks from extreme weather events, transition risks associated with shifting to a low-carbon economy, and reputational risks related to stakeholders' expectations for sustainability. Effective risk management strategies are essential for organizations to mitigate these risks, protect their assets, and ensure long-term profitability. This chapter explores the various types of climate change risks, provides a practical example, and includes an exercise with calculations, examples, and answers to illustrate strategic approaches to managing these risks.

Understanding Climate Change Risks

Climate change risks refer to the potential adverse impacts on businesses resulting from the changing climate, including the increased frequency and severity of extreme weather events, evolving environmental regulations, and growing demand for sustainable practices from stakeholders.

Key Concepts

- **Physical Risks:** Damage to assets and infrastructure due to extreme weather events, such as floods, hurricanes, and wildfires. Physical risks can lead to business interruptions, increased repair costs, and loss of revenue.
- **Transition Risks:** Financial risks associated with the transition to a low-carbon economy. These risks can arise from changes in regulations (e.g., carbon pricing), shifts in market demand towards sustainable products, and technological advancements in renewable energy.
- **Reputational Risks:** The risk of negative public perception due to perceived environmental negligence or failure to address climate change. Reputational risks can result in lost customers, reduced investor confidence, and damage to brand value.
- **Example:** An energy company faces increasing pressure from regulators and investors to reduce its carbon emissions and transition to sustainable energy sources. In response, the company invests $500 million in renewable energy projects, sets ambitious targets to reduce its carbon footprint by 50% over the next decade, and discloses its climate-related risks and strategies through its annual sustainability report. This proactive approach helps the company manage transition risks and enhances its reputation among stakeholders.

Financial Impact of Transition to Renewable Energy

Assume the investment in renewable energy is expected to generate cost savings of $100 million annually due to lower operational costs and reduced carbon taxes.

Payback Period Calculation

Payback Period = Initial Investment / Annual Savings

$$= 500M\ /\ 100M = 5 \text{ years}$$

The investment in renewable energy is expected to pay back in 5 years, after which the company will benefit from ongoing cost savings and improved sustainability credentials.

Practical Example: Developing a Climate Change Risk Management Strategy for a Manufacturing Company

Scenario

You are the sustainability officer for a global manufacturing company. The company operates several coastal facilities that are increasingly exposed to physical risks from climate change, including more frequent and severe flooding. These risks threaten to disrupt operations, damage assets, and increase costs.

Exercise 2: Creating a Climate Change Risk Management Strategy

Task

Develop a risk management strategy that addresses the physical risks from climate change, including both short-term and long-term actions.

Answer and Explanation

- **Short-Term Actions**
  - **Strengthen Flood Defenses:** Invest in physical barriers such as flood walls, levees, and drainage systems to protect vulnerable coastal facilities from flooding.

    Cost Calculation: Assume strengthening flood defenses costs $10 million per facility, and there are 5 vulnerable facilities.

    Total Cost:

    $\text{Total Cost} = 10\text{M} \times 5 = 50\text{M}$
  - **Purchase Flood Insurance:** Obtain insurance coverage to protect against potential financial losses from flood damage.

Cost Calculation: Assume the annual premium for flood insurance is $500,000 per facility.

Total Annual Insurance Cost:

Total Insurance Cost = 500K × 5 = 2.5M

- **Develop an Emergency Response Plan:** Create a comprehensive emergency response plan to ensure quick and effective action in the event of flooding. The plan should include evacuation procedures, communication protocols, and coordination with local authorities.

  Cost Calculation: Assume the cost of developing and implementing the emergency response plan is $1 million.

- **Long-Term Actions**
  - **Relocate Critical Operations:** Relocate critical operations from highly vulnerable coastal areas to less flood-prone locations. This may involve moving key equipment, personnel, and inventory to inland facilities.

    Cost Calculation: Assume the relocation cost for critical operations is $20 million per facility for 3 facilities.

    Total Relocation Cost:

    Total Relocation Cost = 20M × 3 = 60M

  - **Invest in Climate-Resilient Infrastructure:** Upgrade infrastructure to withstand extreme weather conditions, such as installing higher-grade materials, improving building foundations, and incorporating climate-resilient design features.

    Cost Calculation: Assume the investment in climate-resilient infrastructure is $15 million for the most vulnerable facility.

- **Reduce Carbon Footprint:** Implement measures to reduce the company's carbon footprint, such as transitioning to renewable energy, improving energy efficiency, and optimizing logistics. This can help mitigate long-term climate risks by aligning with global efforts to combat climate change.

  Cost Calculation: Assume the cost of reducing the carbon footprint through energy efficiency measures and renewable energy investments is $30 million, with expected annual savings of $5 million in reduced energy costs and lower carbon taxes.

  Payback Period Calculation:

  Payback Period = 30*M* / 5*M* = 6 years

- **Total Cost of Climate Change Risk Management Strategy**

  Total Cost = 50M + 2.5M + 1M + 60M + 15M + 30M = 158.5M

Example Calculation: Cost-Benefit Analysis of Climate Risk Management

Scenario

The manufacturing company estimates that without implementing the risk management strategy, the potential cost of flood-related damage, operational disruptions, and regulatory fines could be $200 million over the next 10 years. The probability of severe flooding affecting multiple facilities in any given year is estimated to be 20%.

- **Expected Cost Without Risk Management**

  Expected Cost = 0.2 × 200M = 40M annually

- **Expected Cost with Risk Management**

  Assume the risk management strategy reduces the probability of severe flooding impact to 5%.

Expected Cost with Risk Management = 0.05 × 200M = 10M annually

- **Net Benefit of Risk Management Investment**
  - **Annual Cost of Risk Management Measures:**

    Annual Cost of Short-Term Measures (Insurance and Maintenance) =

    2.5M + 1M = 3.5M
  - **Reduction in Expected Cost:**

    Cost Reduction = 40M – 10M = 30M annually
  - **Net Annual Benefit Calculation:**

    Net Annual Benefit = 30M – 3.5M = 26.5M
  - **Return on Investment (ROI):**

    ROI = Net Annual Benefit / Total Initial Investment Cost × 100

    ROI = 26.5*M* / 158.5*M* × 100 ≈ 16.7%
- **Conclusion**

  The positive ROI of 16.7% demonstrates that the risk management strategy is a sound investment, reducing potential losses from climate-related risks while supporting the company's long-term sustainability objectives.

Geopolitical and Economic Risks

Geopolitical and economic risks are critical concerns for multinational organizations operating in a globalized economy. These risks arise from political instability, changes in government policies, trade disputes, and conflicts between nations. Managing these risks is essential for ensuring business continuity, protecting assets, and maintaining competitive advantage. This chapter provides a detailed understanding of geopolitical risks, offers practical examples, and includes an exercise with calculations, examples, and answers to illustrate strategic risk management approaches.

Understanding Geopolitical Risks

Geopolitical risks are uncertainties and potential disruptions to business operations resulting from political instability, changes in government policies, trade disputes, and international conflicts. These risks can impact supply chains, create regulatory challenges, and affect global market conditions.

Key Concepts

- **Political Instability:** Risks associated with changes in government, civil unrest, or conflicts that can disrupt business operations. For example, a change in government might lead to nationalization of assets or restrictions on foreign investments.
- **Trade Risks:** Risks related to changes in trade policies, tariffs, and trade agreements that can affect the cost and availability of goods and services. Trade tensions between major economies can result in increased tariffs, import/export bans, and other trade barriers.
- **Sanctions and Regulatory Risks:** Risks associated with the imposition of economic sanctions, export controls, and other regulatory measures that can limit market access or increase compliance costs. Sanctions may restrict a company's ability to do business in certain countries or with certain entities.
- **Example:** A technology company based in the U.S. faces geopolitical risks due to escalating trade tensions with China, a key export market. The company's supply chain is disrupted as tariffs on its products increase costs, and new regulatory requirements restrict the export of certain technologies. To mitigate these risks, the company diversifies its supply chain by sourcing components from other countries, establishes new partnerships in Asia and

Europe, and actively lobbies for favorable trade policies in its home country.

Financial Impact of Geopolitical Risks

- Assume the increased tariffs on exports to China result in additional costs of $50 million annually.
- The cost of diversifying the supply chain and establishing new partnerships is estimated at $30 million.
- Net Financial Impact Calculation:

  Net Financial Impact = Increased Costs + Mitigation Costs = 50M + 30M = 80M

By implementing mitigation strategies, the company aims to reduce the potential long-term impact of geopolitical risks.

Practical Example: Developing a Risk Management Plan for Geopolitical Risks in the Automotive Industry

Scenario

You are the risk manager for a global automotive company. The company relies heavily on raw materials sourced from a politically unstable region. The instability threatens to disrupt the supply chain, increase costs, and delay production. A strategic risk management plan is required to address these potential impacts.

Exercise 3: Creating a Geopolitical Risk Management Plan

Task

Develop a risk management plan that addresses the potential impact of geopolitical risks on the company's supply chain. Consider strategies for supply chain diversification, inventory management, and insurance coverage.

Answer and Explanation

- **Supply Chain Diversification**
  - **Identify Alternative Suppliers:** Research and identify alternative suppliers in more politically stable regions. Establish contracts with multiple suppliers to reduce dependency on a single source.
  - **Cost Calculation:** Assume diversifying the supply chain to include three new suppliers costs $10 million in upfront investments and contract negotiations.
  - **Ongoing Costs:** Additional annual costs for diversified supply contracts are $2 million.

- **Inventory Management**
  - **Increase Inventory Levels:** Maintain higher inventory levels of critical raw materials to buffer against potential supply disruptions caused by geopolitical instability.
  - **Cost Calculation:** Assume the cost of increasing inventory levels by 30% involves an additional $5 million annually for storage, insurance, and handling.

- **Political Risk Insurance**
  - **Purchase Political Risk Insurance:** Obtain insurance coverage to protect against losses related to political instability, such as expropriation, currency inconvertibility, or government interference.
  - **Cost Calculation:** Assume the cost of political risk insurance is $1 million annually, covering up to $50 million in potential losses.

- **Total Cost of Risk Management Plan**

  Total Cost = Upfront Diversification Cost + Ongoing Diversification Cost + Increased Inventory Cost + Insurance Cost

  Total Cost = 10M + 2M + 5M + 1M = 18M annually

Example Calculation: Cost-Benefit Analysis of Geopolitical Risk Management

Scenario

The automotive company estimates that without implementing the risk management plan, the potential cost of supply chain disruptions due to geopolitical instability could be $100 million over the next 5 years. The probability of a significant disruption affecting production in any given year is estimated to be 15%.

- **Expected Cost Without Risk Management**

  Expected Cost = 0.15 × 100M = 15M annually

- **Expected Cost with Risk Management**

  Assume the risk management plan reduces the probability of a significant disruption to 5%.

  Expected Cost with Risk Management = 0.05 × 100M = 5M annually

- **Net Benefit of Risk Management Investment**

  - **Reduction in Expected Cost**

    Cost Reduction = 15M – 5M = 10M annually

  - **Net Annual Benefit Calculation**

    Net Annual Benefit = 10M – 18M = –8M

- **Analysis**

  The net annual benefit appears negative; however, the calculation does not consider potential long-term benefits and reduced volatility in production costs. Additionally, the company must evaluate non-financial benefits, such as maintaining customer trust and protecting market share, which could outweigh the direct financial costs in the long run.

- **Conclusion**

  While the initial cost of the geopolitical risk management plan is high, the reduced probability of supply chain disruptions ensures more stable production and less volatility in operations. The company may consider further cost optimization or a phased implementation approach to balance immediate costs with long-term benefits.

Strategic Implications of Emerging Risks

Emerging risks such as cybersecurity threats, climate change, and geopolitical instability present significant challenges and opportunities for organizations. These risks can profoundly impact a company's business strategy, requiring a proactive approach to safeguard long-term success and maintain competitive advantage. This chapter explores the strategic implications of emerging risks, offers practical examples, and includes an exercise with calculations, examples, and answers to illustrate how organizations can integrate these risks into their overall business strategy.

Impact on Business Strategy

Emerging risks can disrupt business operations, affect market dynamics, and alter the competitive landscape. To manage these risks effectively, organizations must integrate risk considerations into their strategic planning, decision-making processes, and operational activities.

Key Considerations

- **Adaptability:** Organizations must be agile and adaptable, continuously reassessing their strategies in light of emerging risks and changing external conditions. This may involve shifting focus to new markets, revising product lines, or adopting new technologies.
- **Resilience:** Building resilience into business operations is essential for withstanding the impact of emerging risks. This includes developing contingency plans, diversifying revenue streams, and investing in robust risk management capabilities.

- **Sustainability:** Companies must consider the long-term sustainability of their strategies, particularly in the face of environmental and social risks. Integrating sustainability into business models can enhance corporate reputation, reduce regulatory risks, and attract environmentally conscious customers.
- **Example:** A global logistics company recognizes the strategic implications of climate change, such as increased regulatory pressure, higher fuel costs, and changing customer preferences. The company integrates sustainability into its core business strategy by investing in green technologies, such as electric vehicles and renewable energy. This reduces its carbon footprint and appeals to environmentally conscious customers, positioning the company as a leader in sustainable logistics.

Financial Impact of Sustainability Investments

Assume the company invests $50 million in electric vehicles and $20 million in renewable energy projects, with expected annual savings of $15 million due to lower fuel costs and reduced carbon taxes.

- **Payback Period Calculation**

  Payback Period = Initial Investment / Annual Savings = $50M + 20M / 15M \approx 4.67$ years

  The investment is expected to pay back in approximately 4.67 years, after which the company will benefit from ongoing cost savings and enhanced sustainability credentials.

Practical Example: Integrating Emerging Risks into Business Strategy for a Consumer Goods Company

Scenario

You are the CEO of a consumer goods company facing emerging risks related to cybersecurity, climate change, and geopolitical instability. To ensure long-term success, it is crucial to integrate these risks into the company's overall business strategy.

Exercise 4: Developing a Risk-Integrated Business Strategy

Task

Develop a business strategy that addresses the emerging risks of cybersecurity, climate change, and geopolitical instability. Outline specific actions to integrate these risks into the company's strategy.

Answer and Explanation

- **Cybersecurity**
  - **Invest in Robust Cybersecurity Measures:** Allocate resources to enhance cybersecurity infrastructure, including firewalls, encryption, and multi-factor authentication, to protect the company's digital assets and customer data.
  - **Cost Calculation:** Assume an annual investment of $3 million in cybersecurity measures, including software, hardware, and employee training.
  - **Integrate Cybersecurity Risk Assessments:** Regularly conduct cybersecurity risk assessments and integrate findings into strategic planning to identify vulnerabilities and develop mitigation strategies.
  - **Financial Impact of Cybersecurity Investment**

    Assume a potential cost of a major data breach is $30 million, with a 10% probability of occurrence without robust cybersecurity measures.

    - **Expected cost without investment:**
      Expected Cost Without Investment = 0.1 × 30M = 3M annually
      Assume the cybersecurity investment reduces the probability of a breach to 1%.

- **Expected cost with investment**

  Expected Cost With Investment = 0.01 × 30M = 0.3M annually

- **Net Benefit of Investment**

  Net Benefit = (3M–0.3M) – 3M = 2.7M – 3M = –0.3M annually

The net benefit appears negative initially, but this calculation does not consider non-financial benefits such as maintaining customer trust and protecting brand reputation.

- **Climate Change**
  - **Develop a Sustainability Strategy:** Reduce carbon emissions by investing in energy-efficient technologies, improving supply chain efficiency, and sourcing sustainable materials.
  - **Cost Calculation:** Assume the cost of these initiatives is $10 million annually, with expected savings of $4 million per year from reduced energy consumption and waste management costs.
  - **Align Brand with Environmental Responsibility:** Rebrand products to highlight sustainability efforts, attract environmentally conscious customers, and meet regulatory requirements.
  - **Net Financial Impact of Sustainability Strategy**

    Net Financial Impact = Annual Savings – Annual Cost = 4M – 10M = –6M

    While the immediate financial impact is negative, the strategy positions the company for long-term growth and compliance with evolving regulations.

- **Geopolitical Instability**
  - **Diversify Market Presence and Supply Chain:** Enter new markets and diversify suppliers to reduce dependence on politically unstable regions.
  - **Cost Calculation:** Assume the cost of diversification includes a \$5 million investment in entering new markets and \$3 million annually for maintaining diversified supplier contracts.
  - **Establish Partnerships in Stable Regions:** Form strategic partnerships in regions with stable political environments to mitigate risks from geopolitical instability.
  - **Expected Benefits from Diversification:**

    Assume diversification reduces potential supply chain disruption costs by 50%, from \$10 million to \$5 million annually.

  - **Net Benefit Calculation**

    Net Benefit = (10M–5M) – (5M + 3M) = 5M – 8M = –3M

    The net benefit is negative initially, but long-term benefits include enhanced stability and reduced exposure to geopolitical risks.

Example Calculation: Overall Cost-Benefit Analysis of Risk-Integrated Strategy

Scenario

The company integrates cybersecurity, climate change, and geopolitical risks into its strategy, incurring costs and savings as follows:

- **Cybersecurity**

  Net annual cost: -\$0.3 million

- **Climate Change**

  Net annual cost: -$6 million

- **Geopolitical Instability**

  Net annual cost: -$3 million

- **Total Annual Net Cost**

  Total Net Cost = −0.3M – 6M – 3M = −9.3M

- **Analysis**

  While the total net cost is negative, this calculation does not capture the strategic benefits such as enhanced market positioning, regulatory compliance, and brand reputation. These benefits can lead to increased market share, customer loyalty, and long-term profitability.

- **Conclusion**

  Integrating emerging risks into the company's strategy may have short-term costs, but it positions the company for long-term success by enhancing resilience, adaptability, and sustainability. The company should continue monitoring the external environment, adjust its strategy as needed, and communicate its risk management efforts to stakeholders to maximize the strategic benefits.

Chapter

10

Risk Communication and Reporting

Effective risk communication and reporting are vital components of an organization's risk management framework. They ensure that all stakeholders, from employees to investors, are well-informed about the risks the organization faces, the potential impacts, and the strategies in place to manage them. Transparent and accurate risk communication builds trust, supports informed decision-making, and enhances the organization's reputation. This chapter explores the principles of effective risk communication, reporting standards and practices, and the strategic implications of risk disclosure. It also provides case studies illustrating best practices and lessons learned in risk communication.

Effective Communication of Risks to Stakeholders

Effective risk communication is crucial for ensuring that stakeholders understand the risks faced by an organization and how these risks are managed. Clear, concise, and transparent communication builds trust, promotes informed decision-making, and enhances the organization's resilience by engaging stakeholders in a collaborative risk management process. This chapter explores the key principles of effective risk communication, provides practical examples, and includes an exercise to illustrate how organizations can communicate risks to different stakeholder groups.

The Importance of Risk Communication

Risk communication involves conveying information about potential risks to stakeholders, such as employees, investors, customers, and regulators, in a way that is clear, concise, and understandable. The objective is to ensure that stakeholders are aware of the risks the organization faces, understand the potential impacts, and know how these risks are being managed.

Key Concepts

- **Clarity:** Use clear and straightforward language, avoiding technical jargon that may confuse stakeholders. Ensure that the message is easy to understand for all stakeholder groups.
- **Relevance:** Tailor the communication to the specific concerns and interests of different stakeholder groups. For example, employees may need to know how a risk could impact their roles, while investors are interested in the financial implications.
- **Transparency:** Be open and honest about the risks, including potential impacts and uncertainties. This builds trust and

credibility, especially when communicating difficult or sensitive information.

- **Engagement:** Encourage dialogue with stakeholders, allowing them to ask questions and provide feedback. This helps address their concerns and fosters a collaborative approach to risk management.
- **Example:** A financial services company faces a potential cybersecurity threat. The company communicates this risk to stakeholders by issuing a public statement that:
- Outlines the nature of the threat (e.g., a detected phishing campaign targeting customer accounts).
- Describes the measures being taken to prevent a breach (e.g., enhanced monitoring, employee training, and collaboration with cybersecurity experts).
- Provides actionable steps customers can take to protect their information (e.g., changing passwords, enabling two-factor authentication).
- Offers contact information for further inquiries, including a dedicated hotline and email for concerned stakeholders.
- By providing clear, transparent, and actionable information, the company builds trust with its stakeholders and demonstrates a proactive approach to risk management.

Practical Example: Developing a Risk Communication Plan for a Global Manufacturing Company

Scenario

You are the Chief Risk Officer (CRO) of a global manufacturing company that has identified a significant supply chain risk due to escalating geopolitical tensions in a region where key suppliers are located. This risk could lead to delays, increased costs, and potential disruptions to production. To mitigate these risks, a communication plan must be developed to inform internal and external stakeholders.

Exercise 1: Creating a Risk Communication Plan

Task

Develop a risk communication plan to inform internal and external stakeholders, including employees, suppliers, and investors. Consider the specific concerns each group may have and how you will address them.

Answer and Explanation

- **Employees**

  Concerns: Employees may be worried about potential impacts on production, job security, and workplace safety.

  Communication Strategy

  - **Message:** Clearly explain the nature of the supply chain risk and its potential impacts on production schedules. Reassure employees that contingency plans are in place to mitigate disruptions, including alternative sourcing strategies and inventory management.
  - **Communication Channels:** Use internal communication tools, such as town hall meetings, emails, and company intranet, to provide regular updates. Encourage feedback and questions through designated communication channels.
  - **Engagement:** Offer opportunities for employees to participate in risk management activities, such as brainstorming sessions to identify further mitigation strategies.

- **Suppliers**

  Concerns: Suppliers may be concerned about potential delays, changes in order volumes, and the continuity of the supply chain.

  Communication Strategy

  - **Message:** Inform suppliers of the geopolitical tensions and their potential impact on supply chain operations. Discuss

collaborative solutions, such as adjusting delivery schedules, exploring alternative routes, or identifying substitute suppliers.
  - **Communication Channels:** Use direct communication, such as emails, phone calls, and virtual meetings, to maintain open lines of communication and build trust.
  - **Engagement:** Encourage suppliers to share their risk management plans and explore joint strategies to ensure continuity.

- **Investors**

  Concerns: Investors may be concerned about the financial impact of the supply chain risk, including potential cost increases, revenue loss, and effects on profitability.

  Communication Strategy

  - **Message:** Provide a comprehensive overview of the supply chain risk, its potential financial impacts, and the company's strategies to mitigate these risks. Highlight actions taken, such as diversifying supply sources, increasing inventory levels, and maintaining financial reserves to absorb potential shocks.
  - **Communication Channels:** Use investor communication tools, such as quarterly earnings calls, investor presentations, press releases, and the company website, to provide transparent updates.
  - **Engagement:** Offer a Q&A session during investor calls and provide a dedicated contact point for investor inquiries.

Example: Implementation of a Risk Communication Plan

Scenario

The global manufacturing company implements the risk communication plan to address the supply chain risks. The company estimates the potential impact on production costs to be $15 million annually if the risk materializes. By effectively communicating the risk to stakeholders, the company aims to mitigate these impacts through collaboration and proactive measures.

Communication to Employees

- **Action:** Conduct a town hall meeting to explain the risk and answer employee questions. Distribute a follow-up email summarizing key points and outlining next steps.
- **Outcome:** Employees feel informed and reassured, reducing the risk of low morale or productivity loss.

Communication to Suppliers

- **Action:** Host virtual meetings with key suppliers to discuss the risk and potential solutions. Establish a joint task force to explore alternative sourcing options.
- **Outcome:** Suppliers collaborate on risk mitigation measures, such as adjusting delivery schedules and identifying substitute materials, reducing the potential impact on supply continuity.

Communication to Investors

- **Action:** Include a detailed risk assessment in the quarterly investor presentation, explaining the potential impact on costs and outlining the company's mitigation strategies.
- **Outcome:** Investors are reassured by the company's proactive approach, resulting in maintained investor confidence and a stable stock price.

Calculations and Analysis

Assume effective communication and collaboration with stakeholders reduce the potential cost impact by 40%.

- **Expected Cost Impact After Mitigation**

  $$\text{Reduced Cost Impact} = 15M \times (1 - 0.4) = 15M \times 0.6 = 9M$$

- **Net Benefit of Effective Risk Communication**

  Net Benefit = Initial Expected Cost – Reduced Cost Impact = 15M – 9M = 6M

Conclusion

By effectively communicating the risks to stakeholders, the company reduces the potential cost impact by $6 million, demonstrating the value of transparent and proactive risk communication.

Reporting Standards and Practices

Adhering to reporting standards is crucial for organizations to communicate risk information consistently, transparently, and comparably. This chapter explains the importance of risk reporting standards, highlights key frameworks, and provides practical examples and exercises to demonstrate how organizations can effectively disclose risks in their annual reports. It also discusses the strategic implications of risk disclosure for maintaining stakeholder confidence, enhancing market perception, and achieving competitive advantage.

Understanding Reporting Standards

Reporting standards provide a framework for how organizations should disclose information about risks to stakeholders. Adherence to these standards ensures that risk information is presented consistently and transparently, facilitating better decision-making by stakeholders and enhancing trust in the organization.

Key Standards

- **International Financial Reporting Standards (IFRS):** IFRS requires companies to disclose risks that could have a material impact on their financial performance, including market risks (like interest rate risk and foreign exchange risk), credit risks (like default risk), and liquidity risks (such as the inability to meet short-term obligations).

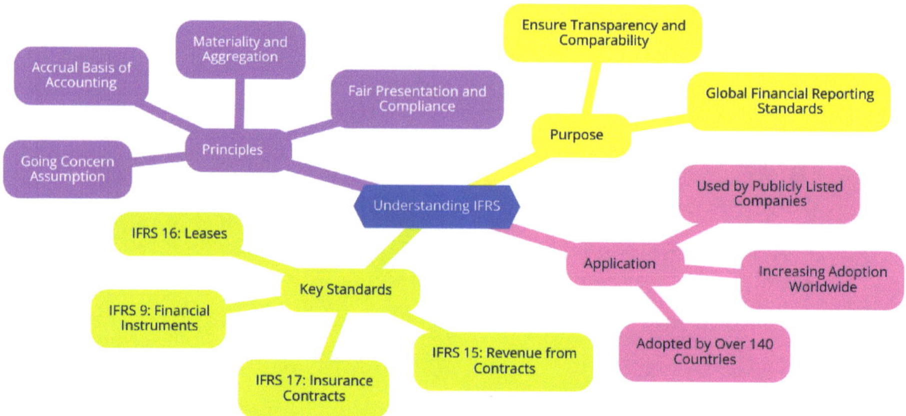

- **Committee of Sponsoring Organizations of the Treadway Commission (COSO):** The COSO Enterprise Risk Management (ERM) framework provides guidelines for risk reporting. It emphasizes integrating risk information into the overall governance, strategy, and performance of the organization, ensuring that risk management is aligned with business objectives.

- **Global Reporting Initiative (GRI):** GRI standards provide a comprehensive framework for sustainability reporting, which includes the disclosure of environmental, social, and governance

(ESG) risks. Companies using GRI standards must disclose information about their sustainability practices, potential environmental impacts, and social and governance-related risks.

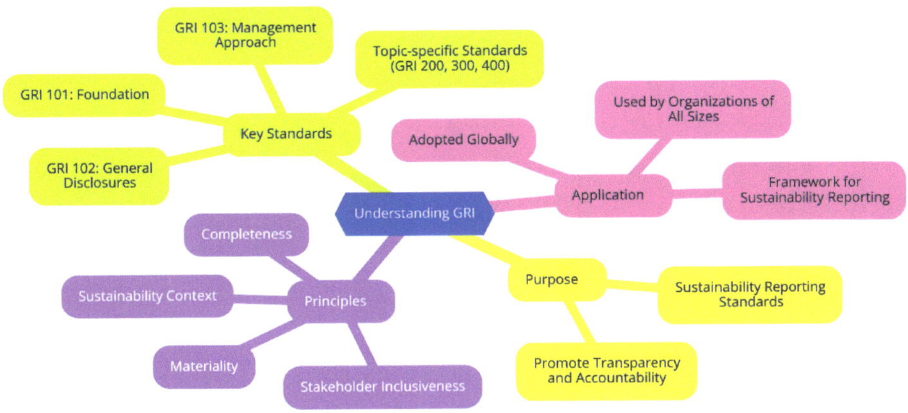

- **Example:** A large multinational corporation adheres to both IFRS and GRI standards in its annual report. It discloses detailed information about its exposure to climate change risks, including potential regulatory changes (transition risks), physical impacts (like floods and droughts), and market shifts (such as changing consumer preferences toward greener products). The report includes qualitative narratives and quantitative data, such as carbon emission metrics and cost estimates for potential regulatory compliance, giving stakeholders a comprehensive view of the company's risk profile.

Practical Example: Preparing the Risk Section of an Annual Report

Scenario

You are responsible for preparing the risk section of the annual report for a publicly traded company. To ensure compliance with relevant reporting standards and provide stakeholders with a clear understanding of the company's risk profile, you must outline the key risks, explain the rationale for their inclusion, and demonstrate how the disclosures align with IFRS, COSO ERM, and GRI standards.

Exercise 2: Creating the Risk Section of the Annual Report

Task

Outline the key risks that should be disclosed in the annual report, the rationale for their inclusion, and how you would ensure compliance with relevant reporting standards.

Answer and Explanation

Market Risk

- **Disclose Risks Related to Market Fluctuations**

  Explain risks arising from fluctuations in commodity prices, currency exchange rates, and interest rates, as these factors can significantly impact the company's financial performance.

  - **Rationale for Inclusion:** Market risks are critical for investors to understand as they affect revenue, cost structures, and overall profitability. Disclosure is required under IFRS to provide transparency about potential financial volatility.
  - **Compliance:** Include quantitative information (e.g., sensitivity analysis of currency fluctuations or interest rate changes) and qualitative descriptions of how these risks are managed (e.g., hedging strategies).

Regulatory Risk

- **Highlight Risks from Potential Changes in Regulations**

  Discuss potential changes in regulations that could affect the company's operations, such as new environmental laws, trade tariffs, or data protection rules.

  - **Rationale for Inclusion:** Regulatory risks can have substantial financial and operational impacts. Clear disclosure helps investors and regulators understand the company's preparedness for regulatory changes.

- **Compliance:** Align disclosures with COSO ERM by describing how the company integrates regulatory risk management into its overall strategy and governance framework.

Operational Risk

- **Discuss Risks Related to Operational Challenges**

  Include risks related to supply chain disruptions, cybersecurity threats, and workforce challenges.

  Rationale for Inclusion: Operational risks can disrupt the company's ability to deliver products and services, affecting financial performance and reputation. Transparency about these risks is crucial for stakeholder trust.

  Compliance: Use both IFRS and GRI guidelines by providing quantitative metrics (e.g., downtime costs or supply chain exposure) and qualitative insights into how operational risks are managed.

Environmental, Social, and Governance (ESG) Risks

- **Disclose ESG Risks and Opportunities**

  Report on environmental risks (like climate change), social risks (like labor practices), and governance risks (like board diversity and ethical practices).

  - **Rationale for Inclusion:** ESG risks are increasingly relevant to investors, regulators, and consumers. Clear disclosure enhances the company's reputation and aligns with sustainability trends.
  - **Compliance:** Follow GRI standards for sustainability reporting, providing both qualitative descriptions (e.g., policies and initiatives) and quantitative data (e.g., emissions, waste, diversity statistics).

Example: Implementation of Reporting Standards in Practice

Scenario

The company's annual report includes a comprehensive risk section that aligns with IFRS, COSO ERM, and GRI standards. The report aims to enhance transparency and build trust with stakeholders by clearly communicating the company's risk profile and management strategies.

Market Risk Disclosure

- **Action:** Include a sensitivity analysis showing how a 10% change in exchange rates would affect net profit.
- **Outcome:** Provides investors with a clear understanding of potential financial volatility, supporting informed decision-making.

Regulatory Risk Disclosure

- **Action:** Describe potential regulatory changes in key markets and the company's preparedness, such as establishing compliance teams and investing in technology.
- **Outcome:** Reassures investors and regulators that the company is proactive in managing regulatory changes, enhancing credibility and reducing compliance risks.

Operational Risk Disclosure

- **Action:** Provide quantitative data on supply chain exposure (e.g., percentage of suppliers in high-risk regions) and qualitative descriptions of mitigation strategies (e.g., diversification of suppliers, inventory management).
- **Outcome:** Demonstrates a comprehensive approach to managing operational risks, boosting stakeholder confidence.

ESG Risk Disclosure

- **Action:** Report on the company's carbon footprint, reduction targets, and progress towards achieving them. Include a discussion on social initiatives, such as diversity and inclusion programs, and governance practices like board independence.
- **Outcome:** Enhances the company's sustainability credentials, appealing to ESG-focused investors and consumers.

Calculations and Analysis

Assume the enhanced risk disclosures result in a 5% reduction in the company's cost of capital due to improved investor confidence.

- Cost of Capital Reduction Calculation:

  Initial cost of capital: 10%

- New cost of capital:

  New Cost of Capital = 10% – (10% × 0.05) = 9.5%

- Annual Savings Calculation:

  Assume the company's total capital is $1 billion.

  Annual Savings = (10% – 9.5%) × 1B = 0.5% × 1B = 5M

Conclusion

By adhering to reporting standards and enhancing transparency, the company achieves a $5 million annual saving in its cost of capital, demonstrating the financial benefits of effective risk disclosure.

Strategic Implications of Risk Disclosure

Risk disclosure is not merely a compliance exercise; it has profound strategic implications for an organization. Transparent risk disclosure can build trust, enhance the company's reputation, and support long-term strategic objectives.

Key Considerations

- **Investor Confidence:** Transparent risk disclosure demonstrates that the organization has a robust risk management framework and is proactive in managing potential threats, boosting investor confidence.
- **Market Perception:** Effective risk communication can positively influence market perception, potentially stabilizing or increasing the company's stock price and market value.
- **Competitive Advantage:** Companies that disclose risks related to innovation, sustainability, or emerging markets can position themselves as forward-thinking, proactive, and potentially gain a competitive edge.
- **Example:** A tech company discloses its strategic risks related to the rapid pace of technological change, including the potential for disruption from new entrants and evolving consumer preferences. The company outlines its investment in research and development, strategic partnerships, and talent acquisition as part of its risk mitigation strategy. This disclosure reassures investors and enhances the company's reputation as an innovator.

Exercise 3: Strategic Risk Disclosure for a Consumer Goods Company Facing Environmental Risks

Task

Assume you are the CEO of a consumer goods company facing significant environmental risks due to climate change. Develop a risk disclosure strategy that aligns with your company's sustainability initiatives and enhances your market position.

Answer and Explanation

- **Transparency**

  Clearly outline the environmental risks, including physical impacts like extreme weather events and regulatory risks related to emissions reduction.

  - **Action:** Provide quantitative data on carbon emissions, water usage, and waste, and qualitative descriptions of the potential impacts on operations and supply chains.

- **Strategic Alignment**

  Highlight the company's sustainability initiatives, such as reducing carbon emissions, investing in renewable energy, and adopting sustainable sourcing practices.

  - **Action:** Include a section in the annual report that describes the company's progress towards achieving its sustainability goals and how these initiatives mitigate identified risks.

- **Market Positioning**

  Emphasize how these initiatives not only mitigate risks but also position the company as a leader in sustainability, appealing to environmentally conscious consumers and investors.

  - **Action:** Use sustainability certifications, endorsements from environmental organizations, and partnerships with eco-friendly suppliers to strengthen the company's market positioning.

Outcome

By effectively disclosing environmental risks and aligning with sustainability strategies, the company enhances its market position, builds stakeholder trust, and attracts ESG-focused investors.

Case Studies in Risk Communication

Effective risk communication is critical for managing crises, maintaining stakeholder trust, and protecting a company's reputation. This chapter explores real-world case studies of risk communication, highlighting both successes and failures. It provides key lessons and insights into best practices for communicating risks during a crisis. The chapter also includes an exercise that encourages readers to analyze a recent corporate crisis and evaluate the effectiveness of the company's risk communication strategy.

Case Study: BP's Deepwater Horizon Oil Spill

Background: The Deepwater Horizon oil spill in 2010 was one of the largest environmental disasters in history, releasing approximately 4.9 million barrels of oil into the Gulf of Mexico. The spill resulted in severe environmental damage, loss of marine and wildlife habitats, and significant economic impact on the local fishing and tourism industries. BP, the company responsible for the spill, faced intense public scrutiny and legal penalties.

BP's Initial Communication: BP's initial communication was widely criticized for downplaying the severity of the spill and providing inaccurate information about the amount of oil leaking into the Gulf. The company's CEO, Tony Hayward, made statements that appeared dismissive of the disaster's impact, such as saying, "I want my life back," which was seen as insensitive to those affected by the crisis. Additionally, BP was slow to release accurate data on the spill's extent, causing frustration among regulators, the public, and stakeholders.

Key Lessons

- **Importance of Transparency:** Accurate and timely communication is critical during a crisis. BP's failure to provide transparent information led to a significant loss of credibility and trust.
- **Stakeholder Engagement:** Engaging with all stakeholders, including regulators, the public, and investors, is essential for

effective crisis management. BP's initial lack of engagement and communication with stakeholders exacerbated the crisis.

- **Financial and Reputational Damage:** BP faced approximately $65 billion in cleanup costs, fines, and legal settlements. The company's stock price fell by nearly 50%, and its reputation suffered long-term damage.

How BP Could Have Improved Communication

- **Early Acknowledgment and Transparency:** BP should have promptly acknowledged the severity of the spill and provided regular, accurate updates on the situation.
- **Stakeholder Collaboration:** Engaging more proactively with regulators, environmental organizations, and the public could have helped manage perceptions and reduce misinformation.
- **Clear and Empathetic Messaging:** BP's communication should have been more empathetic and focused on the impact on affected communities, demonstrating genuine concern for those impacted.

Case Study: Johnson & Johnson's Tylenol Crisis

Background: In 1982, Johnson & Johnson faced a major crisis when several people died after consuming cyanide-laced Tylenol capsules. The company immediately halted production conducted a nationwide recall of Tylenol products (costing over $100 million), and communicated openly and transparently with the public about the risks.

Johnson & Johnson's Response: Johnson & Johnson took swift action by recalling 31 million bottles of Tylenol, halting production, and cooperating fully with authorities. The company provided frequent updates to the public, media, and healthcare professionals, explaining the steps being taken to ensure safety. Johnson & Johnson also introduced tamper-evident packaging to prevent future incidents and launched a new advertising campaign to rebuild trust in the Tylenol brand.

Key Lessons

- **Proactive Communication:** Johnson & Johnson's swift and transparent communication helped mitigate the impact of the crisis and restore public trust. The company's decision to put customer safety first, even at significant financial cost, was seen as a commitment to ethical standards.
- **Long-Term Focus:** Johnson & Johnson prioritized long-term reputation over short-term financial considerations, which ultimately helped rebuild the brand's reputation and customer loyalty.
- **Innovative Solutions:** Introducing tamper-evident packaging not only addressed the immediate crisis but also set a new industry standard, positioning the company as a leader in product safety.

Outcomes

- Johnson & Johnson's stock price quickly recovered, and Tylenol regained its market share within a year.
- The company's handling of the crisis is still cited as a textbook example of effective risk communication and crisis management.

How Johnson & Johnson's Communication Was Effective

- **Transparency and Timeliness:** Johnson & Johnson provided timely updates and openly communicated the risks, actions taken, and future safety measures.
- **Engagement with Stakeholders:** The company engaged with the public, media, and regulatory authorities, demonstrating commitment to consumer safety.
- **Building Trust:** By prioritizing customer safety and implementing innovative safety measures, Johnson & Johnson rebuilt trust and loyalty.

Exercise: Analyzing a Recent Corporate Crisis

Task

Research a recent corporate crisis and analyze the effectiveness of the company's risk communication. What strategies were used, and what were the outcomes? How could the company have improved its communication?

Answer and Explanation

- **Analysis of Communication Strategy**

  Example: Consider the Boeing 737 Max crisis in 2018-2019, where two crashes resulted in 346 deaths and led to the global grounding of the aircraft. Boeing faced intense scrutiny over its handling of the crisis and its communication with stakeholders.

  - **Communication Strategy:** Boeing initially downplayed the severity of the situation, was slow to accept responsibility, and provided limited information about the software issues contributing to the crashes.
  - **Outcome:** The delayed and non-transparent communication led to a loss of trust among regulators, airlines, and the public. Boeing's reputation was severely damaged, and its stock price fell by more than 25%.

- **Outcomes**

  - **Impact on Reputation and Trust:** Boeing's reputation suffered significantly, and the company faced multiple lawsuits, regulatory penalties, and order cancellations.
  - **Financial Performance:** Boeing incurred more than $20 billion in direct costs related to the grounding, compensation to airlines, and legal settlements.

- **Recommendations for Improvement:**
    - **More Transparent Communication:** Boeing could have been more transparent and proactive in communicating the risks and accepting responsibility for the software issues.
    - **Engage Stakeholders Early:** Engaging with regulators, airlines, and passengers early in the crisis would have helped build trust and demonstrate a commitment to safety.
    - **Frequent Updates and Clear Messaging:** Providing regular updates on investigation progress, corrective actions, and safety improvements could have reassured stakeholders and mitigated damage to Boeing's reputation.

Conclusion

The analysis shows that timely, transparent, and stakeholder-focused communication is essential for managing crises effectively. Boeing's initial communication strategy could have been improved by embracing these principles, which might have reduced the negative impact on its reputation and financial performance.

Chapter 11

Behavioral Finance and Risk Perception

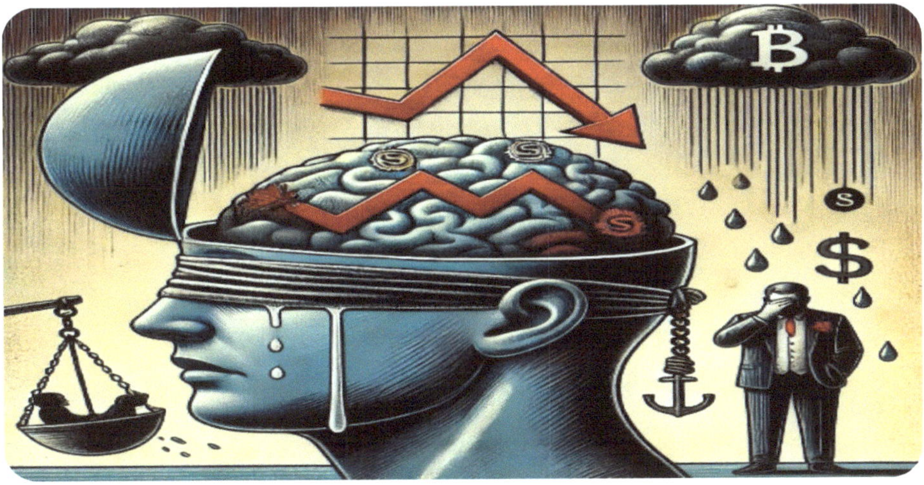

Behavioral finance explores the psychological factors that influence how individuals perceive and respond to risk. Traditional financial theories often assume that people make rational decisions based on all available information. However, behavioral finance acknowledges that cognitive biases and emotional responses can lead to irrational decision-making, particularly when it comes to assessing and managing risk. This chapter delves into the cognitive biases that affect risk perception, how these biases influence strategic decision-making, and the implications for financial risk management. Practical examples and exercises are provided to help readers recognize and manage the psychological aspects of risk in strategy.

Cognitive Biases in Risk Perception

Cognitive biases are systematic patterns of deviation from rational judgment that affect how individuals perceive and respond to risk. These biases can lead to misjudgment or irrational decisions, impacting risk management and strategic planning. This chapter explores key cognitive biases that influence risk perception, provides practical examples, and offers strategies to mitigate these biases in decision-making processes.

Understanding Cognitive Biases in Risk Perception

Cognitive biases are mental shortcuts or tendencies that can distort rational decision-making, especially in uncertain or complex situations. In the context of risk management, these biases can affect how risks are identified, assessed, and prioritized, often leading to flawed risk management strategies.

Key Biases Affecting Risk Perception

- **Overconfidence Bias**

  The tendency to overestimate one's ability to predict outcomes or control events, leading to an underestimation of risks.

  - **Impact on Risk Perception:** Overconfidence can cause decision-makers to take on excessive risks or disregard potential threats, believing that they have more control over outcomes than they actually do.
  - **Example:** An investor assumes they can consistently predict stock market movements and makes aggressive investments without adequately considering potential risks. During a market downturn, this overconfidence leads to significant losses.

- **Availability Heuristic**

  The tendency to judge the likelihood of events based on how easily examples come to mind. This often leads to overestimating the risks of more memorable or recent events.

  - **Impact on Risk Perception:** Decision-makers may give undue weight to recent events or dramatic occurrences, neglecting less salient but potentially more significant risks.
  - **Example:** After a recent financial crisis, a financial institution's board focuses heavily on preventing another similar crisis, while ignoring other emerging risks, such as cybersecurity threats.

- **Anchoring Bias**

  The tendency to rely heavily on the first piece of information encountered (the "anchor") when making decisions, even if it is irrelevant or outdated.

  - **Impact on Risk Perception:** Anchoring can cause decision-makers to underreact to new information or fail to adjust their risk assessments appropriately.
  - **Example:** A company bases its risk management strategy on outdated data about market conditions, failing to adjust its approach when new data suggests a shift in risk factors.

- **Loss Aversion**

  The tendency to prefer avoiding losses over acquiring equivalent gains, leading to risk-averse behavior even when taking calculated risks could be beneficial.

  - **Impact on Risk Perception:** Decision-makers may avoid taking necessary risks that could lead to long-term gains due to fear of potential losses.
  - **Example:** A company avoids investing in a new technology that could yield significant future benefits because of the

upfront costs and perceived risks, potentially missing out on strategic opportunities.

Practical Example: Cognitive Biases in Strategic Risk Assessment

Scenario

You are part of a strategic planning team for a financial institution that is developing a risk management strategy for the upcoming fiscal year. The team is responsible for assessing various risks, including market volatility, regulatory changes, and cybersecurity threats. However, several cognitive biases could potentially affect the team's risk assessment process.

Exercise 1: Identifying and Mitigating Cognitive Biases

Task

Identify potential cognitive biases that might affect the team's risk assessment during the planning process. Suggest strategies to mitigate the impact of these biases on decision-making.

Answer and Explanation

Potential Biases

- **Overconfidence Bias**

  Risk: Team members may believe they can accurately predict market trends or interest rate changes based on past performance, leading to underestimating potential market risks.

- **Availability Heuristic**

  Risk: The team may focus heavily on recent financial crises or dramatic market events that are more memorable, neglecting less obvious but equally important risks (e.g., geopolitical risks or operational risks).

- **Anchoring Bias**

  Risk: The team may base its assessments on initial forecasts or previous year's data, even if current market conditions have changed significantly.

- **Loss Aversion**

  Risk: The team may avoid taking strategic risks, such as entering a new market, due to fear of potential short-term losses, even if the long-term benefits outweigh the risks.

Mitigation Strategies

- **Use a Structured Decision-Making Process**

  Implement a formal risk assessment framework that requires team members to justify their assumptions, evaluate multiple scenarios, and consider a range of potential outcomes.

- **Involve Diverse Perspectives**

  Include team members from different departments and backgrounds to provide diverse viewpoints and challenge prevailing assumptions. This can help counteract individual biases, such as overconfidence or anchoring.

- **Encourage Data-Driven Analysis**

  Use quantitative data and statistical models to assess risks objectively. For example, use Monte Carlo simulations to estimate the probability of different outcomes, reducing reliance on intuition or heuristics.

- **Conduct Regular Reviews and Updates**

  Regularly update risk assessments based on the latest data and market conditions. Encourage the team to revisit initial assumptions and adjust strategies as necessary.

- **Implement "Pre-Mortem" Analysis**

  Conduct a pre-mortem analysis where team members imagine a scenario in which the risk management strategy fails and work backward to identify potential causes. This approach helps highlight overlooked risks and biases.

Example Calculation: Impact of Cognitive Biases on Decision-Making

Scenario

The strategic planning team initially estimates that the probability of a significant market downturn is 5%, based on recent market trends and historical data (anchoring bias). However, new economic indicators suggest a higher probability of 15%.

Calculating the Impact of Anchoring Bias

- **Initial Expected Loss Calculation**

  Assume the potential loss in a market downturn is estimated at $50 million.

  Expected Loss with Anchoring Bias = $0.05 \times 50M = 2.5M$

- **Revised Expected Loss with Updated Probability**

  Expected Loss without Anchoring Bias = $0.15 \times 50M = 7.5M$

- **Impact of Anchoring Bias**

  The anchoring bias led to an underestimation of expected losses by $5 million ($7.5M - $2.5M).

Mitigation Impact

- **Revised Decision Process**

  If the team used updated economic indicators and revised their assumptions, they could allocate additional resources to mitigate the increased risk of a downturn (e.g., diversifying investments or increasing liquidity reserves).

Conclusion

The cognitive bias of anchoring led the team to underestimate the risk of a market downturn, potentially resulting in inadequate preparation. By recognizing this bias and adjusting their approach, the team can better align their risk management strategy with current conditions, reducing the potential impact of a market downturn.

Behavioral Influences on Strategic Decision-Making

Behavioral influences can significantly impact strategic decision-making, particularly in how risks are assessed and managed. Understanding these behavioral factors can help organizations make more informed, balanced decisions and avoid common pitfalls. This chapter explores key behavioral factors, provides practical examples, and offers strategies to mitigate their effects on strategic decision-making processes.

Behavioral Factors in Decision-Making

Behavioral influences are psychological factors that affect how individuals make decisions, especially under uncertainty or in high-stakes situations. These influences can cause decision-makers to deviate from rational analysis, leading to suboptimal or irrational choices.

Key Concepts

- **Herd Behavior**

  The tendency of individuals to mimic the actions of a larger group, often leading to irrational decisions driven by social influence rather than objective analysis.

  - **Impact on Decision-Making:** Herd behavior can lead companies to make strategic decisions based on what competitors or market peers are doing, rather than on their own thorough analysis.

- **Example:** A company decides to enter a new market simply because its competitors are doing so, without fully evaluating the market's potential or aligning the decision with its own strategic objectives. This herd behavior leads to financial losses when the market turns out to be less profitable than anticipated.

- **Framing Effect**

  The way information is presented (framed) can influence decision-making. People tend to react differently depending on whether potential outcomes are presented as gains or losses.

  - **Impact on Decision-Making:** Decision-makers may take on more risk when outcomes are framed as avoiding losses and become more risk-averse when outcomes are framed as gains.
  - **Example:** A healthcare company is presented with two options for a new treatment. When framed as "a 90% survival rate," executives are more likely to approve it than when framed as "a 10% mortality rate," even though the statistics are identical.

- **Status Quo Bias**

  The preference for maintaining the current situation or state of affairs, leading to resistance to change and underestimation of risks associated with inaction.

  - **Impact on Decision-Making:** Status quo bias can prevent organizations from pursuing potentially beneficial changes or innovations, leading to missed opportunities.
  - **Example:** A technology company remains focused on its existing product lines due to the status quo bias, failing to invest in emerging technologies that could provide new revenue streams. Over time, the company loses market share to more innovative competitors.

Practical Example: Behavioral Influences in Strategic Decision-Making

Scenario

You are advising the executive team of a healthcare company on a major strategic decision, such as entering a new market with a novel medical device. The decision involves substantial investment and carries significant risks and rewards. However, several behavioral influences could potentially affect the team's decision-making process.

Exercise 2: Identifying and Addressing Behavioral Influences

Task

Identify potential behavioral influences that could affect the executive team's decision-making process and propose methods to address these influences.

Answer and Explanation

- **Potential Behavioral Influences**
    - **Herd Behavior**
        - Risk: The executive team may feel compelled to enter the new market because competitors are doing so, without conducting a comprehensive analysis of the market's specific conditions and alignment with the company's strategic goals.
    - **Framing Effect**
        - Risk: The decision to enter the new market might be influenced by how the opportunity is presented (e.g., emphasizing potential profits rather than potential risks). This framing could lead to a skewed perception of the risks and benefits.

- **Status Quo Bias**
  - Risk: The team may prefer to continue focusing on their existing markets and products, underestimating the risks of not innovating or expanding into new areas.

- **Proposed Methods to Address Behavioral Influences**
  - **Comprehensive Risk Analysis**
    - Method: Conduct a detailed risk assessment of entering the new market, considering various scenarios, potential barriers to entry, regulatory challenges, competitive dynamics, and market demand.
    - Outcome: Provides an objective basis for decision-making, reducing the impact of herd behavior by focusing on the company's specific context and strategic objectives.
  - **Balanced Presentation of Information**
    - Method: Present information in a balanced way, highlighting both potential gains and risks. Use neutral language to avoid framing bias, and include quantitative data (e.g., potential market size, estimated return on investment, and risk-adjusted net present value).
    - Outcome: Helps the team evaluate the decision from multiple perspectives, reducing the framing effect and promoting a more balanced assessment of risks and rewards.
  - **Encourage Independent Thinking**
    - Method: Involve external experts or consultants to provide independent insights and challenge internal assumptions. Encourage team members to voice differing opinions and explore alternative strategies.
    - Outcome: Counteracts herd behavior by fostering a culture of independent thought and critical analysis, ensuring that

decisions are based on objective analysis rather than social influence.

- **Decision-Making Framework**
  - Method: Use a structured decision-making framework that incorporates both qualitative and quantitative factors, such as a SWOT analysis (Strengths, Weaknesses, Opportunities, Threats) and decision trees.
  - Outcome: Helps identify the key drivers of success or failure for the market entry and reduces status quo bias by systematically evaluating the pros and cons of various options.

Example Calculation: Impact of Behavioral Bias on Strategic Decision-Making

Scenario

The executive team of the healthcare company initially estimates that the probability of success in the new market is 70%, influenced by the fact that several competitors have recently entered the market (herd behavior). However, a more comprehensive risk assessment suggests the probability of success is closer to 50%.

Calculating the Impact of Herd Behavior

- **Initial Expected Value Calculation**

  Assume the potential profit from entering the market is estimated at $10 million.

  Expected Value with Herd Behavior = 0.7 × 10M = 7M

- **Revised Expected Value with Comprehensive Risk Assessment**

  Expected Value without Herd Behavior = 0.5 × 10M = 5M

- **Impact of Herd Behavior**

  Herd behavior led to an overestimation of the expected value by $2 million ($7M - $5M).

Mitigation Impact

- **Revised Decision Process**

  After conducting a comprehensive risk assessment, the team revises its strategy to allocate additional resources for market research and risk mitigation, such as regulatory compliance and local partnerships.

Conclusion

The herd behavior bias caused the team to overestimate the potential benefits of entering the new market, which could have led to a suboptimal decision. By recognizing this bias and adjusting their approach, the team makes a more balanced decision that better aligns with the company's strategic goals.

Managing Psychological Aspects of Risk in Strategy

Understanding and managing the psychological aspects of risk is essential for developing effective strategies. Emotions and cognitive biases can significantly influence risk perception and decision-making, leading to suboptimal strategic outcomes.

The Role of Psychology in Risk Management

Psychological factors, such as emotions and cognitive biases, can distort how risks are perceived and assessed. These factors can lead to irrational decision-making, where decisions are based more on intuition or emotional responses rather than objective analysis. Recognizing and managing these psychological aspects is crucial for making balanced and informed strategic decisions.

Key Approaches

- **Risk Awareness Training**

  Educating employees and decision-makers about common cognitive biases and how they can affect risk perception. Raising awareness of these biases can help individuals recognize when their judgment is being influenced by non-rational factors.

  - **Example:** Training sessions for a manufacturing company's leadership team focus on common biases such as overconfidence (the belief that one's judgment is more accurate than it is) and loss aversion (the tendency to prioritize avoiding losses over acquiring equivalent gains). This training helps leaders recognize these biases and adopt a more balanced approach to risk management, such as incorporating diversification strategies to reduce exposure to any single market or supplier.

- **Scenario Analysis and Stress Testing**

  Techniques that involve exploring different scenarios and stress-testing the organization's strategic plans under varying conditions. These methods help decision-makers visualize potential outcomes, reducing reliance on intuition and providing an objective basis for decision-making.

  - **Example:** A bank conducts stress testing to evaluate its capital adequacy under different economic conditions, such as a severe recession or a market crash. The results provide insights into the bank's resilience and highlight areas where risk exposure needs to be reduced, encouraging data-driven decision-making rather than emotional reactions to market events.

- **Diversification and Hedging**

  Strategies that involve spreading risk across different assets, markets, or operations to minimize the impact of any single adverse event.

Diversification and hedging can counteract psychological biases by providing a more balanced risk exposure.

- **Example:** An investment firm adopts a diversified portfolio strategy to manage market volatility. By spreading investments across various asset classes (stocks, bonds, commodities), the firm reduces the impact of market swings on the overall portfolio, counteracting biases like overconfidence and ensuring a more stable performance over time.

Practical Example: Psychological Aspects of Risk in Strategic Decision-Making

Scenario

A manufacturing company recognizes that its leadership team often makes strategic decisions based on intuition and emotion rather than data-driven analysis. The company decides to implement risk awareness training to address common cognitive biases, such as overconfidence and loss aversion, which have led to overly aggressive expansion strategies in the past.

Exercise 3: Developing a Risk Management Training Program

Task

Imagine you are responsible for developing a risk management training program for the senior leadership of an insurance company. Outline the key components of the program, focusing on how it will address the psychological aspects of risk perception.

Answer and Explanation

Key Components of the Training Program

- **Education on Cognitive Biases**
  - **Content:** Develop modules on common cognitive biases, such as overconfidence, loss aversion, anchoring, and status

quo bias. Use examples specific to the insurance industry to illustrate how these biases can affect decision-making.

  - **Objective:** Help leaders recognize when their judgment is being influenced by biases and provide strategies to counteract these effects.
  - **Example Activity:** Present a case study where overconfidence led to underestimating risks in underwriting, resulting in substantial financial losses. Discuss how recognizing this bias could have led to a more conservative and balanced approach.

- **Scenario Analysis Workshops**
  - **Content:** Conduct interactive workshops where leaders practice scenario analysis to explore potential risks and outcomes in different market conditions, such as economic downturns, regulatory changes, or catastrophic events.
  - **Objective:** Encourage leaders to think critically about potential risks and use data to assess their impact rather than relying on intuition or recent experiences.
  - **Example Activity:** Use a hypothetical scenario where a sudden increase in claims occurs due to a natural disaster. Have leaders work in groups to identify potential impacts, develop response strategies, and present their findings.

- **Decision-Making Frameworks**
  - **Content:** Introduce structured decision-making frameworks, such as decision trees, SWOT analysis (Strengths, Weaknesses, Opportunities, Threats), and Monte Carlo simulations, which help reduce the influence of biases and encourage data-driven analysis.
  - **Objective:** Provide leaders with tools to make more objective and balanced decisions, considering all potential outcomes and uncertainties.
  - **Example Activity:** Apply a decision tree framework to evaluate whether to enter a new insurance market, considering

factors like regulatory risk, market competition, and potential profitability.

- **Behavioral Coaching and Feedback**
    - **Content:** Incorporate one-on-one coaching sessions and feedback loops where leaders can reflect on past decisions, understand how biases influenced their thinking, and develop strategies for future decisions.
    - **Objective:** Reinforce learning and encourage continuous improvement in risk management practices.
    - **Example Activity**: Analyze a previous strategic decision where biases may have played a role, such as underestimating a new market's risks. Discuss alternative approaches and the importance of challenging assumptions.

Example Calculation: Quantifying the Impact of Psychological Biases on Decision-Making

Scenario

An insurance company plans to launch a new product line, estimating an initial investment of $5 million. Due to overconfidence bias, the leadership team assumes a high probability of success (80%) without considering potential market risks and regulatory challenges. A more realistic probability assessment, incorporating market data and risk factors, suggests a success rate of 50%.

Calculating the Impact of Overconfidence Bias

- **Initial Expected Return Calculation (Overconfidence Bias)**

  Assuming potential profits from the new product line are estimated at $15 million.

  Expected Return with Overconfidence Bias = 0.8 × 15M − 5M = 7M

- **Revised Expected Return with Realistic Probability**

  Expected Return without Overconfidence Bias = 0.5 × 15M – 5M = 2.5M

- **Impact of Overconfidence Bias**

  The overconfidence bias led to an overestimation of the expected return by $4.5 million ($7M - $2.5M).

Mitigation Impact

- **Revised Decision Process**

  After recognizing the overconfidence bias, the leadership team revises its approach, incorporating additional market research, regulatory analysis, and competitive benchmarking to refine its probability estimates. This more balanced assessment leads to a decision to either adjust the investment amount or modify the product launch strategy.

Conclusion

Overconfidence bias led the insurance company to overestimate the potential return on investment, which could have resulted in a poor strategic decision. By recognizing this bias and adopting a more data-driven approach, the company can make more balanced decisions that align with its strategic objectives.

Implications for Financial Risk Management

Behavioral finance plays a crucial role in financial risk management by highlighting how psychological factors influence risk perception, communication, and decision-making. Understanding these influences can lead to more effective strategies for managing risk, enhancing the stability and resilience of financial institutions. This chapter explores the key implications of behavioral finance for risk management, provides practical examples, and outlines a plan for addressing behavioral biases in investment decisions.

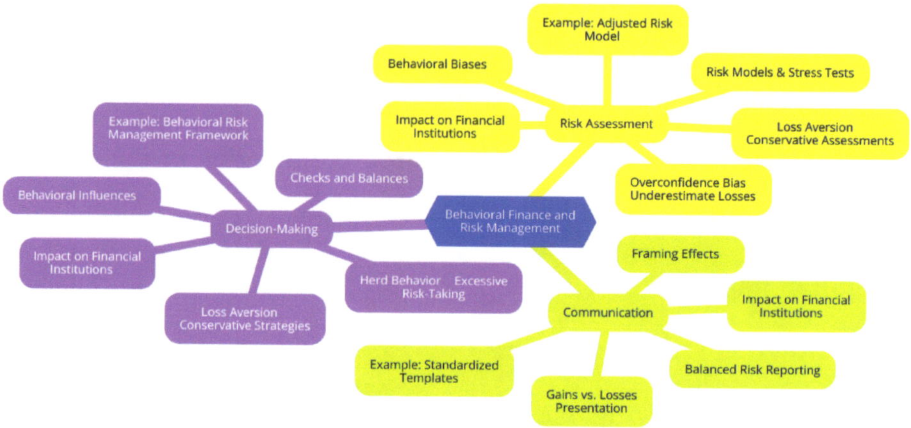

Behavioral Finance and Risk Management

Behavioral finance examines how cognitive biases and emotions affect financial decision-making. These biases can lead to suboptimal choices, such as underestimating or overestimating risks, miscommunicating risks, and making decisions based on herd behavior or overconfidence.

Key Implications

- **Risk Assessment**

  Behavioral biases can affect how risks are assessed, leading to inaccurate risk evaluations. For instance, overconfidence bias might cause decision-makers to underestimate potential losses, while loss aversion might result in overly conservative risk assessments.

  - **Impact on Financial Institutions:** Financial institutions must account for these biases when developing risk models, conducting stress tests, and assessing capital adequacy. Failure to do so can lead to inadequate risk management strategies, potentially jeopardizing financial stability.
  - **Example:** A bank adjusts its risk assessment model to account for cognitive biases by incorporating a wider range of stress

scenarios, including unlikely but severe events, to ensure a more comprehensive evaluation of its risk exposure.

- **Communication**

  The way risks are communicated within an organization can be influenced by framing effects and other biases. For example, presenting risk information in a way that emphasizes gains (e.g., "95% success rate") rather than losses (e.g., "5% failure rate") can alter how risks are perceived and acted upon.

  - **Impact on Financial Institutions:** Clear, balanced, and unbiased communication of risks is essential to ensure that all stakeholders have a correct understanding of the organization's risk profile. Misleading framing can lead to misinformed decision-making.
  - **Example:** A financial institution creates standardized templates for risk reporting that emphasize both potential gains and losses, ensuring a balanced presentation of information that minimizes framing bias.

- **Decision-Making**

  Behavioral influences, such as herd behavior, overconfidence, and loss aversion, can lead to suboptimal decisions. For example, herd behavior may drive excessive risk-taking during bull markets, while loss aversion may result in overly conservative strategies during downturns.

  - **Impact on Financial Institutions:** Implementing checks and balances, such as independent reviews and structured decision-making frameworks, can help mitigate these biases and ensure that decisions are based on objective analysis.
  - **Example:** A bank adopts a behavioral risk management framework that includes regular reviews of decision-making processes, helping avoid excessive risk-taking during periods of

market exuberance and contributing to more stable financial performance.

Practical Example: Addressing Behavioral Biases in Financial Risk Management

Scenario

An investment firm notices a trend of herd behavior among its portfolio managers, leading to an overconcentration in technology stocks. This overconcentration increases the firm's exposure to sector-specific risks, such as market downturns or regulatory changes, which could significantly impact its overall performance.

Exercise 4: Developing a Plan to Address Behavioral Biases

Task

Develop a plan to address herd behavior and diversify the firm's investments to reduce risk.

Answer and Explanation
Plan to Address Behavioral Biases

- **Risk Awareness Training**
  - **Action:** Conduct regular training sessions for portfolio managers to educate them about the dangers of herd behavior and the importance of diversification in risk management.
  - **Objective:** Increase awareness of cognitive biases and encourage more independent decision-making based on thorough market analysis rather than following the crowd.
  - **Example Activity:** Use historical case studies, such as the Dot-com bubble or the 2008 financial crisis, to illustrate the consequences of herd behavior and the benefits of diversification.

- **Investment Guidelines**
    - **Action:** Establish formal investment guidelines that limit exposure to any single sector, asset class, or geographic market. For example, the guidelines might specify that no more than 20% of the portfolio can be allocated to technology stocks.
    - **Objective:** Ensure a more balanced portfolio by reducing concentration risk and encouraging a broader asset allocation strategy.

Example Calculation

- Assume the firm's total investment portfolio is $500 million, with 40% currently allocated to technology stocks ($200 million).
- Under the new guidelines, the maximum allocation to technology stocks would be 20%, or $100 million.

Reallocation Calculation

- Excess Investment in Technology Stocks = 200M – 100M = 100M
- The firm needs to reduce its exposure by $100 million, reallocating these funds to other sectors or asset classes to achieve a diversified portfolio.

Independent Review

- **Action:** Implement an independent review process for major investment decisions. A committee or external advisors can provide an objective assessment of potential risks and diversification opportunities.
- **Objective:** Provide checks and balances to ensure that investment decisions are not solely based on internal consensus or biases.
- **Example Activity:** Require all major investment decisions, especially those involving significant sector allocations, to be reviewed by an independent risk management team that evaluates potential biases and suggests alternative strategies if necessary.

Example Calculation: Impact of Behavioral Bias on Portfolio Risk

Scenario

Before implementing the diversification plan, the firm's portfolio is heavily concentrated in technology stocks, which increases its risk exposure. To understand the potential impact of diversification, the firm decides to calculate the portfolio's risk (standard deviation) before and after reallocation.

Calculating Portfolio Risk Before Diversification

- **Initial Portfolio Allocation**

  Technology Stocks: 40% ($200 million)

  Other Sectors: 60% ($300 million)

- **Assume**

  Standard deviation of technology stocks = 15%

  Standard deviation of other sectors = 8%

  Correlation between technology stocks and other sectors = 0.6

- **Portfolio Variance Calculation**

  Portfolio Variance = $(0.4^2 \times 0.15^2) + (0.6^2 \times 0.08^2) + 2 \times 0.4 \times 0.6 \times 0.15 \times 0.08 \times 0.6 = (0.16 \times 0.0225) + (0.36 \times 0.0064) + 2 \times 0.4 \times 0.6 \times 0.15 \times 0.08 \times 0.6$

  $= 0.0036 + 0.0023 + 0.00432 = 0.01022$

- **Portfolio Standard Deviation (Risk)**

  Portfolio Standard Deviation = $\sqrt{0.01022} \approx 10.1\%$

Calculating Portfolio Risk After Diversification

- **Revised Portfolio Allocation**

  Technology Stocks: 20% ($100 million)

  Other Sectors: 80% ($400 million)

- **Revised Portfolio Variance Calculation**

  Portfolio Variance = $(0.2^2 \times 0.15^2) + (0.8^2 \times 0.08^2) + 2 \times 0.2 \times 0.8 \times 0.15 \times 0.08 \times 0.6 = (0.04 \times 0.0225) + (0.64 \times 0.0064) + 2 \times 0.2 \times 0.8 \times 0.15 \times 0.08 \times 0.6 = 0.0009 + 0.0041 + 0.00288 = 0.00788$

- **Revised Portfolio Standard Deviation (Risk)**

  Portfolio Standard Deviation = $\sqrt{0.00788} \approx 8.87\%$

- **Impact of Diversification**

  The diversification strategy reduces the portfolio's risk from 10.1% to 8.87%, reflecting a decrease in overall risk exposure due to reduced concentration in technology stocks.

Chapter

12

The Future of Financial Risk Management

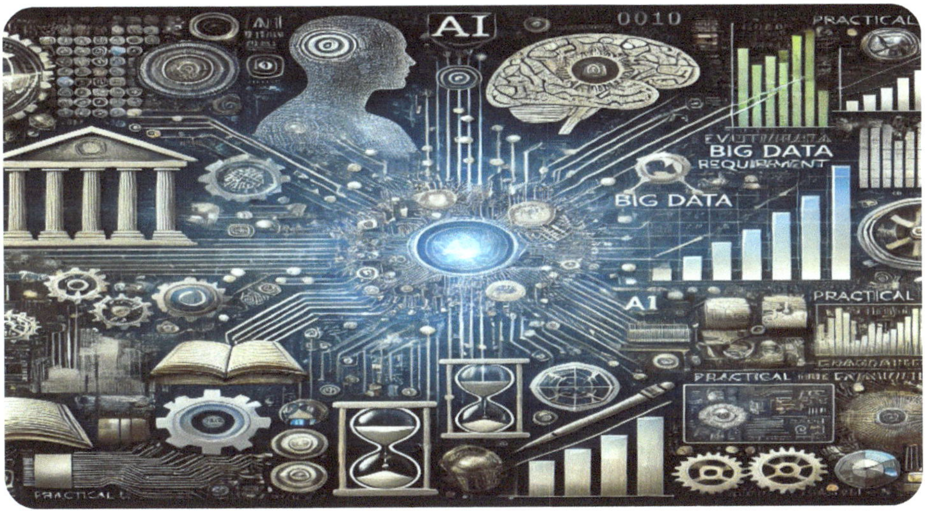

The financial risk management landscape is undergoing rapid transformation driven by technological innovations, the growing role of artificial intelligence (AI) and big data and evolving regulatory requirements. As these changes reshape the industry, organizations must strategically adapt to future risks and adjust their risk management frameworks to remain resilient and competitive. This chapter explores the future of financial risk management, focusing on the impact of technological advancements, AI, big data, and regulatory changes. Through practical examples and exercises, readers will gain insights into how they can prepare for and navigate the challenges and opportunities that lie ahead.

Technological Innovations and Risk Management

Technological advancements are reshaping financial risk management by providing innovative tools and techniques for identifying, assessing, and mitigating risks. Technologies such as blockchain, cloud computing, and real-time analytics are enabling more accurate and efficient risk management processes, enhancing the ability of organizations to respond to emerging threats proactively. This chapter explores key technological innovations in risk management, provides practical examples, and outlines a plan for integrating these technologies into a financial services firm's risk management framework.

The Impact of Technological Innovations on Risk Management

Technological innovations have significantly transformed how organizations manage risks. They offer new capabilities for data collection, analysis, and storage, allowing for more comprehensive and real-time risk management approaches. Leveraging these technologies can enhance an organization's ability to detect, assess, and respond to risks efficiently.

Key Innovations

Blockchain Technology

Blockchain is a decentralized and immutable ledger that records transactions securely across a network of computers. It provides a transparent and tamper-proof system that reduces the risk of fraud and enhances the traceability of assets.

- **Impact on Risk Management**
  - **Transparency:** Blockchain's transparency allows all participants in a transaction to view the same data, reducing discrepancies and the potential for fraudulent activities.
  - **Security:** The decentralized nature of blockchain makes it difficult for hackers to alter data, thereby enhancing security in financial transactions.
  - **Smart Contracts:** Blockchain enables the use of smart contracts, which automatically execute and enforce agreements when predefined conditions are met, reducing counterparty risk.
  - **Example:** A global bank adopts blockchain technology to enhance the security and transparency of its cross-border payment systems. By using blockchain, the bank reduces the risk of fraud, lowers transaction costs, and ensures that all transactions are securely recorded and easily traceable.

Cloud Computing

Cloud computing provides scalable and cost-effective platforms for storing and processing large volumes of data. It enables organizations to access computing resources on-demand, facilitating real-time risk analysis and improving responsiveness to emerging risks.

- **Impact on Risk Management**
  - **Scalability:** Cloud-based solutions can easily scale up or down based on demand, supporting dynamic risk management needs.
  - **Cost Efficiency:** Cloud services reduce the need for costly on-premises infrastructure, lowering overall IT expenses

and freeing up resources for other risk management initiatives.

- **Collaboration:** Cloud platforms enable better collaboration among risk management teams, regardless of location, by providing secure and centralized access to data and tools.
- **Example:** An insurance company leverages cloud computing to manage large datasets for its actuarial models. This allows the company to perform complex risk assessments more quickly and efficiently, improving its ability to price policies accurately and respond to market changes.

Real-Time Analytics

Real-time analytics involves using advanced tools and algorithms to analyze data as it is created or received. This enables organizations to monitor key risk indicators and detect emerging threats as they occur.

- **Impact on Risk Management**
  - **Proactive Monitoring:** Real-time analytics allows for continuous monitoring of risk indicators, enabling quicker responses to potential threats.
  - **Enhanced Decision-Making:** By providing up-to-date insights, real-time analytics supports more informed decision-making and reduces the likelihood of adverse outcomes.
  - **Customization:** Real-time analytics tools can be customized to focus on specific risk factors relevant to the organization, such as credit risk or market volatility.
  - **Example:** A hedge fund uses real-time analytics to monitor market movements and portfolio risk exposure continuously. This allows the fund to adjust its positions rapidly in response to market changes, reducing the potential for significant losses.

Practical Example: Integrating Technological Innovations in Risk Management

Scenario

As the Chief Technology Officer (CTO) of a financial services firm, you are tasked with integrating blockchain and real-time analytics into the firm's risk management framework. The goal is to enhance the firm's ability to monitor, assess, and mitigate risks while maintaining compliance with regulatory requirements.

Exercise 1: Developing a Plan to Integrate Blockchain and Real-Time Analytics

Task

Develop a plan to integrate blockchain and real-time analytics into your firm's risk management framework. Consider the potential benefits and challenges of implementing these technologies.

Answer and Explanation
Plan for Blockchain Integration

Objective: Leverage blockchain technology to enhance transaction security, transparency, and efficiency, particularly in high-risk areas such as cross-border payments, trade finance, and asset management.

Steps

- **Identify High-Risk Areas:** Start with areas where blockchain can provide the most value, such as cross-border payments that require secure and transparent processing.
- **Develop a Pilot Program:** Launch a pilot program to test blockchain applications in these areas. Evaluate the effectiveness in terms of reducing fraud, improving transaction speed, and enhancing data integrity.

- **Address Regulatory Compliance:** Work with legal and compliance teams to ensure that blockchain applications meet all relevant regulations, such as data privacy laws and anti-money laundering (AML) requirements.
- **Ensure Interoperability:** Focus on integrating blockchain with existing systems and processes. Address challenges related to interoperability, such as standardizing data formats and establishing protocols for data exchange.

Challenges

- **Regulatory Compliance:** Navigating different regulatory environments and ensuring compliance with local and international standards.
- **Interoperability:** Integrating blockchain with legacy systems and ensuring compatibility with existing technologies.
- **Adoption Resistance:** Overcoming resistance from stakeholders who may be unfamiliar with or skeptical of new technologies.

Plan for Real-Time Analytics Integration

Objective: Utilize real-time analytics tools to monitor key risk indicators across the firm's portfolio, enabling faster identification and mitigation of emerging risks.

Steps

- **Select Appropriate Tools:** Choose advanced analytics tools that align with the firm's risk management objectives, such as platforms that offer real-time data visualization, anomaly detection, and predictive modeling.
- **Data Integration:** Ensure seamless integration of real-time analytics tools with existing data sources, such as transaction records, market data feeds, and customer information databases.

- **Develop Risk Dashboards:** Create risk dashboards that display key risk indicators (e.g., credit exposure, liquidity metrics, market volatility) in real-time, enabling managers to make informed decisions quickly.
- **Establish Governance Protocols:** Define governance protocols to ensure data quality, security, and privacy. Regularly review and update these protocols to keep pace with evolving risks and regulatory requirements.

Challenges

- **Data Quality:** Ensuring that the data used in real-time analytics is accurate, complete, and up to date.
- **Cybersecurity:** Protecting data and analytics tools from cyber threats, such as hacking and data breaches.
- **Scalability:** Scaling the analytics infrastructure to handle large volumes of data and support real-time processing.

Example Calculation: Evaluating the Impact of Technological Integration on Risk Management

Scenario

A financial services firm plans to integrate blockchain technology for secure cross-border payments and real-time analytics to monitor market risks. The firm estimates that these technologies will reduce its annual fraud losses and enhance its risk management capabilities.

Calculating the Impact of Blockchain Integration on Fraud Losses

- Current Annual Fraud Losses: $10 million
- Estimated Reduction in Fraud Losses Due to Blockchain: 30%

Reduced Fraud Losses = Current Losses × Reduction Percentage = 10M × 0.3 = 3M

New Annual Fraud Losses

- New Fraud Losses = 10M – 3M = 7M
- Impact: By integrating blockchain technology, the firm reduces its annual fraud losses by $3 million, improving its financial stability and risk management efficiency.

Evaluating the Impact of Real-Time Analytics on Market Risk Management

- Current Loss from Market Volatility: $5 million
- Estimated Reduction in Losses Due to Real-Time Analytics: 20%
  Reduced Market Losses = Current Losses × Reduction Percentage
  = 5M × 0.2 = 1M
- New Annual Market Losses
  New Market Losses = 5M – 1M =4M

Impact

By using real-time analytics to monitor market risks more effectively, the firm reduces its losses from market volatility by $1 million annually.

The Role of Artificial Intelligence and Big Data

AI and Big Data technologies provide significant advantages in risk management by offering advanced analytical capabilities that traditional methods cannot match. They allow organizations to process vast amounts of structured and unstructured data, identify trends, and predict potential risks with greater accuracy.

Key Concepts

- **Predictive Analytics**

  AI-powered predictive models analyze historical and real-time data to forecast potential risks, such as credit defaults, market fluctuations, or cyber threats. These models help organizations anticipate adverse events and take preventive actions.

Impact on Risk Management

- **Early Warning Systems:** Predictive analytics provide early warning signs of emerging risks, enabling organizations to respond proactively.
- **Optimized Decision-Making:** By forecasting future risks, organizations can make better-informed decisions regarding risk mitigation strategies.
- **Example:** A hedge fund uses AI and Big Data to develop a predictive model that forecasts market volatility based on diverse data sources, including economic indicators, social media sentiment, and geopolitical events. The model helps the fund adjust its investment strategy to minimize losses during periods of high volatility.

- **Machine Learning**

  Machine learning algorithms continuously learn from new data, improving their accuracy over time. These algorithms can be used to detect anomalies, assess credit risk, and optimize investment strategies.

Impact on Risk Management

- **Anomaly Detection:** Machine learning models identify unusual patterns that may indicate fraudulent activity, operational risks, or compliance breaches.
- **Credit Risk Assessment:** Algorithms analyze vast datasets to determine the likelihood of credit defaults, improving the accuracy of credit scoring models.
- **Example:** A bank implements machine learning algorithms to monitor transactions for signs of fraud. The algorithms detect suspicious patterns and flag potentially fraudulent activities for further investigation, reducing financial losses.

- **Natural Language Processing (NLP)**

  NLP enables AI systems to analyze unstructured data, such as news articles or social media posts, to assess sentiment and detect emerging risks.

  Impact on Risk Management

  - **Sentiment Analysis:** NLP tools analyze public sentiment to gauge market reactions to news, political events, or corporate announcements.
  - **Risk Identification:** By analyzing large volumes of text data, NLP helps identify emerging risks that may not be immediately apparent through traditional data sources.
  - **Example:** A financial institution uses NLP to analyze social media posts and news articles about its brand. The AI system detects negative sentiment trends, prompting the institution to investigate potential reputational risks and take corrective actions.

Practical Example: AI-Driven Predictive Analytics in Underwriting

Scenario

As a risk analyst at an insurance company, you are tasked with exploring the use of AI to improve the underwriting process. The goal is to enhance the accuracy of risk assessments, reduce underwriting time, and minimize losses.

Exercise 2: Implementing AI-Driven Predictive Analytics in Underwriting

Task

Outline the steps you would take to implement AI-driven predictive analytics in underwriting, including the data sources you would use and the potential risks associated with AI implementation.

Answer and Explanation
Steps for Implementing AI-Driven Predictive Analytics

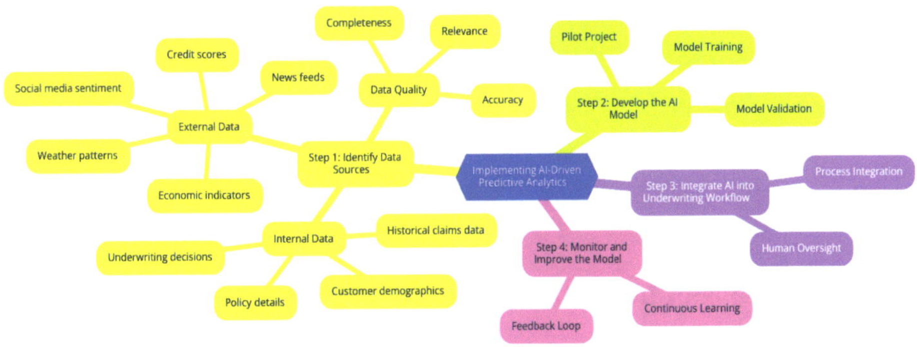

- **Step 1: Identify Data Sources**
  - **Internal Data:** Use historical claims data, customer demographics, policy details, and underwriting decisions.
  - **External Data:** Incorporate external data sources such as economic indicators, weather patterns (for property insurance), credit scores, social media sentiment, and news feeds.
  - **Data Quality:** Ensure that all data sources are accurate, complete, and relevant to the underwriting process to enhance the model's effectiveness.

- **Step 2: Develop the AI Model**
  - **Pilot Project:** Begin with a pilot project focusing on a specific insurance product line (e.g., auto insurance).
  - **Model Training:** Use historical data to train the AI model, enabling it to recognize patterns and predict risk factors associated with underwriting decisions.
  - **Model Validation:** Test the model against a validation dataset to ensure its accuracy and reliability. Adjust the model parameters based on the validation results.

- **Step 3: Integrate AI into Underwriting Workflow**
    - **Process Integration:** Integrate the AI model into the existing underwriting system, allowing it to provide real-time risk assessments and recommendations to underwriters.
    - **Human Oversight:** Establish protocols for human oversight to review AI-generated outputs and ensure that underwriting decisions align with regulatory requirements and ethical standards.
- **Step 4: Monitor and Improve the Model**
    - **Continuous Learning:** Implement machine learning algorithms that continuously learn from new data and improve their accuracy over time.
    - **Feedback Loop:** Create a feedback loop where underwriters provide input on AI-generated decisions, helping refine the model.

Potential Benefits

- **Improved Accuracy:** AI-driven predictive analytics can improve the accuracy of risk assessments by analyzing vast amounts of data quickly and efficiently.

- **Reduced Underwriting Time:** Automating parts of the underwriting process reduces the time required to assess risks and make decisions.
- **Cost Efficiency:** Enhanced accuracy and reduced underwriting time translate to lower operational costs and minimized losses.

Potential Risks

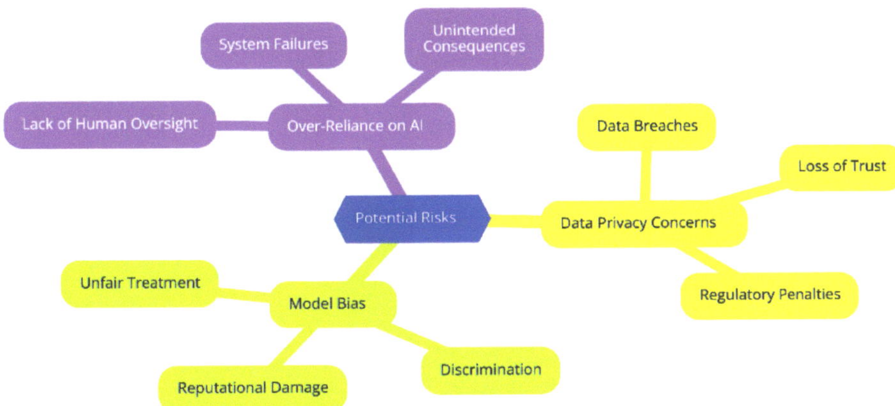

- **Data Privacy Concerns:** The use of personal data for AI-driven underwriting must comply with data protection regulations, such as GDPR or CCPA.
- **Model Bias:** AI models can inadvertently introduce bias if the training data is not representative or contains inherent biases. This can result in unfair underwriting decisions.
- **Over-Reliance on AI:** Over-reliance on AI-driven decisions can lead to errors if the model fails to account for unique or unforeseen factors.

Example Calculation: AI-Driven Predictive Analytics in Underwriting

Scenario

An insurance company implements an AI-driven predictive model to assess the risk of auto insurance policies. The model uses historical claims data, customer demographics, and external data sources to predict the probability of claims for each policyholder.

Calculating Risk Score Using AI

- **Data Inputs**
  - Historical claims frequency and severity
  - Customer demographics (age, location, driving history)
  - External factors (traffic data, weather conditions)
- **Model Output**
  - The AI model assigns a risk score to each policyholder based on the likelihood of a claim. A higher score indicates a higher risk.

Example Calculation

- **Assumptions**
  - The AI model assigns a risk score between 0 and 100.
  - A risk score of 60 or above indicates a high-risk policyholder.
- **Policyholder Data**
  - Age: 45, Location: High traffic area, Driving history: 2 minor accidents in the past 5 years, Weather data: Frequent adverse conditions
- **Model Prediction**
  - Historical data indicates that policyholders with similar profiles have a 30% higher likelihood of filing a claim.

Risk Score Calculation

Risk Score = Base Score + Increment for High Traffic Area + Increment for Adverse Weather + Increment for Driving History = 50 + 5 + 3 + 7 = 65

Outcome

The policyholder is classified as high-risk, prompting the underwriter to consider a higher premium or additional terms for the policy.

Strategic Adaptation to Future Risks

As the risk landscape evolves, organizations must adapt their strategies to address new and emerging risks proactively. This requires a forward-looking approach to risk management, incorporating techniques such as scenario planning, stress testing, and continuous monitoring of the external environment. By preparing for future risks, organizations can build resilience, maintain stability, and achieve long-term success.

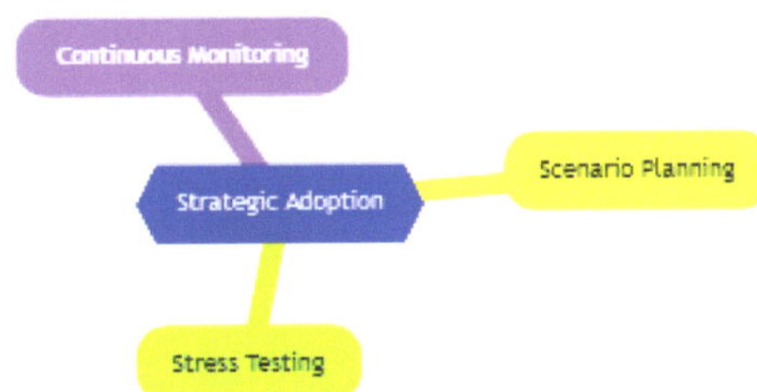

Preparing for Future Risks

The nature of risks facing organizations is constantly changing due to factors such as technological advancements, geopolitical tensions, regulatory shifts, and climate change. Adapting to these evolving risks requires organizations to adopt a strategic approach that anticipates potential future risks and prepares for them in advance.

Key Approaches

- **Scenario Planning**

  Scenario planning involves developing hypothetical scenarios that consider various potential future risks, such as climate change, geopolitical instability, or technological disruption. These scenarios help organizations assess the potential impact of these risks and develop contingency plans to mitigate them.

Impact on Risk Management

- **Proactive Preparation:** Enables organizations to anticipate potential risks and prepare for different possible futures.
- **Strategic Flexibility:** Helps organizations remain flexible and adaptable, ready to pivot their strategies as needed.
- **Example:** A multinational corporation conducts scenario planning to assess the potential impact of climate change on its global supply chain. The company identifies regions vulnerable to extreme weather events and develops strategies to diversify its suppliers and relocate critical operations to less risky areas.

- **Stress Testing**

Stress testing involves evaluating an organization's resilience under extreme conditions, such as market crashes, cyberattacks, or natural disasters. It helps identify vulnerabilities and areas where risk management frameworks need to be strengthened.

Impact on Risk Management

- **Resilience Building:** Stress tests help organizations identify weaknesses and develop strategies to improve their resilience to adverse events.
- **Risk Awareness:** Increases awareness of potential risks and their impact, prompting organizations to prioritize risk mitigation efforts.
- **Example:** A bank conducts stress tests to evaluate its capital adequacy under scenarios of economic recession, cyberattacks, and regulatory changes. The tests reveal vulnerabilities in its loan portfolio and cybersecurity defenses, prompting the bank to increase capital reserves and enhance cybersecurity measures.

- **Continuous Monitoring**

  Continuous monitoring involves implementing systems that track key risk indicators in real time, enabling the organization to detect and respond to emerging risks as they arise.

  Impact on Risk Management

  - **Early Detection:** Helps organizations detect potential risks early, allowing for quicker responses and mitigation efforts.
  - **Dynamic Adjustment:** Enables organizations to adjust their risk management strategies dynamically as new risks emerge.
  - **Example:** A technology company uses continuous monitoring tools to track cybersecurity threats and market volatility. The company receives real-time alerts about potential threats and adjusts its security protocols and investment strategies accordingly.

Practical Example: Developing a Strategic Risk Management Plan

Scenario

As the Chief Risk Officer (CRO) of a financial institution, you are tasked with developing a strategic risk management plan that includes scenario planning and stress testing to address future risks, such as economic recessions, cyber threats, and regulatory changes. The goal is to ensure the institution's resilience and ability to adapt to an uncertain risk environment.

Exercise 3: Implementing a Strategic Risk Management Plan

Task

Develop a strategic risk management plan that includes scenario planning and stress testing. Explain how you would implement this plan and monitor its effectiveness.

Answer and Explanation
Plan Components

- **Scenario Planning**
    - **Objective:** Develop scenarios for different types of risks, including:
    - **Global Economic Recession:** A prolonged economic downturn characterized by high unemployment, reduced consumer spending, and declining asset values.
    - **Major Cyberattack:** A significant cyberattack targeting the institution's financial systems, leading to data breaches and service disruptions.
    - **Significant Regulatory Changes:** New regulations that impose stricter capital requirements, data protection rules, or transaction monitoring obligations.
    - **Impact Assessment:** Evaluate the potential impact of each scenario on the institution's financial performance, operations, and compliance.
    - **Contingency Plans:** Develop contingency plans for each scenario, such as increasing capital reserves, enhancing cybersecurity measures, and adjusting the business model to comply with new regulations

- **Stress Testing**
- **Objective:** Conduct stress tests to evaluate the institution's resilience under each scenario.
- **Steps**

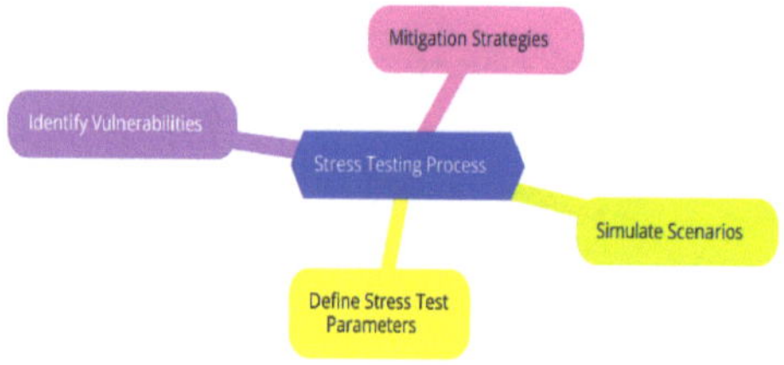

    - **Define Stress Test Parameters:** Determine the assumptions and parameters for each stress test, such as the duration of the economic recession, the scale of the cyberattack, and the extent of regulatory changes.

- **Simulate Scenarios:** Use financial models to simulate the impact of each scenario on key risk indicators, such as capital adequacy, liquidity, credit risk, and operational risk.
- **Identify Vulnerabilities:** Analyze the results to identify vulnerabilities and areas where risk management frameworks need to be strengthened.
- **Mitigation Strategies:** Develop mitigation strategies based on the stress test results, such as increasing capital reserves, diversifying the loan portfolio, investing in cybersecurity infrastructure, and enhancing compliance programs.

Implementation Steps

- **Integration with Existing Frameworks**
    - **Embed Scenario Planning and Stress Testing:** Integrate scenario planning and stress testing into the institution's regular risk management activities, ensuring they are conducted at least annually or whenever significant changes occur in the external environment.
    - **Use Real-Time Data and Analytics**: Implement real-time data analytics tools to continuously monitor key risk indicators and detect emerging risks. Ensure that these tools are integrated with existing risk management systems for seamless data flow and analysis.
    - **Allocate Responsibilities:** Assign responsibility for conducting scenario planning, stress testing, and continuous monitoring to specific teams or individuals within the risk management function. Establish clear reporting lines to ensure accountability.
- **Monitoring Effectiveness**
    - **Regular Review and Updates:** Review the strategic risk management plan regularly (at least quarterly) to assess its effectiveness in addressing emerging risks. Update the plan

based on new risk data, stress test results, and changes in the external environment.

- **Performance Metrics:** Develop performance metrics to measure the effectiveness of risk management activities, such as the accuracy of risk forecasts, the speed of response to emerging risks, and the effectiveness of mitigation strategies.
- **Stakeholder Engagement:** Communicate the results of scenario planning and stress testing to key stakeholders, including the board of directors, senior management, and regulators. Engage stakeholders in discussions on risk management priorities and adjustments to the plan.

Example Calculation: Stress Testing for Economic Recession Scenario

Scenario

A financial institution wants to evaluate its resilience to a global economic recession scenario. The stress test assumes a 30% decline in asset values, a 15% increase in loan defaults, and a 20% drop in consumer spending.

Calculating Impact on Capital Adequacy Ratio (CAR)

- **Initial Data**

  Total Assets: $100 billion
  Risk-Weighted Assets (RWA): $80 billion
  Tier 1 Capital: $8 billion
  Current CAR:
  CAR = Tier 1 Capital / RWA × 100 = 8 / 80 × 100 = 10%

Impact of Economic Recession Scenario

- **Assumptions**
  - Asset Value Decline: 30% reduction in asset values leads to a $30 billion decrease in total assets.

  - Increase in Loan Defaults: 15% increase in loan defaults results in an additional $5 billion in loan loss provisions.

- **New Total Assets and Tier 1 Capital**

  New Total Assets = 100 – 30 = 70 billion

- **New Tier 1 Capital**

  New Tier 1 Capital = 8 – 5 = 3 billion

- **New Risk-Weighted Assets (RWA)**

  New RWA = 80 - (30×0.6) = 80 – 18 = 62 billion

- **New CAR**

  New CAR = 3 / 62 × 100 ≈ 4.84%

Interpretation and Action

- **Outcome:** The stress test shows that the institution's CAR would drop from 10% to approximately 4.84% under the recession scenario, falling below the regulatory minimum of 8%.
- **Mitigation Strategy:** To address this vulnerability, the institution may need to increase its capital reserves, reduce risk-weighted assets by tightening lending criteria, or divest certain assets.

Evolving Regulatory Landscape and Strategic Adjustments

The regulatory environment for financial institutions is continually evolving due to technological advancements, market dynamics, and global economic conditions. Organizations must remain vigilant and adapt their risk management strategies to stay compliant and minimize regulatory risk. This chapter outlines the key considerations for adapting to regulatory changes, provides practical examples, and offers exercises to help organizations integrate regulatory requirements into their risk management frameworks.

Adapting to Regulatory Changes

Regulatory changes can significantly impact an organization's operations, financial performance, and strategic direction. Staying ahead of these changes and proactively adapting risk management strategies is crucial for maintaining compliance, avoiding penalties, and building stakeholder trust.

Key Considerations

- **Regulatory Compliance**

  Organizations must stay informed about new and emerging regulations that may affect their operations, such as data privacy laws, anti-money laundering (AML) requirements, or environmental, social, and governance (ESG) regulations.

  Impact on Risk Management

  - **Compliance Frameworks:** Compliance frameworks must be updated regularly to reflect new regulatory requirements. This involves revising internal policies, procedures, and controls to ensure they align with current laws.
  - **Monitoring and Reporting:** Establish systems for monitoring regulatory developments and reporting compliance status to regulators and other stakeholders.
  - **Example:** A financial institution prepares for the implementation of new data privacy regulations by overhauling its data management practices. The institution invests in data encryption, strengthens its cybersecurity measures, and trains employees on data privacy compliance. These strategic adjustments not only ensure compliance but also enhance customer trust.

- **Engagement with Regulators**

  Building strong relationships with regulators helps organizations stay informed about upcoming changes, influence regulatory developments, and ensure a smooth transition to new requirements.

Impact on Risk Management

- **Regulatory Intelligence:** Regular communication with regulators provides insights into potential changes, allowing organizations to anticipate and prepare for regulatory shifts.
- **Advocacy:** Organizations can engage in advocacy efforts to influence the design and implementation of regulations, ensuring they are fair, transparent, and conducive to business growth.
- **Example:** A multinational bank engages with regulators to understand new AML regulations. The bank provides feedback on the proposed rules, helping shape regulations that are practical and effective.

- **Strategic Adjustments**

  Organizations may need to adjust their business models, products, or services to align with new regulatory requirements. This could involve developing new compliance processes, investing in technology, or shifting to more sustainable practices.

Impact on Risk Management

- **Business Model Evolution:** Regulatory changes may require adjustments to pricing, product offerings, or market strategies.
- **Technology Investments:** Investments in technology, such as data analytics tools or compliance management systems, can help organizations meet new regulatory standards more efficiently.
- **Example:** A financial institution facing new ESG reporting requirements develops a framework for collecting and reporting ESG data. This includes tracking metrics related to environmental impact, social responsibility, and governance practices.

Practical Example: Ensuring Compliance with AML and ESG Regulations

Scenario

As the head of compliance at a large multinational bank, you are tasked with developing a plan to ensure the bank's compliance with new AML and ESG regulations. The goal is to integrate these requirements into the bank's risk management framework, minimize regulatory risk, and maintain strong relationships with regulators and stakeholders.

Exercise 4: Developing a Compliance Plan for AML and ESG Regulations

Task

Develop a plan to ensure the bank's compliance with new AML and ESG regulations, including the steps you would take to integrate these requirements into the bank's risk management framework.

Answer and Explanation

Plan Components

- **AML Compliance**
    - **Objective:** Ensure compliance with new AML regulations to prevent money laundering, terrorism financing, and other illicit activities.
    - **Steps**
        - **Implement Advanced Transaction Monitoring Systems:** Invest in AI-driven transaction monitoring systems that can detect suspicious activities in real-time. These systems should be capable of flagging unusual transaction patterns, high-risk jurisdictions, and potential shell companies.
        - **Enhance Customer Due Diligence (CDD):** Strengthen CDD processes by conducting thorough background

checks, risk assessments, and ongoing monitoring of customers. This includes implementing Know Your Customer (KYC) procedures to verify customer identities and assess their risk profiles.

- **Timely Reporting:** Develop protocols for reporting suspicious transactions to regulatory authorities within the required timeframes. Ensure that all reports are complete, accurate, and filed using the appropriate channels.
- **Continuous Training:** Provide regular training sessions for employees on AML compliance, including updates on new regulations, red flags for suspicious activities, and reporting requirements.

- **ESG Reporting Compliance**
  - **Objective:** Develop a comprehensive framework for ESG reporting that aligns with new regulatory requirements and stakeholder expectations.
  - **Steps**
    - **Identify Key ESG Metrics:** Determine the key metrics that need to be reported, such as carbon emissions, energy consumption, diversity and inclusion, and board governance practices.
    - **Data Collection and Management:** Implement systems for collecting, verifying, and managing ESG data across the organization. This may involve investing in data analytics tools, establishing data governance protocols, and integrating ESG metrics into the bank's overall performance reporting.
    - **Develop an ESG Risk Management Framework:** Integrate ESG risks into the bank's existing risk management framework. This includes assessing ESG risks, setting risk tolerance levels, and developing mitigation strategies.

- **Engage with Stakeholders:** Regularly communicate ESG performance to stakeholders, including investors, customers, employees, and regulators. Provide transparency on ESG initiatives, progress toward goals, and any challenges encountered.

Integration into the Risk Management Framework

- **Incorporate AML and ESG Compliance into Risk Assessments**
  - **Risk Identification:** Identify AML and ESG risks during regular risk assessments. Consider factors such as customer profiles, transaction patterns, geopolitical developments, and market conditions.
  - **Risk Assessment and Prioritization:** Assess the likelihood and impact of these risks on the bank's operations, reputation, and financial performance. Prioritize risks based on their potential impact and likelihood of occurrence.
  - **Mitigation Strategies:** Develop specific strategies to mitigate AML and ESG risks. For AML, this could involve enhancing transaction monitoring and due diligence processes. For ESG, this could include setting clear targets for reducing carbon emissions and improving governance practices.
- **Monitoring and Reporting**
  - **Continuous Monitoring**: Implement systems for continuously monitoring key AML and ESG risk indicators. Use data analytics tools to detect early warning signs of potential risks and take proactive measures.
  - **Regular Reporting:** Develop a reporting schedule to provide regular updates to senior management and the board on AML and ESG compliance. This includes reporting on key metrics, risk assessments, mitigation efforts, and any regulatory developments.

- **Audits and Reviews:** Conduct regular internal audits and reviews to ensure compliance with AML and ESG regulations. Engage external auditors if necessary to provide an independent assessment of the bank's compliance efforts.

Example Calculation: Estimating the Cost of Compliance with New Regulations

Scenario

A large multinational bank needs to estimate the cost of complying with new AML and ESG regulations, including investments in technology, training, and additional staffing.

Cost Estimation for AML Compliance

- **Assumptions**
  - Transaction Monitoring System Investment: $2 million (one-time cost)
  - Annual Maintenance and Upgrades: $500,000
  - Training Costs for Employees: $200 per employee for 5,000 employees = $1 million (annual)
  - Additional Staff for AML Compliance: 20 new hires at $100,000 per employee = $2 million (annual)
- **Total Annual AML Compliance Cost**

  Total AML Cost = 2 million (system) + 0.5 million (maintenance) + 1 million (training) + 2 million (staffing) = 5.5 million per year

Cost Estimation for ESG Compliance

- **Assumptions**
  - Data Management System Investment: $1 million (one-time cost)
  - Annual Data Collection and Reporting Costs: $300,000

- Training Costs for Employees on ESG Practices: $150 per employee for 5,000 employees = $750,000 (annual)
- Consultancy Fees for ESG Strategy Development: $250,000 (annual)

- **Total Annual ESG Compliance Cost**

  Total ESG Cost = 1 million (system) + 0.3 million (data) + 0.75 million (training) + 0.25 million (consultancy) = 2.3 million per year

- **Total Cost of Compliance**

  Combined Total

  Total Compliance Cost = AML Cost + ESG Cost = 5.5 million + 2.3 million = 7.8 million per year

Interpretation and Action

- **Outcome:** The bank estimates that complying with the new AML and ESG regulations will cost approximately $7.8 million per year. This cost should be considered in the bank's strategic planning and budgeting processes.
- **Mitigation Strategy:** The bank may explore ways to reduce costs, such as leveraging technology more effectively, optimizing training programs, or negotiating better terms with external consultants.

www.ingramcontent.com/pod-product-compliance
Lightning Source LLC
LaVergne TN
LVHW071221220926
848486LV00038B/288
* 9 7 9 8 8 9 6 3 2 3 7 0 9 *